Foreign exchange markets

Foreign exchange markets

A guide to foreign currency operations

HEINZ RIEHL, *Citibank*

RITA M. RODRIGUEZ, *Harvard University*

McGraw-Hill Book Company

*New York   St. Louis   San Francisco   Auckland   Bogotá
Düsseldorf   Johannesburg   London   Madrid   Mexico
Montreal   New Delhi   Panama   Paris   São Paulo
Singapore   Sydney   Tokyo   Toronto*

Library of Congress Cataloging in Publication Data

Riehl, Heinz.
Foreign exchange markets.

Bibliography: p.
Includes index.
1. Foreign exchange.   2. International finance.
3. Money market.   I. Rodriguez, Rita M., date,
joint author.   II. Title.
HG3851.R47   332.4'5   77-24909
ISBN 0-07-052670-2

34567890   HDHD   7654321098

The editors for this book were W. Hodson Mogan and Joan Zseleczky,
the designer was Elliot Epstein, and the production supervisor
was Teresa F. Leaden. It was set in Baskerville
by J. C. Meyer & Son, Inc.

Printed and bound by Halliday Lithograph Corporation.

To our mothers

ROSEMARIE MOELLER

and

ADELA MEDEROS DE RODRIGUEZ

Contents

PART II

A few days in the life of a funds manager 123

Preface

Foreign exchange markets have long ceased to be the concern of only a few people whose dealings in international trade required exchanging one currency for another. The spread of the multinational enterprise and the growing interdependence among nations have made foreign exchange markets the concern of almost everyone.

In spite of the growing importance of exchange markets, the interested reader will find only two major sources of information. One source is provided by economists; the other, by exchange traders. The economists with a theoretical approach and generalized conclusions are likely to leave the uninitiated with a general sense of bewilderment. At the other extreme, the exchange trader, who encapsules his or her general understanding of prevailing market conditions into a single number, without providing any further explanation, will leave most people fully mystified.

The object of this book is to bridge the gap between the camps of the economist and the trader. We intend to provide a practical, down-to-earth understanding of the nature of exchange markets and their close relationship to money markets. After dissecting the links among participants and segments of the market, this generalized knowledge is used to discuss extensively many specific problems encountered in exchange market operations. This approach should enable the reader to operate in international financial markets with an understanding of the situation—including the risks involved.

The presentation does not assume any background in the field; we want the book to be accessible to those who do not have any previous acquaintance with financial markets. Therefore, it begins with essentials that probably will be familiar to many readers. This is particularly true in Chapter 1. The reader who feels some of the introductory section to be too elementary will be well advised to skip these sections. However, it should be noted that the discussion moves quickly from these essentials to more specialized areas. For example, even though we start Chapter 1 with a discussion of the nature of interest rates and how they are expressed in percentage terms, by the end of the chapter we have moved the discussion to the field of Eurodollar markets.

We wish to apologize to the non-U.S. Americans for our use of the word "American" to refer to the United States. Since the United States is the largest financial market on the American continents, the use of "American" to refer to the United States is very prevalent in practice, and we have followed this practice here. On the other hand, to make the discussion more accessible to the reader, the language of the book departs at times from common trading-room usage when it involves specialized trading jargon. Although all specialized terminology is discussed in detail, some of the jargon peculiar to trading rooms has been avoided.

It should also be kept in mind that the examples presented in the text use rates that can vary widely. Therefore, no effort was made to use current rates, which might well change before the reader sees this book. However, the points made by these examples remain valid regardless of the prevailing rates.

We wish to express our deepest appreciation to Adam Blistein, hereby named "honorary editor" of this book. Although ostensibly only a secretary who impatiently typed and retyped an unending number of drafts of the manuscript, he did much more. He saw to it that the traces of German and Spanish in the authors' English were properly translated to make a coherent manuscript. He also made sure that even a Ph.D. candidate in Classics, such as himself, could understand the content of the book. This book is proof that Classical Greek and Latin have a contribution to make in the modern world.

Special thanks are given to Mr. Hugh Conway, Staff Member of the Board of Governors of the Federal Reserve Bank, to David Darst, of Goldman, Sachs & Co., to Dr. Yoon S. Park, of the World Bank, and to Edwin L. Pomeroy, of Citibank in New York, for valuable comments on the manuscript.

Mr. Riehl wishes to thank Citibank in New York for the encouragement it provided in the preparation of this book. In particular, he wishes to thank Mr. Freeman H. Huntington, Senior Vice President, for his continuous support of the project. Both authors wish to thank Citibank for granting permission to adapt slides from its videotaped presentations on foreign exchange markets.

Finally, Ms. Rosemarie Bou of Citibank typed portions of the manuscript. We thank her for this job as well as for working as a courier between the authors—something which at times required her performing above and beyond the call of duty.

Heinz Riehl
Rita M. Rodriguez

Foreign exchange markets

PART I
What are currency markets about?

When we enter the world of financial management in the foreign exchange market, we should first go through a brief period of initiation. This is what Part 1 of this book is all about.

We need to know who the main participants are in this area where we intend to operate. Thus, the cast of characters is introduced in Chapter 1. Then, we must understand the language which these characters speak. The language is one that expresses the price of money, and it does so through the use of quotes. The mechanics of understanding market quotes are discussed in Chapter 2. Finally, we introduce the leading actor in our story, the funds manager. The problems of this individual, who must manage funds in both the money market and the foreign exchange market, lead us (in Chapter 3) to an understanding of the interdependence of these two markets. Chapters 4 and 5 introduce the reality of quotes, including both bid and offer rates, which funds managers must use in their operations. Finally, Chapter 6 discusses the general economic and political factors which affect exchange rates.

The six chapters in Part 1 of this book provide the foundations of the world in which the funds manager operates. When we understand its structure, we shall look at some specific examples which illustrate efficient operations in the money and foreign exchange markets.

CHAPTER 1
Who's who in the money and foreign exchange markets

Do you remember the first time that you visited an Arab bazaar or a cattle auction? Do you remember the first time that you entered the visitors' gallery at the New York Stock Exchange or a foreign exchange trading room? Your reaction to these experiences is likely to have been one of bafflement combined with a bit of amusement. However, if you stop to think what all these experiences had in common, you soon realize that in every case people were just buying and selling whatever was at hand in the given place. This is what a market is all about; the foreign exchange market is no exception. The degree of colorfulness and noise may be different from market to market. However, the basic fact remains that in every market people buy and sell certain articles; they make a market in those articles. In the foreign exchange room, the traders are just making a market in foreign exchange, pieces of paper denominated in foreign currencies. Never mind that at the cattle auction, buyers and sellers face one another in a given physical place, whereas, in the foreign exchange trading room, all transactions are made via the telephone or telex throughout a geographical area that covers the world. In both situations there is an ongoing market.

No market exists in isolation. In addition to the interactions among the participants in each market, there are other markets that have a bearing on the performance of the given market. In the case of the foreign exchange market, the other market which it is essential to understand is the money market. The money market and the foreign exchange market are so interlocked that it is impossible to understand one without understanding the other. In the following sections we shall introduce these two markets, as well as the foreign sister of the money market, in some detail. However, the discussion of how these markets are related is reserved for Chapter 3.

3

Money market

What the money market is

We begin with the money market because it is the one in which we all have operated at one time or another. Anybody who has a checking account is a participant in the money market. The article that is bought and sold in this market is "money" or "near-money." Money or near-money is nothing more than financial paper representing a sum of money that one person (or enterprise) owes to another. In the case of currency, that is, cash in your pocket, it is the government that owes the money to you as the bearer of the currency.[1] In the case of a Treasury bill, it is also the government that owes an equivalent value to the owner of the bill. Here, however, a specified time has to elapse before the piece of financial paper—the Treasury bill—becomes payable in hard cash by the government, i.e., before the date of the maturity of the document. In the first case, the government currency is actually money. In the second instance, the Treasury bill is only near-money. It would not be very hard to sell the Treasury bill to another person; however, the government itself is not liable for the payment of the money represented by the bill until the instrument matures. This last example also points to another characteristic of the goods traded in the money market: marketability. The fact that a financial instrument has a short maturity does not in itself guarantee that it is marketable. (Who wanted to buy a 30-day commercial paper of the Penn Central in June 1970?)

The bulk of the financial assets traded in the money market have a maturity of less than a year. However, active trading is carried on in documents of up to five years' maturity. Anything above five years is pretty much the domain of the investors in the capital markets where these longer-term securities are traded.

Actors in the money market

Listed in order of importance as reflected by the volume of transactions they execute in this market, the major actors are commercial banks, central banks, large corporations, institutions that make a market in specialized instruments such as commercial paper, and the public at large which uses money for various purposes. Let's have a glimpse at what makes each of these actors tick.

[1] Money is money is money . . . ! Presenting a two-dollar bill to the U.S. Treasury for redemption will meet with one of two responses: The Treasury will exchange a two-dollar bill for either another two-dollar bill or two one-dollar bills.

Commercial banks. The large role of these institutions in the money market can be easily envisioned by looking at their assets and liabilities. A major portion of their liabilities are demand deposits, which, by definition, are money itself. Another large portion of banks' liabilities are time deposits, which are considered to be near-money. On the asset side, in addition to loans, banks have part of their assets invested in marketable securities of short maturity (money-market instruments) which guarantee the liquidity of the bank.

If one asks why commercial banks operate in the money market, one can rank the objectives in the following order:

1. To maintain the liquidity, and therefore the solvency, of the bank

2. To use excess funds so that they produce the highest possible return, given the constraints imposed by the first objective

3. To borrow necessary funds at the lowest possible cost

From the previous two paragraphs it is easy to have an intuitive feeling that commercial banks must wheel and deal a lot in the type of paper that we call money market instruments. Let's see, in more detail, how these institutions are triggered to enter the money market. Without trying to be comprehensive, let's take one example.

Energetic Corp., which keeps its cash balances with commercial bank ABC, makes a payment to Creditor Corporation in the amount of $10 million. Creditor Corp. deposits the check drawn on commercial bank ABC in the bank that it usually deals with, commercial bank XYZ.

Assuming that both commercial banks ABC and XYZ were happy with their cash positions before the Energetic Corp. decided to pay its creditor, and that Creditor Corp. deposited the check in the XYZ bank, we see that each of the two banks now has a problem. Bank ABC will feel that its liquidity has been impaired by the loss of $10 million. On the other hand, bank XYZ has to find a profitable use for the $10 million it has received. These are the forces that will send the two banks into the money market. In this simplified example, where no other changes take place, the easiest solution will be for bank XYZ to lend its excess funds to bank ABC. This transaction will bring the money position of the two banks back into balance.

Central banks. In most countries, the government regulates the nation's monetary system and banking operations through a central bank such as the U.S. Federal Reserve System. These institutions not only print the pieces of paper that are called money; they also operate directly in the money market.

The objectives of the central bank of any country are the well-known goals that every politician has promised and that every policymaker has wrestled with: economic growth, price stability, external balance of payments equilibrium, and full employment. The occasional inconsistency of these goals is a separate issue which will be discussed in Chapter 6 (for example, how to assure full employment in an inflationary environment). When these objectives are translated into policy decisions at the central bank, they are called monetary policy. (This is in contrast with fiscal policy, which is the set of policies based on government taxation and expenditure.) Monetary policy is usually phrased in terms of some desired level of money supply and interest rates.[2] To achieve the desired monetary objectives, such as an increase or a decrease in the money supply, the central bank has a whole battery of tools at its command. These tools include the following:

1. Buying and selling money market instruments (primarily Treasury bills), an activity known as open market operations

2. Voluntarily purchasing and selling foreign exchange against local currency

3. Changing the interest rate at which commercial banks can get money from the central bank (the discount rate)

4. Changing the amount of reserves that commercial banks are required to keep against deposits

5. Issuing other specific regulations pertaining to the rate and type of assets and liabilities that commercial banks are allowed to hold

It is clear from the above that the central bank not only operates directly in the money market through open market operations, but that it also controls the commercial banks, which are the major institutions in the market.

---

[2] According to the most frequently used definition, money supply represents money in circulation and demand deposits in banks. This is referred to as M_1. As you can gather from the subscript of M, economists have generated a whole family of M's which are distinguished from one another according to the type of deposits, e.g., savings deposits, and money-market instruments included in each definition.

Large corporations. The treasury department of any large corporation often operates in a fashion very similar to a commercial bank. It has a liquidity position to maintain, but it also has to make sure that every penny is invested at the highest possible return. In this sense we can say that the objectives of large corporations, when operating in the money market, are similar to those of commercial banks.

To see the forces that trigger the participation of these companies in the money market, we can pursue the example of the Energetic Corp., presented earlier. In that case, after the payment was made, the amount of liquid assets, or cash, of the Energetic Corp. decreased, and that of Creditor Corp. increased. Assuming other things remained constant, if the payment had not been fully anticipated (which, in a way, is the function of the treasurer), Energetic Corp. will now need to replenish its inventory of liquid assets. Creditor Corp. will have to find a profitable use for its newly acquired funds. However, in contrast with the commercial banks, a corporation may, but need not, consummate its adjustment transactions in the money market. Energetic Corp. may replenish its liquid balances with payments from products it sold on credit in the past, and Creditor Corp. may use its newly acquired funds to purchase a piece of equipment.

Other financial institutions. The problems of other financial institutions are similar to those of commercial banks, except that these other institutions tend to concentrate their borrowings and investments in other instruments, such as commercial paper. However, the rationale for the participation by these institutions in the money market is very like that of commercial banks.

Individuals. As mentioned before, anybody who owns a checking account is a participant in the money market. So is the person who owns a time deposit or a Treasury bill. The buying and selling of these instruments (by writing a check or by actually acquiring or disposing of the relevant piece of paper) constitute participation in the money market.

The participation of individuals in the money market depends on their attitude toward holdings of cash and near-cash. The traditional motives for holding cash and near-cash instruments are as follows:

1. For transaction purposes to make payments for desired articles

2. For precautionary purposes, in case some unforeseen event takes place

3. For speculation purposes, to profit from expected changes in interest rates

Foreign money market

The money and near-money instruments that are traded in a domestic money market are denominated in terms of the currency which is legal tender in that country.[3] When money market instruments are bought and sold outside the country where their currency of denomination is legal tender, then we have a foreign money market. This is the case when United States dollars are traded outside the United States. This type of transaction is the core of the so-called Eurodollar market, which is centered in London. When speaking of all the currencies traded in foreign markets, one usually refers to them as the Euro-currency markets; these include Euro-French francs, Euro-German marks, and so on.

Before going any further in the description of Euro-markets, let's make a few comments on terminology. The word "Euro" indicates only a geographical area where these markets exist; it does not identify the exact country where the foreign money market transaction occurs. However, the specific country where the transaction takes place, particularly the country of a borrower, is important inasmuch as it affects the interest rate charged. For example, a U.S. dollar deposit with the Swiss branch of an American bank and a deposit with another branch of the same bank in a less stable country command different rates because of the difference in sovereign risk.[4] It would be more exact to talk about external dollars on deposit in Switzerland or external dollars on deposit in the less stable country. However, "Euro" has become a generic term, and we have to live with it. It is for that reason that we shall continue to use the word "Euro" in this book.

We should note, too, that, in addition to the Euro-currency markets, foreign money markets have also emerged in Asia and, to a much lesser extent, in other regions. These other markets are identified by names such as the Asian dollar market. The kinds of limitations on the term "Euro" also apply to terms such as "Asian."

---

[3] Legal tender money is money which the law requires a creditor to accept in payment of a debt.

[4] Sovereign risk is the risk that the local government will take measures that will make it impossible for the borrower to repay the loan. Differences in interest rates reflecting the sovereign risk of different countries can range from ⅛ percent to 2 percent. Obviously, the country considered to be a smaller risk will be charged a smaller sovereign risk premium.

Why did Euro-currency markets come into being, and why do they continue to exist? For illustration purposes, we shall use the Eurodollar market, the largest of all the Euro-currency markets.

Why a Eurodollar market?

Historically, the Eurodollar market was first created to reduce the perceived sovereign risk. After World War II, the Eastern Bloc countries found themselves with foreign exchange reserves denominated largely in U.S. dollars. The natural way to hold these reserves would have been to keep them in bank deposits and other securities in the United States. However, in the midst of the cold war that came to dominate the postwar period, the danger that the United States might expropriate or otherwise control these reserves became unacceptable to the communist countries. As an alternative, these countries began placing their deposits in banks outside the United States. The deposits were still denominated largely in U.S. dollars; however, the immediate legal liability fell outside the United States, often in London.

The largest impetus to this market came from regulations designed to control the banking system and to support the foreign exchange value of currencies. The regulations to control the banking system establish, among other things, levels of reserve requirements and maximum interest rates payable on deposits. Reserve requirements and other costs, such as deposit insurance, reduce the amount of interest a bank is willing to pay for its deposits. An explicit limit on the interest that the governmental authorities allow to be paid to depositors discourages these individuals during periods when market rates surge above the limits the bank is permitted to pay. The combination of these factors means that, to the extent that banks can operate outside the jurisdiction of these regulations, the interest received by a depositor can be higher than otherwise. This is the situation that came to prevail in the Eurodollar market where none of the above regulations exists. The flight of deposits to the Euro-markets, where higher interest can be earned, was a natural development under these circumstances.

The other type of regulation that governments impose on the money market is designed to support the foreign exchange value of their currencies. When under heavy pressures from the market to appreciate or depreciate a given currency, governments have often responded by imposing controls on foreign capital movements. These controls, of course, apply only to transactions within the boundaries of jurisdiction of the country. As a result, two segmented markets in the same currency evolve:

the domestic market and the Euro-currency market. Let's look at two Euro-currency markets whose functioning has been greatly aided by the establishment of controls on capital movements in their domestic counterparts: markets in the Europound sterling and in the Euro-German mark.

In the case of sterling, the pressures in the market in the late 1960s and the 1970s have often been toward a depreciation of that currency. To avoid capital outflows from the country, the government of England has established controls that restrict the amount of sterling that foreigners can borrow in England. Because of the often-anticipated depreciations in sterling, many participants in the market have wished to borrow sterling either to convert it into other currencies or to use it as a balance against the assets they already hold in sterling. The Europound sterling market caters to the demands of these individuals. As a result, the interest rates on the Europound market are above those prevailing in the domestic pound market where the demand for borrowed funds is controlled.

In the case of the German mark, the pressures in the market during the late 1960s and 1970s have usually been toward an appreciation of that currency. To avoid the capital inflows that the expected appreciation of the mark produced in West Germany,[5] the national government introduced controls on these flows. These controls were designed to limit the amount of funds that nonresidents could deposit in West Germany and to restrict the amount of funds that its residents could borrow abroad. Any non-German resident wishing to hold deposits denominated in marks had only the alternative of the Euro-German marks. With a number of individuals wishing to purchase marks either to benefit from the expected appreciation or to protect the value of liabilities already contracted in marks, the rate on Euro-German marks fell considerably below the one prevailing in the domestic money market in West Germany.

The factors that affect the rates in the foreign money markets, as opposed to domestic markets, will be explored further in the next chapter. As a result of the factors discussed above, financial centers where Euro-currencies are traded share three characteristics: an acceptable political risk, no regulation affecting the cost of Euro-currency deposits, and no restrictions on the inflow and outflow of the Euro-currencies. All three of these conditions have prevailed for a time in the major "Euro" financial centers, such as London, Singapore, Nassau, and Bahrain.

---

[5] West Germany refers to the Federal Republic of Germany, established in 1949. Its currency, officially the deutsche mark (DM), is commonly called the mark.

Actors in the foreign money markets

The actors in the foreign money markets are mainly commercial banks and corporations. Their objectives in these markets are the same as in the domestic money market.

Central banks also participate in the foreign money markets when they invest their foreign exchange reserves. We should note, however, that no central bank exercises a supervisory or controlling function in the foreign money markets. This fact has been the subject of much discussion among central bankers whenever an international financial crisis has erupted. The problem is that a foreign money market may move to any country which combines a favorable regulatory environment with an acceptable political risk. In particular, the Bank of England has refused to regulate the external money market in London unless all other countries eligible for the development of external money markets agree to implement similar regulations.

Individuals typically do not participate in the foreign money markets. Transactions in these markets are usually of a wholesale nature, too large for average individuals. The financial institutions in these markets consider the handling of smaller transactions to be too expensive operationally.

Foreign exchange market

What the foreign exchange market is

Like the money market, the foreign exchange market is a market where financial paper with a relatively short maturity is traded. However, unlike the money market, the financial paper traded in the foreign exchange market is not all denominated in the same currency. In the foreign exchange market, paper denominated in a given currency is always traded against paper denominated in another currency. One justification for the existence of this market is that nations have decided to keep their sovereign right to have and control their own currency. If every country in the world used the same currency, there would not be a foreign exchange market.

Like the money market, the foreign exchange market considers the time when the transaction is closed to be one of the elements in the market. In describing the money market, we made this point by comparing currency and a Treasury bill. Currency provides immediate aquisitive power, whereas a Treasury bill provides this purchasing power at some specified future date (assuming the bill is held to maturity and not sold in the secondary market). In the foreign exchange market this time element is taken into account by dividing the market into spot and forward markets. The *spot market* is for foreign exchange delivered within two business days; the *forward market* is for foreign exchange to be delivered at some specified future date. The date of delivery is technically called the *value date*.[6]

Let's consider some examples of how transactions in the foreign exchange market arise. When a United States company exports to a foreign country, Japan, for example, foreign exchange is required. The people manufacturing and performing services in the United States must be paid in local currency, U.S. dollars. The people consuming the goods and services in Japan have only their local currency, yen, with which to pay. There are now two possibilities for settling the account between the United States and Japan. The American exporter bills the Japanese importer either in U.S. dollars or in yen.

1. If the American exporter bills in dollars, the Japanese must sell yen to purchase U.S. dollars in the foreign exchange market.

2. If the American exporter bills in yen, the exporter must sell yen to purchase U.S. dollars.

As we can see, whatever the currency for invoicing is, somebody has to go into the foreign exchange market to sell yen and purchase U.S. dollars.

To offset this transaction in the market, there must be a supply of dollars and a demand for yen. This could be brought about by an American importing goods from Japan. The situation would be the reverse of that created by the American exporter. Here, either the American importer or the Japanese exporter must purchase yen and sell dollars. Whether the importer or the exporter makes the exchange transaction, it takes place in the foreign exchange market.

It does happen that transactions between two countries are sometimes settled in a third currency, that is, a currency that is neither the exporter's nor the importer's own local currency. This means of payment is particularly popular if both countries have infrequently traded or weak curren-

---

[6] The concept of "value date" and its central role in the management of flow of funds is discussed in more depth in Chap. 3.

cies. Again, there is a need for the foreign exchange market in which the importing agency, say, will purchase the third currency against (sell) its own currency, and the exporting agency will sell the third currency against (purchase) its own.

Actors in the foreign exchange market

In principle, anyone who exchanges currency of a given country for currency of another country participates in the foreign exchange market. However, it is useful if we concentrate on the major actors in this market. Under any priority system, commercial banks are the main participants in the foreign exchange market. Indeed, one can say that it is the commercial banks that "make a market" in foreign exchange. Next in importance are the large corporations with foreign trade activities or direct investment abroad. Finally, the central bank is always omnipresent in the foreign exchange market.

Commercial banks. Obviously, when we talk of the commercial bank as the leading actor in the foreign exchange scene, we are speaking mostly of large commercial banks with many clients engaging in imports and exports which must be paid for in foreign currencies or of banks which specialize in the financing of certain trade.

Commercial banks participate in the foreign exchange market as an intermediary for their corporate customers who wish to operate in the market. They also operate on their own account. The intermediation process usually leaves the commercial bank with a net position in each of the currencies involved. If the new position is different from the desired one, then the bank will deal on its own account to achieve the desired goal. For example, if a bank's clientele includes more importers than exporters dealing in a given currency, the bank will tend to have its sales of that currency to importers exceed its purchases from exporters. This imbalance will affect the inventory position that the bank wishes to maintain in that currency. As a result, the bank will deal with other banks until the imbalance is corrected. Specifically, the bank will purchase the currency which its customers are demanding against other currencies of which the bank has an inventory higher than desired. The avenues open to accomplish this goal are discussed in Chapter 7.

From the previous description of the role of commercial banks in the foreign exchange market, one can easily see the goals which the bank tries to achieve when operating in this market:

1. To give the best possible service to customers

2. To manage the bank's position so that inventory in each foreign currency is kept at the desired level

3. To produce a profit for the bank while accomplishing the first two objectives

To give the best possible service to customers means providing easy accessibility (an adequate number of well-attended phones and telexes), sound counsel about pertinent economic developments, competitive rates, and, wherever possible, capability to transact the entire amount suggested by the customer. For example, if a customer calls the bank on, say, February 18 and indicates a need to sell 5 million pounds sterling against U.S. dollars for delivery on April 20, the bank should advise its customer of the price of the pound vis-à-vis the U.S. dollar for delivery on April 20. Moreover, if the service is to be provided fully, the bank should also quote a "reasonable" rate for the transaction and, if agreeable to the customer, close the transaction at this rate.

The previous example also illuminates how the bank gets involved in its second goal, that of managing the foreign exchange position of the bank itself. The bank wishes to maintain certain inventories of foreign ex-change to serve its clients. However, every time that a transaction with a customer is closed, the inventory for the currencies involved is affected. First, let's visualize what an inventory of foreign exchange looks like. In our example of pounds sterling and dollars, the inventory for these currencies consists of a list of the inflows and outflows which the bank expects for that currency for every value date for which the bank trades. When the bank accepts the transaction of the customer who wishes to sell 5 million pounds against dollars for delivery on April 20, the impact on the bank's inventory is as follows: inflow of pounds sterling, value date April 20, 5 million pounds; outflow of U.S. dollars, value date April 20, U.S. dollars equivalent to 5 million pounds. In the absence of any other counteracting transaction, the bank will have to enter the foreign ex-change market and possibly also the money market (and here is part of the relationship between these two markets) so that on April 20 there will be an outflow of pounds sterling and an inflow of U.S. dollars. This will "square off" the bank's inventory.

The two previously stated objectives of a foreign exchange trader, serving the customer and keeping the bank's foreign currency accounts balanced, must be performed in such a way that the bank is properly compensated. The profits will come from exchange rate differentials, exchange commissions and fees, and "float." The float is created when the bank receives deposits from a customer who wishes to exchange funds into another currency. The bank will sometimes take a day or two before crediting the desired currency to the client's account. Thus, the bank has the use of the funds for the two intervening days.

Each bank with an active international department maintains an account with a correspondent bank in each financially important country. This account with, say, a bank in France is the "storage room" for the foreign exchange trader's working balances (inventory) in French francs. The number of accounts depends on how active a bank is in international business. Some banks have accounts in as many as fifty countries. Very often, banks also maintain more than one account for any given currency; they do so to facilitate payments for different geographical areas within a country. The balances in each account vary depending on the number and size of the transactions involved. These balances should be large enough to compensate the corresponding banks for their services, but not unnecessarily large, because they are typically non-interest-bearing and represent a cost of doing foreign exchange business. (The trader is usually told by management what minimum balance should be kept with each bank, and the trader acts accordingly.) Banks that are particularly active in international business often have branches in foreign countries with which they and their customers do business. These banks obviously will use their own branches as "correspondents." Still, these banks will also keep accounts with the respective countries' leading banks if they, in turn, maintain accounts and balances with the bank in the United States. International banking is very much a business of reciprocity.

Finally, there are thousands of very fine domestic banks whose volume of international business does not warrant an account abroad. They will ask one of the banks with international departments to handle their international business for them. In other words, these domestic banks use another bank in the United States as their "correspondent bank abroad."

Nonfinancial businesses. The involvement of business in the foreign exchange market originates from two primary sources: international trade and direct investment. International trade usually involves the payment or receipt of currency other than the one used in the home country of the corporation. In this regard, the concern of a company is not only that foreign currency be paid or received, but also that the transaction be done at the most advantageous price of foreign exchange possible.

Given that the spot rate of a currency may fluctuate between the date when the business transaction is initiated and the date the actual cash flow takes place, management may wish to consider the foreign exchange market as a way to lock in a specific exchange rate.[7]

A business also deals in the foreign exchange market when it engages in foreign direct investment. Foreign direct investment involves not only the acquisition of assets in a foreign country, but also the generation of liabilities in foreign currency. So, for each currency in which a firm operates, an "exposure to foreign exchange risk" is likely to be generated. That is, given that the company will have either a net asset or a net liability position in the operations in a given currency, any fluctuation that occurs in the value of that currency will also occur in the value of the company's foreign operations. In the deliberate acceptance or avoidance of these risks, businesses will keep dealing in the foreign exchange market.

Furthermore, the Eurodollar and Euro-currency markets have stimulated deposits and borrowings in other currencies besides the one actually available or needed. For example, a company which basically needs to borrow marks may decide to borrow U.S. dollars instead. The company then has to sell the dollars in the exchange market for marks, the currency needed.[8] Likewise, some holders of U.S. dollars may prefer to keep their money in Swiss francs; consequently, they exchange the dollars in the foreign exchange market for Swiss francs and put the Swiss francs on deposit in Switzerland. These financial transactions without an underlying import or export of merchandise add a substantial amount of activity to the trillion dollars' worth of annual commercial business generated by imports and exports.

Central banks. These institutions are not only responsible for the printing of domestic currency and the management of the money supply (as well as all the other objectives of monetary policy discussed earlier in the "Money Market" section), but, in addition, they are often responsible for maintaining the value of the domestic currency vis-à-vis the foreign currencies. This is certainly true under the system of "fixed exchange rates." However, even within systems of "floating exchange rates," the central banks have usually felt compelled to intervene in the foreign exchange market at least to maintain "orderly markets."

Under a system of freely floating exchange rates, the external value of a currency is determined, like the price of any other good in a free market,

---

[7] See Chap. 8, the section "Hedging Exposure to Foreign Exchange Risk."
[8] See Chap. 7, the section "How to Raise Needed Funds in a Given Currency."

by the forces of supply and demand. If, as a result of international transactions between the residents of a given country and the rest of the world, more *domestic* currency is offered than is demanded, that is, if more *foreign* currency is demanded than is offered (as would happen, for example, if imports were to exceed exports), then the value of the currency in terms of foreign currencies will tend to decrease; that is, it will take fewer units of foreign currency to acquire one unit of domestic currency. In this scheme, the role of the central bank should be minimal unless it has certain preferences for what the foreign exchange rate should be, e.g., if it wishes to protect the local export industry. Then, the central bank will try to make the domestic currency cheaper relative to those of other countries by selling its local currency on the exchange markets.

Under a system of fixed exchange rates, the central banks agree to maintain the value of their currencies within an agreed narrow band of fluctuations. Therefore, if pressures like the ones just described develop, and if the price of the domestic currency approaches the lowest price allowed under the system, then the central bank is obliged to intervene and counteract the forces prevailing in the market. This responsibility is discharged by the central bank's acting as a buffer between the forces of supply and demand. In a system of fixed rates, whenever the transactions of the financial and nonfinancial institutions do not produce a balance between supply and demand for foreign exchange, the central bank will usually absorb the difference. In doing so, it must consider three variables:

1. Foreign exchange reserves

2. Domestic money supply

3. Value of the local currency in the foreign exchange market

If there is an *excessive demand* for local currency in the market, the central bank has to provide the shortfall by accumulating foreign exchange and providing local currency, probably at rising prices for the latter. It will sell local currency and purchase foreign currencies. This produces an inflow of foreign currency, an increase of the country's foreign exchange reserves, and pressures to upvalue the local currency or increase domestic prices. (The sale of local currency will increase the domestic money supply, fuel the economy, and stimulate inflation. It could be "involuntary open market policy.")

If there is an *excessive supply* of local currency in the market, the central bank has to absorb the surplus of local currency by selling out its stock of foreign exchange, probably at rising prices. It will purchase local currency and sell foreign currencies. This process produces an outflow of foreign currency, a decrease in the country's foreign exchange reserves, and pressures, or even the need, to devalue the local currency or deflate the domestic economy. (The purchase of local currency will decrease the domestic money supply and help fight inflation; the reduced availability of credit will cool off the economy. The effect is again equal to "involuntary open market policy.")

We can see from this discussion that any action taken in the foreign exchange market by a central bank has domestic and external economic effects. Therefore, it is necessary that a central bank coordinate its behavior in the foreign exchange markets with its overall strategy for the economy of the country.[9]

---

[9] This issue is discussed further in Chap. 6.

CHAPTER 2
Interest rates and foreign exchange rates—what do they mean?

There is a basic fact of life which we must bear in mind: You never get anything for nothing. When you acquire a house, you have to give money in exchange. When you acquire a Treasury bill, you must also give money in exchange. When you operate in the money and foreign exchange markets, you are always giving and taking every time that you enter into a transaction. In this chapter we shall discuss how the price, or rate of exchange, in this giving and taking is expressed.

As in any other market, prices in the money market and the foreign exchange markets depend on whether one is buying or selling. Traders in these markets will always offer two prices: the one at which they are willing to buy, and the one at which they are willing to sell. Actually, this is one of the ways in which traders in these markets make a profit. However, in this chapter, we shall talk about market sales in general, leaving our discussion of the complications involved in two-way rates until Chapter 4.

The money market

The prices in the money market are usually expressed in terms of percentage rates. These rates represent the return associated with the use of money for a specified period of time. The actors in the money market are called, in general, borrowers and lenders. The borrower is the individual who buys the right to use the funds for a predetermined period of time. The lender is the individual who sells the right to use the funds for that time. The price that the lender receives for relinquishing the use of the given funds is the interest rate. For example, in a loan of $100, if the lender receives $108 at the end of the year, the $8 return for the use of the

19

money is expressed in terms of an 8 percent annual return on the money. In physical terms, the lender gives up currency in exchange for a piece of financial paper that establishes the amount of principal and interest that the lender will receive in exchange for the services rendered to the borrower.

In reading interest rate quotations, one must be careful to understand the period of time involved. The figure 8 percent alone does not convey the necessary information to evaluate the cost of money. Usually, these rates are expressed on a per annum basis. This designation facilitates comparing the rates charged by various suppliers of funds.

Sometimes a rate will specify the period of time over which the interest rate will be applied. For example, in countries with high interest rate levels, interest rates are often quoted on a per month basis, for example, 2 percent per month. Obviously, any rate applicable for any period of time can be converted to a per annum basis. Thus, a 2 percent per month rate is equivalent to 24 percent (2 percent × 12 months) per annum. Whatever the unit of time involved, the important fact to remember is that if one wants to compare interest rates among themselves or with other percentage returns, all the numbers must be based on the *same* unit of time, usually per annum. Otherwise, one will reach erroneous conclusions.

The alternative to interest rates quoted for a specific period of time, such as per annum, per quarter, or per month, is a *flat interest rate*. For example, 4 percent flat of $100 is $4. In this calculation the time factor does not play a role. The 4 percent flat is always simply 4 percent of the amount in question. Of course, it is possible to convert a flat interest rate into a per annum (p.a.) interest rate. For example, if the flat charge of 4 percent covers a two-month period, then 4 percent flat would be equal to 24 percent per annum. On the other hand, per annum interest rates may be converted into flat interest rates. A charge of 10 percent p.a. covering two years would be equal to a 20 percent flat rate.

The price paid for the use of funds can be paid either at the beginning, at the end, or at intervals during the life of the loan. When the interest payment takes place at the beginning of the transaction, it is called "discounting." For example, a one-year loan of $100 (the principal amount) at 8 percent p.a. is discounted if the borrower receives only $92 at the beginning of the transaction while contracting an obligation to pay $100 at the end of the year. When the loaned amount is received in its entirety at the beginning and returned with interest only at the end of the loan period, it is called a "balloon payment." When taking out a $100 loan, the borrower would receive $100 at the beginning of the transaction and pay back $108 at the end of the year. Finally, arrangements can be made for payment of interest as well as the principal at various intervals within the life of the loan.

Because of the various alternatives available as to the time when principal and interest payments are due, there may be a difference between the *explicit interest rate* (the one quoted) and the *effective interest rate* (the interest payment as a percentage of the amount borrowed, adjusted for time). One popular example of this situation is the interest paid on time deposits. Here, the effective interest rate will be different from the explicit interest rate, depending on whether interest payments are compounded daily, monthly, or whenever. The faster the interest is paid, the larger the effective interest rate. For example, $100 at 8 percent for one year earns $8 if the interest is paid at the end of the year. However, if the interest is payable quarterly, and we assume a reinvestment rate of, again, 8 percent for the $2 of interest collected each quarter, the total interest earned at the end of one year is $8.24, or almost ¼ percent more than when interest is compounded annually. (See Exhibit 2.1.) The higher the interest rate levels are, the greater is this impact of fast compounding.

Money market transactions among banks with a maturity of a year or less will usually be of the "balloon" type; that is, both the principal and the interest will be paid back at the end of the period. For transactions with a maturity greater than a year in the interbank market, the interest payments will be made on an annual basis, the principal according to pre-negotiated agreements. When banks deal with customers who hold time deposits, the interest on those deposits is paid on predetermined conditions—daily, quarterly, etc., as mentioned earlier. When the bank deals with a customer who is borrowing from the bank, the payments of interest on the loan and the terms of the repayment of the principal are negotiated. However, interest payments on loans from banks are usually paid on a quarterly basis.

At this point we should note that in bank parlance, the acquisition of deposits is called *purchase of funds*. The lending operation is called *placement of funds*. Unfortunately, bankers have developed a tendency to use the word *buy* for both transactions, as in *buy deposits* and *buy loans*, which may lead to misunderstandings. To avoid this confusion, we propose the following terminology: banks *accept* or *take* deposits; they *lend* money to clients; and they *place* money with other banks. Nonbanks *make* deposits with banks and *borrow* from banks.

Exhibit 2.1
EFFECTIVE INTEREST RATE ON AN 8 PERCENT P.A. DEPOSIT, COMPOUNDED QUARTERLY

AMOUNT OF TIME DEPOSIT: $100

Interest Collected		Interest Reinvested at 8%	Earnings on Reinvested Income
After three months	$2.00	for nine months	$0.12
After six months	$2.00	for six months	$0.08
After nine months	$2.00	for three months	$0.04
After twelve months	$2.00	—	—
	$8.00		$0.24

Total interest earned $8.24

EFFECTIVE INTEREST RATE: 8.24%

Foreign money market

As discussed in Chapter 1, a foreign money market exists whenever short-to medium-term funds are lent and borrowed outside the country where the currency of denomination of the funds is legal tender. An example is U.S. dollars traded outside the United States. The price of funds in the foreign money market is expressed in terms of interest rates, as in the domestic market. In the absence of governmental controls which affect the cost and availability of funds in the domestic market, and with comparable political stability, the interest rate on funds traded in the foreign money market should be the same as in the domestic market. In this situation, the interest rate on 90-day U.S. dollar deposits should be the same whether the deposit is made in a bank's New York office or in its London branch. However, we know that the major incentive for the development of Euro-currency markets has been the presence of such regulations as reserve requirements on deposits with domestic commercial banks, foreign exchange controls, and other restrictions.

Spread between domestic and Euro-rates

If a country of relatively large economic importance in the world has regulations affecting the cost of funds, we can expect that the currency of that country will most likely be traded in the Euro-currency markets. In addition, we can say that interest rates in the Euro-currency market will be slightly higher than in the domestic market for funds of comparable maturity and credit risk. When they are, banks will be able to pay a higher rate for deposits in the Euro-currency market because they thus do not have to incur certain costs that are required in the domestic market, e.g., reserve requirements.

A typical example is the Eurodollar market. Even in periods when no foreign exchange controls existed in the United States, interest rates on Eurodollars have often traded at a premium over domestic U.S. dollar interest rates. The premium reflects primarily the cost of maintaining reserve requirements and the cost of insuring deposits with the Federal Depositors Insurance Corporation (FDIC) in the United States. In other words, if a Euro-market exists because of regulations affecting the cost of funds domestically, the Euro-interest rates for that currency will exceed the domestic rates by a "spread." In this case, the spread will be limited to the amount of additional costs associated with operating in the domestic market.

If, in addition to the regulations affecting the domestic cost of funds, a country's government imposes regulations on foreign capital flows, Euro-interest rates may vary substantially from domestic interest rates for the same currency. A currency which is a candidate for devaluation, as sterling has often been, is very much in demand by borrowers. With England maintaining controls on capital outflows from the country, borrowers have had to raise the wanted funds in the Eurosterling market. As a result, interest rates on Eurosterling, which is traded free of controls outside England, have increased substantially over domestic sterling rates. The arbitrage process that would keep interest rates in the domestic and Euro-currency markets in line is not allowed to operate in this case because of the capital outflow controls. (This process is explained in detail in Chapter 3.) Consequently, there is no limit as to how high a Euro-interest rate for a devaluation-prone currency may rise.

In a similar fashion, a currency which the market considers likely to upvalue will often find the local government opposing such a trend by imposing controls on foreign capital inflows. On several occasions, this has been the case for West Germany and the mark. With the prevailing trends in the market, a large demand for investing funds in marks developed. Since the German authorities restricted the inflow of foreign funds into the country, the investors who wished to fulfill their desire to invest in marks were confined to the Euromark market. As a result, the interest rates in Euromarks decreased substantially below those prevailing in the domestic market in West Germany. Again, the usual forces of arbitrage were frustrated by the capital controls that effectively segmented the domestic from the foreign market. (See Exhibit 2.2.)

Finally, there is one more factor that affects Euro-rates as opposed to domestic rates. This is the political or sovereign risk associated with the specific country where the Euro-currency is deposited. As mentioned before, a U.S. dollar deposit with a branch of an American bank in Switzerland earns a lower interest rate than it would if the deposit were kept with a branch of the same bank in a less stable country. The difference in the political situations of the two countries makes it necessary for the branch in the less stable country to pay a premium over the rate paid by the branch in Switzerland.

Revolving Euro-term loan

The instruments used in the Euro-currency markets are essentially the same as the ones used in the domestic money markets. However, there is one lending technique, in particular, which is most popular in the Euro-

Exhibit 2.2
FOREIGN EXCHANGE MARKET PRESSURES AND ASSOCIATED DEVELOPMENTS

Expected Devaluation (£)	*Expected Upvaluation (DM)*
Domestic Markets	
Capital outflow controls	Capital inflow controls
Lower interest rates	Higher interest rates
Euro-Markets	
Higher interest rates	Lower interest rates

currency markets and which deserves special mention here: the revolving Euro-term loan. Under this arrangement a bank agrees to make funds available for a number of years, usually not longer than five or seven years. The interest rate charged on the funds used under this loan are set for three months at a time; after that period the rates are reviewed again. The actual rate charged is a markup over the London Interbank Offered Rate (LIBO) for three months.[1]

For example, if LIBO is 6 percent at the time of the initial "take down" of the loan, and the negotiated markup over LIBO is 1½ percent, then the effective interest rate for the loan will be 7½ percent for the initial three-month interest period. At the end of that interest period, both bank and customer will look at the then-prevailing LIBO rate of, say, 7 percent and arrive at a new effective rate of 8½ percent for the second interest period of three months. Under this procedure, a five-year loan would really consist of 20 three-month loans at a rate of 1½ percent over the LIBO rates prevailing at the times of rate revision. Exhibit 2.3 shows the effective interest rates for the first year of this loan.

The system of revolving Euro-term loans is attractive to borrowers because they obtain medium-term money at a small markup over a short-term rate. The system is also attractive to the lending bank because it can take a matching deposit for each interest period and, in doing so, secure a profit margin equal to the negotiated markup over LIBO. The borrower's risk is a sharp rise in interest rates. The lending bank's risk is its ability to find three-month deposits over a five-year period. Assuming that, at some rate, a bank in good standing will always get money, the liquidity risk to the bank should be bearable. As to the borrowers: In case of very high interest rates, they may choose to repay these loans at the end of any interest period and temporarily not use the loanable funds available from the bank. This does not present any problem to the lending bank because it will usually not take deposits exceeding the end of an interest period.

A variation of the regular revolving Euro-term loan occurs when the borrower is given the right to choose an interest period between one and twelve months instead of the predetermined three-month interest periods. This arrangement enables the borrower to choose a one-month interest period when interest rates are expected to decline. If interest rates indeed are lower after one month, the borrower can then choose a longer interest period of between six and twelve months to secure the

---

[1] LIBO is the rate at which banks located in London borrow Euro-currency from other banks.

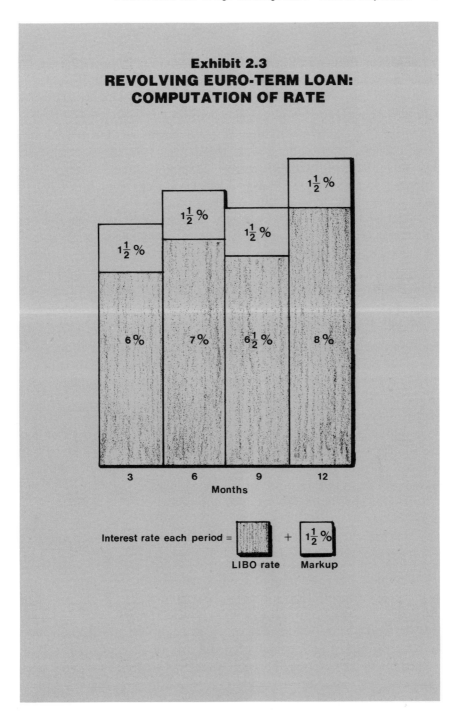

Exhibit 2.3
REVOLVING EURO-TERM LOAN:
COMPUTATION OF RATE

lower interest rates. There is no disadvantage to the bank because the effective lending rate is always equal to the markup over LIBO. The bank can always take a deposit with a maturity matching the one requested by the borrower and secure its profit margin.

A further refinement of the revolving Euro-term loan takes place when a multicurrency feature is added. The bank and the customer then stipulate in the loan agreement that, at the end of each interest period, the customer may borrow other currencies than the currency committed in the loan agreement, subject to mutual agreement and availability of the respective currency. From the bank's viewpoint there is not much difference. It will continue to add the agreed-upon markup to whatever the offered rate for the chosen currency may be. Borrowers like this arrangement because they can incorporate this multicurrency feature in their hedging strategies[2] or use it to minimize overall borrowing costs.[3]

Foreign exchange market

Prices of foreign exchange in a given country are expressed in the same way as the price of any good or service in that country—in terms of local currency. For example, in the United States, one expresses the price of goods and services in U.S. dollars. This applies to cars, dishwashers, medical services, and everything else; it also applies to foreign exchange. For example, one can say the price of a car is $3800 or the price of one French franc is $0.23. In contrast to the money market, where quotations are expressed in percentage form, the prices in the foreign exchange market are expressed in terms of local currency.

Every price quotation answers two questions:

1. What are we trying to price (houses, tomatoes, foreign currency)?

2. What unit of account or currency are we using to express the price? (Usually, it is the domestic currency.)

When one asks for a quotation of the price of foreign exchange, one must be careful to understand what the unit of account used is. The French will quote in terms of French francs, the Venezuelans in terms of

[2] See Chapter 8, pp. 180–188.
[3] See Chapter 8, pp. 172–176.

bolivars, and in Singapore the quotes will be in terms of Singapore dollars. In the rest of the book, we shall refer to the unit of account as "terms." Thus, when quotations are given in terms of French francs per unit of foreign currency, they are called "French terms." When quotations are given in terms of U.S. dollars per unit of foreign currency, they are called "American terms."[4]

We can see in Exhibit 2.4 how the prices of cars, tomatoes, and a one-dollar bill are expressed in four different cities. In New York, using American terms, the price of a certain car is $3800, the price of a tomato is $0.30, and the price of a one-dollar bill is $1.00. In Paris, using French terms, the prices of these three items are FF16,830, FF1.30, and FF4.40, respectively. The exhibit also shows these prices using bolivars, Venezuelan terms, and using Singapore dollars, Singaporean terms.

The column to the right in Exhibit 2.4 is of particular interest in our discussion. In this column we have shown that the price of a one-dollar bill is $1.00, FF4.40, B4.30, or S$2.30, depending on what terms we use. By pricing a one-dollar bill, we have actually provided the exchange rates between the dollar and the currencies used as the unit of account in the other cities.

The exchange rates in the right column of Exhibit 2.4 are given in local terms. However, by making use of some simple arithmetic, we can change the terms in which the quote is given. For example, if we know that the price of $1 is FF4.40, we can find the price of FF1 in terms of dollars, i.e., express the price of one French franc in American terms. The price of FF1 in American terms is $0.2273 ($1/FF4.40). The relationship is one of reciprocity. Exhibit 2.5 shows on the left side the price of one U.S. dollar bill in terms of French francs, bolivars, and Singapore dollars. These numbers are the same as those shown in Exhibit 2.4. In addition, Exhibit 2.5 shows on the right side the price of one French franc, one bolivar, and one Singapore dollar in terms of U.S. dollars. The last three numbers are the respective reciprocals of the first three numbers.

The tourist, let's say an American, will continue thinking in terms of his home currency, U.S. dollars. However, when one starts looking at price tags in any foreign country, those prices are in the currency of the country, French francs, guilders, pesetas, or some other unit. For the American to understand the price of an article in terms of U.S. dollars, which is what he "understands," a mental translation has to be made. If the price of an article is £50, the American tourist is likely to want to know

---

[4] Here we are adopting standard trading-room usage. Our apologies to South Americans and other Americans outside the United States.

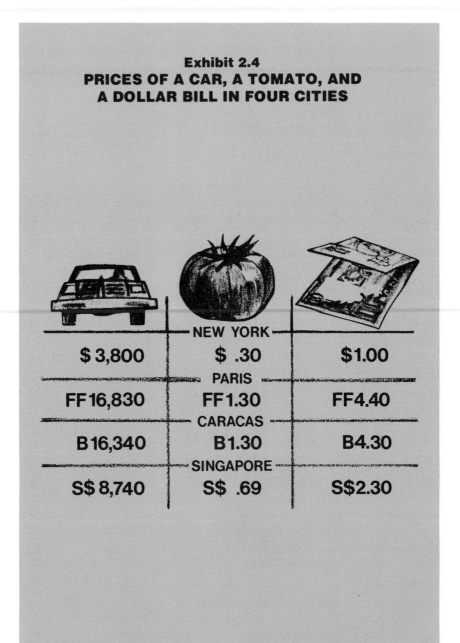

Exhibit 2.4

**PRICES OF A CAR, A TOMATO, AND
A DOLLAR BILL IN FOUR CITIES**

	NEW YORK	
$ 3,800	$ .30	$1.00

	PARIS	
FF 16,830	FF 1.30	FF 4.40

	CARACAS	
B 16,340	B 1.30	B 4.30

	SINGAPORE	
S$ 8,740	S$ .69	S$ 2.30

Exhibit 2.5
EXCHANGE RATES—
RECIPROCAL RELATIONSHIPS

Foreign Terms | *American Terms*

US$1 = FF4.40   FF1 = US$0.2273

$$\frac{1}{4.40} = 0.2273$$

US$1 = B4.30   B1 = US$0.2326

$$\frac{1}{4.30} = 0.2326$$

US$1 = S$2.30   S$1 = US$0.4348

$$\frac{1}{2.30} = 0.4348$$

what that means in terms of U.S. dollars. In this case the article may cost about $100 if the price of one pound sterling at the time is $2 (50 pounds × $2 per pound = $100).

The fact that prices of foreign currency are given in terms of local currency in each country can also be confusing to the uninitiated. Thus, our American tourist, after leaving England, goes to Germany. At the airport in Frankfurt he wishes to exchange $100 of traveler's checks into German marks. When presenting the checks to be exchanged, he asks what the going exchange rate is. The reply is 2.50. The tourist is used to prices expressed in terms of U.S. dollars. However, the quote he has been given is expressed in terms of German marks, the local currency in Germany. Specifically, the quote means DM2.50/$. Can the tourist convert the quote from German terms to American terms? Yes.

If we want to convert the 2.50 quote from German into American terms, we just take the reciprocal of 2.50. So, we can express the quote in two ways:

German terms	American terms
DM2.50/$	$0.40/DM

The quote given in American terms is the *reciprocal rate* of the quote given in German terms. So, for the American tourist who insists on thinking in terms of U.S. dollars, the quote given by the German trader in German terms implies $0.40/DM in American terms. Now we can see how our tourist's initial question, "What is the price of marks?" is imprecise unless he specifies the currency "against" which he wants the quotation. We have just used the word "against" to indicate the other currency involved in the quotation. This very vividly states the fact that it is impossible to buy one currency without selling another. "Against" says, in a very literal sense of the word, that the opposite transaction (buy versus sell) is being quoted for each currency.

The correct complete question for our tourist to ask, then, would be, "What is the price of German marks against U.S. dollars?" Then, one should also specify what "terms" one wants. Does one want the price expressed in German terms or in American terms? When the German trader answered 2.50, the tourist assumed that the desired price was against U.S. dollars; that is, he was looking at his dollar-denominated traveler's checks. Since no special terms were requested, the trader gave the quote in the terms most familiar to him—in German terms.

Let's take as another example the American businesswoman who sits on the Champs-Elysées with a French newspaper and tries to find out what has happened to the German mark since she left the United States. She finds that the price of German marks in the newspaper is 1.75. When she left Chicago, the German mark was near 0.40. Her immediate reaction is one of bafflement; could the German mark have moved up that much from 0.40 to 1.75 during her brief vacation? After the initial shock, the search for potential explanations reminds her that 1.75 is the amount of French francs required to buy one German mark. The French newspaper expresses the price of foreign currency, like any other good in France, in terms of French francs; that is, it quotes foreign currency in French terms. The quote for German marks which the businesswoman remembers from the United States, 0.40, is a quote given in American terms, $/DM. The newspaper also carries the price of U.S. dollars at FF4.00/$, again in French terms.

The businesswoman is interested in translating today's quote for German marks from French terms into American terms so that she can compare the figure with the $0.40/DM that she remembers. As discussed previously, to change the terms in a quote, one just takes the reciprocal of the rates. Thus, we can say the following:

French terms	American terms	German terms
FF4.00/$	$0.25/FF	
FF1.75/DM		DM0.57/FF

The figures given under American terms and German terms are the *reciprocal rates* of the rates given in French terms. However, we still do not have a rate of German marks in American terms, i.e., $/DM, which we can compare with the rate $0.40/DM which the businesswoman remembers. But, from the previous calculations of reciprocal rates, we know the following:

$$1 \text{ FF} = \$0.25/\text{FF} = \text{DM0.57/FF}$$

or

$$\$0.25 = \text{DM0.57}$$

If we want to find the price of one mark, we solve for DM:

$$\text{DM} = \frac{\$0.25}{0.57} = \$0.44/\text{DM}$$

So, the German mark has gone up about 10 percent ($0.04) against the U.S. dollar since our businesswoman left home. The $/DM rate derived from the other two rates given by the French newspaper, FF/$ and FF/DM, is called a "cross rate."[5]

The system of quoting foreign exchange rates just discussed is called the "price quotation system." Under this system, prices are quoted in local currency for an even amount such as 1, 100, or 1000 units of foreign currency, e.g., $25 per 100 French francs. The even foreign currency amount remains unchanged, and the rate fluctuations are reflected in changes in the price in local currency per unit size of foreign currency.

The British, however, do not have the price quotation system; instead, they use the "volume quotation system." In this system the even unit which does not change is one pound sterling, and the value of foreign currencies is expressed through the amount (volume) of a given foreign currency that is required to purchase one pound sterling. For example, assume the rate for U.S. dollars against pound sterling is $2.40 per pound. In the United States this represents a price quotation because the value of an even amount of foreign currency, such as one pound sterling, is expressed in local currency, as US$2.40. However, in London an even amount of local currency, such as one pound sterling, is equal to a variable amount of foreign currency, that is, US$2.40. If this rate moves from $2.40 to $2.30 per pound, people in the United States will say, "The pound went down," because the value of the pound decreased from US$2.40 to US$2.30. At the same time people in England will say, "The dollar went up," because it now takes only US$2.30 to purchase one pound.

Let's clarify the distinction between the two quotation systems through an example from the supermarket. The price for tomatoes may be 28 cents per pound one day, or 4 pounds for US$1 another day. The first price is a price quotation because changes in the price would be indicated by an increase or decrease in the 28 cents. The price of 4 pounds per US$1 is clearly a volume quotation because, if the price were to change, for example by increasing 25 percent, the volume would move to 3 pounds per dollar. (See Exhibit 2.6.)

Before the U.S. dollar moved into its position as the most frequently used currency for international trade, this position was held by the pound sterling. It is probably for that reason that the British adopted the volume quotation system. This system expresses rates in terms that are readily understood by local traders outside England. Because of the prominence

[5] See Chap. 4, p. 69.

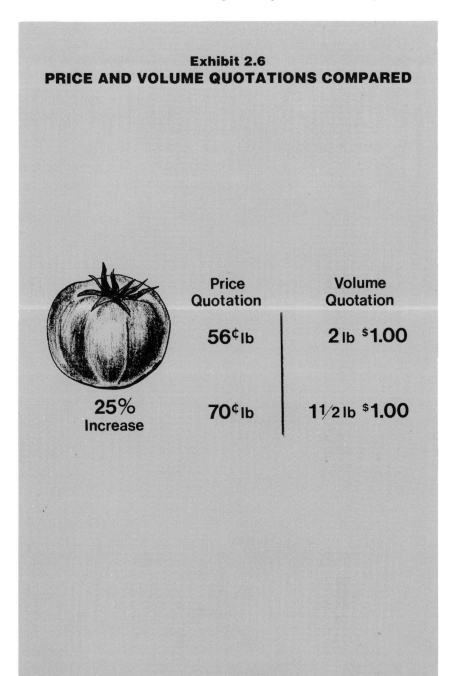

Exhibit 2.6
PRICE AND VOLUME QUOTATIONS COMPARED

	Price Quotation	Volume Quotation
	56¢ lb	2 lb $1.00
25% Increase	70¢ lb	1½ lb $1.00

of the U.S. dollar in the world today, it would probably be desirable for the United States to adopt the volume quotation system for the same reason. The professionals in the international departments of large banks and in the treasury departments of multinational companies already follow the major European currencies in European terms, that is, in volume quotations in the United States. The reason is convenience in using information in the form in which it is provided by the subsidiaries and representatives in Europe, where most of the action for these currencies occurs.

At this point, it is important to warn the reader to try to avoid the term "buy" in the context of the foreign exchange market and, instead, to use "purchase." Thus, one can avoid potential confusion with the loose manner in which the term "buy" has been used by banks, as described in the previous section.

CHAPTER 3
The funds manager and the interaction between money and foreign exchange markets

The problems and opportunities of each participant in the money and foreign exchange markets are all present in the operations of the funds manager. The objective of this individual is to manage the cash flows in various currencies in the most efficient and profitable way. The management of cash flows involves making sure that payments are made when due, and that funds received are invested at the highest possible return. When dealing in international markets, the funds manager also must maintain the appropriate positions in various currencies. The desired position in each currency depends on the currencies of the cash flows involved as well as on the manager's view of their future values.

The funds manager often has to operate within constraints imposed elsewhere in the organization, e.g., a loan payment, while trying to reach a goal of maximizing profits on excess funds or minimizing costs on borrowed funds. In this chapter we shall see how funds managers perform their duties by operating through the money and/or foreign exchange markets. To facilitate the initial presentation, we shall continue to avoid getting involved in discussions of the realities of bid and offer rates and talk only about "the rate" in each market. "The rate" can be thought of as the midpoint between bid and offer rates.

The nature of cash flows

Cash flows are the raw material with which funds managers work. This raw material has certain characteristics which determine the possibilities that are open to the manager. Some of these characteristics are implied by the name "cash flow."

Cash. The stock in trade is money, whether its denomination is U.S. dollars, yen, Turkish liras, or some other currency. However, the cash management will involve the funds manager in the handling of near-cash items as well, such as Treasury bills.

Flow. Our direct concern is not with what the exact stock of funds is at any precise time. Our real concern is with the *flow* that is generated as cash balances increase or decrease. Obviously, there is a relationship between stocks and flows. Flows are the changes which take place in the inventory of stocks from one point in time to another. Still, we must keep in mind that when we are talking about funds management, the direct object to be managed is the *flow*.

Other characteristics of the cash flows are necessary to define clearly the nature of cash flows. They are direction, currency, time, and location.

Direction. Cash flows can be inflows or outflows. The intrinsic nature of a cash flow involves both an inflow and an outflow, though not necessarily at the same point in time. We can relate the meanings of inflows and outflows to the traditional concepts of a balance sheet in the following manner:

Inflow

Increase in liability, e.g., borrowings

Decrease in an asset, e.g., conversion of a noncash asset into cash

Outflow

Decrease in a liability with its payment

Increase in assets, e.g., acquisition of assets with cash

Specific examples for financial and nonfinancial businesses are as follows:

Commercial bank	*Nonfinancial business*
Inflows	
Receipt of a deposit from a customer	Receipt of proceeds from borrowings

Receipt of payment of a loan previously granted to customer	Collection of an account receivable
Termination of a deposit with another bank	Termination of a deposit with a bank

Outflows

Withdrawal of a deposit by a customer	Repayment of borrowings
Granting of a loan to a customer	Payment of account payable
Deposit of excess funds with another bank	Deposit of excess funds with a bank

Currency. This factor is self-explanatory. The problems of dealing in various currencies simultaneously will be explained further when we discuss the operations of the funds manager in the foreign exchange markets.

Time. The identification of a cash flow requires the specification of dates. For example, as a result of borrowings made, we will receive funds (a cash inflow) in Swiss francs in two business days, June 30 (in a so-called spot transaction); they will be payable (a cash outflow) thirty days later, July 30. The specific terminology describing these dates is the term "value date." In this example we could say that the Swiss franc inflow is the result of a borrowing with value date June 30, and maturing (producing an outflow) on value date July 30.

Location. One more characteristic which identifies a cash flow is the place where it is to occur. This place is usually identified in terms of the name of an institution in a given country. For example, we can say that we will have a cash inflow in Swiss francs, value date Friday, to take place in The Union Bank of Switzerland in Zurich. The bank and the city have probably been previously arranged with the party making the payment.

We can visualize the job of a funds manager as that of keeping a set of boxes properly organized. The boxes in each case contain four major identifying characteristics:

1. Currency

2. Date

3. Balance of outflows against inflows

4. Location

Going back to the previous example where we borrowed, say, SF1 million for thirty days, we can identify the transaction in terms of our fictitious boxes as follows:

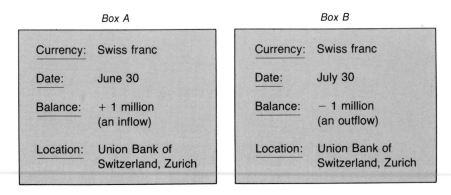

Box A   Box B

Box A		Box B	
Currency:	Swiss franc	Currency:	Swiss franc
Date:	June 30	Date:	July 30
Balance:	+ 1 million (an inflow)	Balance:	− 1 million (an outflow)
Location:	Union Bank of Switzerland, Zurich	Location:	Union Bank of Switzerland, Zurich

Box A describes the receipt of the proceeds from the borrowings. Box B specifies that the loan is payable in thirty days. The other information gives the details of how the transaction is to take place. The responsibility of the funds manager, then, is to see that the highest possible return is obtained on the cash inflows received on June 30 and to make sure that funds are available at an acceptable rate on July 30 to repay the loan.

Value dates

Because of the technicalities involved in expressing the time when a cash flow is to take place, we shall discuss in this section the concept of "value dates" in some detail. From previous discussions, we have established that there are two major time dimensions in the money and foreign exchange markets:

1. *Spot transactions* are for a value date two business days following the day when the transaction is closed.

2. *Forward transactions* are for value dates in the future, usually computed as a number of months from the spot value date at the time of the transaction.

Value dates as of "right now" are also possible; however, this would not be a genuine spot transaction, and the spot rate would not apply, in spite of semantic implications. If we deal for "value today," an adjustment of the spot rate may be necessary to reflect the interest rate differential between the two currencies involved for the two days between today and the value day for spot transactions. Before going into more detail about the application of the rules used by the market in determining "value dates," let's first establish what an eligible value date is.

Eligible value dates

To be an eligible value date, a value date must be a business day in the home countries of the currencies involved in the transaction. In a money market transaction, only one currency and, therefore, one country are involved. However, in transactions in the foreign exchange market, two currencies are involved, the one bought and the one sold; therefore, to be an eligible date, the value date must be a business day in the countries of both the currencies being traded.

Let's first look at a normal business week without holidays in Europe and the United States. On Monday, the spot value date would be Wednesday, on Tuesday it would be Thursday, on Wednesday it would be Friday, on Thursday it would be Monday, and on Friday it would be Tuesday. Whenever there are ineligible days, such as weekends, we see that it is market practice to go forward to the next eligible business day. (See Exhibit 3.1.)

Now, let's assume that Wednesday is a holiday in England. All international money market transactions in sterling on Monday would be for value Thursday because Wednesday is a holiday. Likewise, exchange transactions for U.S. dollars against sterling on Monday would be for value Thursday. However, exchange transactions for U.S. dollars against continental European currencies, such as German marks or Swiss francs, on Monday would be for value Wednesday.

It is important to note that it is quite possible for business in the country in which one or both parties of the transaction are located to be closed on a settlement date. This date is still eligible as a value date as long as businesses in those countries in which the payments have to be made are legally open. Thus, in our example, individuals in England can deal U.S. dollars against continental European currencies on Monday for value Wednesday. The fact that the English financial institutions are not open

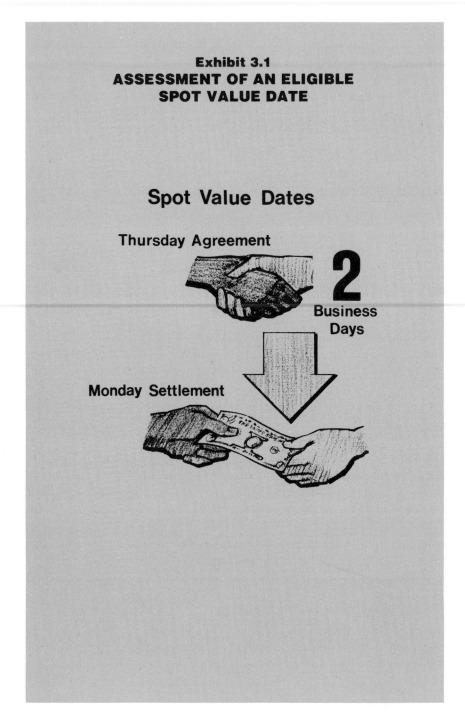

Exhibit 3.1
ASSESSMENT OF AN ELIGIBLE
SPOT VALUE DATE

Spot Value Dates

Thursday Agreement

2 Business Days

Monday Settlement

for business on Wednesday does not interfere with the settlement of U.S. dollars and continental European currencies on that day.

Let's look at the details of the funds transfer to see how the rule of eligible value dates and holidays works. When a British company sells spot German marks against U.S. dollars to a British bank on Monday, the value date will be Wednesday, even though that day is a holiday in England. On Wednesday, the ownership of German marks will be effectively transferred from the British company to the British bank, and the ownership of U.S. dollars will be transferred from the British bank to the British company. Now, where is this done? Not in England. The transfers will be made in Germany and in the United States. Assuming no other financial intermediary, the British company will instruct its German bank to transfer funds out of its account and into the British bank's account in Germany. Similarly, the bank will instruct its American bank to transfer dollars out of its account into the British company's account in the United States.[1] Since, in our example, Wednesday is a holiday in neither the United States nor Germany, Wednesday is an eligible value date for transactions involving marks and dollars. In our example, the British company will gain ownership of dollars and lose ownership of marks on Wednesday even though the company is not open for business on that day. The transfer is done by other parties outside England.

Spot value dates

As discussed previously, the standard spot value date is two business days following the day on which the transaction has been closed. The reasons for this custom are of a practical and administrative nature.

The exchange and money market business is a global business, and, as such, it must overcome time differences of up to twelve hours. Therefore, a standard spot value date of either the same day (today) or the following business day (usually tomorrow) would not be practical. In addition, time must be allowed to process properly all the paper work involved. Banks executing the transfer of funds must be allowed time to check important details, such as

[1] It is possible that the banks involved are Euro-banks and that a bank in the home country of the currency is not involved. For example, Eurodollars are deposited with a French bank. However, this Euro-bank must be given the opportunity to react to the transaction initiated in this example by the two British entities. For this Euro-bank to be able to react, it must have access to the banking system of the home country of the currency—in this case the United States. So, whether the home country for the given currency is open for business or not is the determinant of whether a given date is an eligible value date.

1. The name of the other party to the transaction

2. Whether the specific currency is being purchased or sold

3. The amount involved

4. The location where the money purchased is wanted

5. The location where the other party wants the money it purchased

6. The rate for this transaction

7. The value date

If only one of the above details is incorrect and the error is not discovered in time, it could be very costly to one or both of the parties to the transaction.

Forward value dates

Forward value dates for money market and foreign exchange transactions are usually for one month, or a multiple thereof. It is, of course, possible to deal for any specific value date in the future, but if it does not indicate a number of full months, then it is considered an odd date, and it requires special attention.

The forward value dates for a certain number of months in the future are determined as follows: We first find out what the proper spot value date is for the specific currency in the money market or currencies in the foreign exchange market. Then we add the respective number of calendar months to that spot value date and arrive at the forward value date. For example, if the spot value date is July 10, then the one-month forward value date would be August 10. The two-month forward value date would be September 10, and so on. Note that it is always a full calendar month, regardless of whether that particular month has 28, 29, 30, or 31 days.

Let's consider the example where the one-month forward value date was August 10. If August 10 is not an eligible day, then it is market practice to go forward to August 11, August 12, or a later date until one finds an eligible business day. There is one exception to this rule. If we add one or more full calendar months to the spot value date and find that the forward date is not eligible and that the process of going forward to the next eligible value date carries us over into the next month, then the rule of going forward to the next eligible date does not apply. Instead, we have to go backward until we hit the first eligible date.

Exhibit 3.2
ASSESSMENT OF ELIGIBLE
FORWARD VALUE DATES

Forward Value Dates

Spot Value	Today Date	Friday	Nov. 25, 1977
		Tuesday	Nov. 29, 1977

Value Dates ————————————————

1 Mo	Thursday	Dec. 29, 1977
2 Mo	Monday	Jan. 30, 1978
3 Mo	Tuesday	Feb. 28, 1978

Exhibit 3.2 shows how forward value dates should be determined. The spot value date is November 29, 1977. The one-month forward value date is simply one month later: Thursday, December 29, 1977. A two-month value date would be Sunday, January 29, 1978, which is obviously not eligible; therefore, we move forward to Monday, January 30. The three-month value date would be February 29, but there is no February 29 in 1978. Moving forward would get us to Wednesday, March 1, 1978, which takes us into a new month. Therefore, we have to go backwards and determine Tuesday, February 28, as the proper three-month value date.

The application of this value date system tends to produce an accumulation of rollovers at month-end. For example, a five-year revolving term loan, where the interest rate is being reestablished every three months, consists of 20 interest periods of three months each. Over the years, the forward dates of interest periods will fall on weekends and holidays and thus move closer and closer to the end of the month. Application of the standard rule makes it impossible to go over from one month into a new one. The resulting accumulation of value dates before the end of a month, however, has disadvantages from operational and economic viewpoints. Interest rates tend to be slightly higher before the end of the month, and the uneven distribution of the rollover workload is undesirable. In such a case, it is recommended that both participants discuss the matter and establish one odd interest period (less than a calendar month) with a maturity at the beginning of a month. Thereafter, the rule can again be applied.

Interactions between the money and foreign exchange markets

Suppose that we work in a commercial bank, and that we are told that on value Monday, June 30, the following flows will take place:

1. A three-month deposit in pound sterling in the amount of £1 million will be received.

2. A loan in U.S. dollars in the amount of $2.4 million will be made with a three-month maturity.

We can translate this information in terms of "boxes" (omitting the details of location), as shown in Exhibit 3.3.

Exhibit 3.3
CASH FLOWS IN A BANK:
A POUND DEPOSIT AND A DOLLAR LOAN

Box A

Currency:	Pound sterling
Date:	June 30
Balance:	+ £1 million (inflow from deposit)

Box B

Currency:	U.S. dollars
Date:	June 30
Balance:	− $2.4 million (outflow from loan granted)

Box C

Currency:	Pound sterling
Date:	September 30
Balance:	− £1 million plus interest (outflow from termination of deposit)

Box D

Currency:	U.S. dollars
Date:	September 30
Balance:	+ $2.4 million plus interest (inflow from repayment of loan)

Boxes A and C describe the transaction in pounds sterling. On June 30 we receive the inflow of £1 million (Box A) which is due (becomes an outflow) on September 30 together with the interest due (Box C). Box B describes the outflow on June 30 when we pay $2.4 million because of the transactions originated elsewhere, say, a loan to a customer. Box D shows the termination of that transaction when the loan is paid back together with the interest earned. Notice that the inflow at the present time is accompanied by an outflow some time in the future, and vice versa. Had we been told only that a payment of $2.4 million was required on Monday, June 30, we would have to ask for additional information: either, "When is that money coming back?" (if we are starting from point zero), or, "When did we acquire these funds which we have to return now?" (if the transaction was initiated in the past).

The funds manager, when informed of the cash flows generated by the transactions on June 30, has a specific function that can be defined as having two objectives:

1. Making sure that no idle funds are maintained, and that all payments are made on time. In this case, the funds manager must:
   a. Place for three months the proceeds from the deposit in pounds sterling. On September 30, the proceeds from the placement will be available to pay for the redemption of the initial deposit.
   b. Borrow dollar funds for three months to extend the loan. When the loan is repaid on September 30, the cash thus obtained can be used to repay the initial borrowings.
2. Accomplishing the above at the most profitable terms possible, given risk constraints.

When the funds manager meets the first objective, the balances in each of the boxes will be zero except for net profits. The inflows will roughly equal outflows in every currency for every date. The funds manager can achieve these objectives by operating in either the money market or the foreign exchange market.

Operating in the money market

If the funds manager chooses to operate in the money market, each box will have to be balanced within the same market. That is, the proceeds of the pounds deposit will be invested in pounds, and the payment of dollars

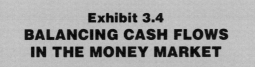

Exhibit 3.4
BALANCING CASH FLOWS
IN THE MONEY MARKET

Box A

Currency:	Pound sterling
Date:	June 30
Balance:	+ £1 million (inflow from deposit) − £1 million (outflow from placement of funds)
Net cash flow	∅

Box B

Currency:	U.S. dollar
Date:	June 30
Balance:	− $2.4 million (outflow from loan granted) + $2.4 million (inflow from borrowings)
Net cash flow	∅

Box C

Currency:	Pound sterling
Date:	September 30
Balance:	− £1 million plus interest (outflow from termination of deposit) + £1 million plus 13% interest (inflow from termination of placement made on June 30)
Net cash flow	∅

Box D

Currency:	U.S. dollar
Date:	September 30
Balance:	+ $2.4 million plus interest (inflow from repayment of loan) − $2.4 million plus 10% interest (repayment of borrowing made on June 30)
Net cash flow	∅

will be met with borrowings made in dollars. Accordingly, the four boxes will now look like the ones in Exhibit 3.4.

These boxes show that at least one of the objectives of the funds manager has been met. The objective to balance the cash flows in each box has been achieved by making inflows roughly equal to outflows for each box. The initial inflow in pounds in Box A was offset by investing (placing) these pounds in the pound sterling money market. The outflow in Box B was met by borrowing in the U.S. dollar money market. As to the two boxes for September 30, the maturity of the placement made on June 30 was designed to match the maturity of the deposit in pounds. Likewise, the maturity of the U.S. dollar borrowings was designed to coincide with the inflow resulting from the loan made earlier, on June 30. Therefore, all cash flows are properly matched. The funds manager has no risk of being unable to meet a required outflow or of having to leave acquired funds idle for any period of time.

What about the second objective of the funds manager: profitability? Extracting from the profitability of the transactions which initiated the example, the loan and the deposit, the profitability of the transactions initiated by the funds manager is measured by the interest differential between the return received on the placement of the pounds and the interest paid on the borrowing of U.S. dollars. Assuming that the interest rate received for pounds is 13 percent, and that the interest rate paid for U.S. dollars is 10 percent, the funds manager has achieved the two cash flow objectives while making a 3 percent profit.

Operating in the foreign exchange market

Continuing with our example, we are dealing with two currencies: pounds sterling and U.S. dollars. If we deal in the foreign exchange market, we shall be dealing in one of these currencies against the other, i.e., purchasing U.S. dollars against pounds sterling. As in the money market, we can deal for a future date. In our example, we can deal either for June 30 or September 30.

The initial situation produces an inflow in pounds sterling and an outflow in U.S. dollars. At an exchange rate of $2.40/£, the amount of the inflow and the outflow are equivalent (£1 million equals $2.4 million). To achieve the cash flow objectives of the funds manager (to have a zero net cash flow in each box), we shall have to produce the following:

Boxes A and B. Initially, we have an inflow of pounds and an outflow of dollars for June 30. To compensate for these flows, we have to sell pounds

Exhibit 3.5
BALANCING CASH FLOWS IN THE FOREIGN EXCHANGE MARKET

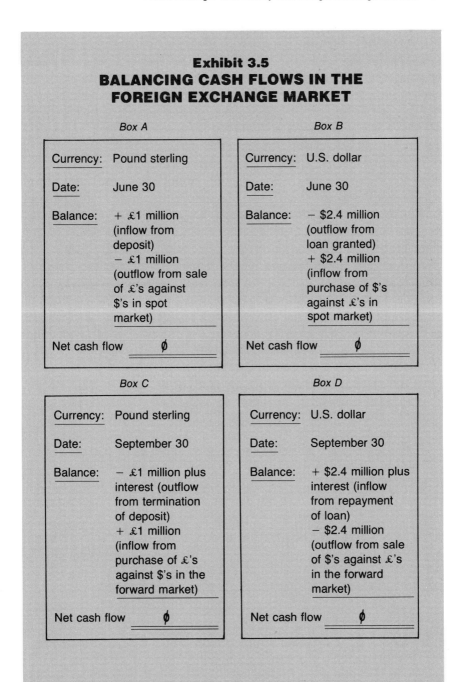

Box A

Currency:	Pound sterling
Date:	June 30
Balance:	+ £1 million (inflow from deposit) − £1 million (outflow from sale of £'s against $'s in spot market)
Net cash flow	∅

Box B

Currency:	U.S. dollar
Date:	June 30
Balance:	− $2.4 million (outflow from loan granted) + $2.4 million (inflow from purchase of $'s against £'s in spot market)
Net cash flow	∅

Box C

Currency:	Pound sterling
Date:	September 30
Balance:	− £1 million plus interest (outflow from termination of deposit) + £1 million (inflow from purchase of £'s against $'s in the forward market)
Net cash flow	∅

Box D

Currency:	U.S. dollar
Date:	September 30
Balance:	+ $2.4 million plus interest (inflow from repayment of loan) − $2.4 million (outflow from sale of $'s against £'s in the forward market)
Net cash flow	∅

(an outflow) against U.S. dollars (acquisition of dollars is an inflow) for value date June 30 in the *spot market.* (Today is June 28.)

Boxes C and D. Initially, we have an outflow in pounds and an inflow in dollars for September 30. To compensate for these flows, we have to purchase pounds (an inflow) against U.S. dollars (sale of dollars is an outflow), value date September 30 in the *forward market.* (We are transacting on June 28 for delivery three months later.)

Let's see how each of the four boxes shows zero net cash flow when we follow the steps indicated. This is seen in Exhibit 3.5. These boxes prove visually that the funds manager has accomplished the first objective: to obtain a net zero cash flow for each box except for profits. However, the previous boxes do not indicate whether the funds manager achieved the profitability objective. We know that if the money market route is followed, the cash flow objective can be achieved at a 3 percent profit. Intuitively, we can say that the foreign exchange approach should yield the same result. (This relationship is explained further in the last section of this chapter.) Then, there must be some relationship between the spot rate and the forward rate which makes for a 3 percent return on the transaction. As we remember, we are:

> *In the spot market:* selling pounds against U.S. dollars

> *In the forward market:* purchasing pounds against U.S. dollars

If we speak in terms of pounds, the sale price in the spot market must be higher than in the forward market; specifically, the price of the pound in the spot market must be 3 percent p.a. above the forward price. In other words, the pound in the forward market must be at a 3 percent discount against the U.S. dollar from the spot rate.

What is the price of the three-month pound in terms of U.S. dollars? Let's continue on an intuitive basis; afterward, we can provide a generalized formula. Earlier, we said that the *spot rate* of the pound against the U.S. dollar is $2.40/£.

> We know that 1 percent of 2.40 is .0240

> However, we wish to know what 3 percent is;
>   So, if 1 percent is .0240, then 3 percent is (3 × .0240) .0720

> As we explained in Chapter 2, these percentages are based on a per annum base; they apply to a twelve-month period.

If we wish to know the amount which corresponds to one month, we would multiply the above numbers by 1/12; if we wish to know the amount which corresponds to three months, we would multiply the above numbers by 3/12.

Therefore, 3 percent of 2.40 for three months is

$$(.0720 \times 3/12) = .0180$$

What we have just done is convert an interest differential (3 percent p.a.) into an exchange rate differential ($0.0180/£). The formula for converting interest differentials into exchange rate differentials is, in generalized terms:

$$\frac{\text{Spot rate} \times \text{interest rate differential} \times \text{time}^2}{100 \times \text{time}}$$

In terms of our example, it is:

$$\frac{2.4000 \times 3 \times 3}{100 \times 12} = \frac{21.6}{1200} = 0.0180$$

We determined that the exchange rate differential between the spot rate and the three-month forward rate for the pound against the U.S. dollar must be 0.0180. This figure (0.0180) is called the *swap rate,* and we shall discuss it at some length in future chapters. To determine the actual rate for the three-month pound against the U.S. dollar, we subtract (the forward pound is selling at a discount) the swap rate from the spot rate:

Spot rate	$2.4000/£
Swap rate	−0.0180
Three-month forward rate	$2.3820/£

Thus, if the foreign exchange market approach to the funds manager's problems yields the same rate of profit as the money market approach, 3 percent, the forward transactions shown in Box C and Box D before

---

[2] Obviously, the time factor can be expressed in days, weeks, or months as the case may be. The denominator would be 360/365, 52, or 12 respectively, and the numerator would be equal to the number of days, weeks, or months in the specific situation.

(three-month purchase of pounds against U.S. dollars or sale of U.S. dollars against pounds) will be done at the forward rate of $2.3820.

Let's make sure that, if we deal at a forward rate of $2.3820/£ for three-month delivery, we are making a 3 percent return. To do that, we have to develop another formula, this time the conversion of an exchange rate differential ($0.0180/£) into an interest rate differential (3 percent p.a.). We know that we are making $0.0180 every three months. Since we are interested in a per annum rate, .0180 every three months is the same as .0720 every year (4 × .0180). If we are making $.0720/£ per year, what percentage is this of the spot rate, $2.40/£? It is 3 percent p.a. = [(.0720 ÷ 2.40) × 100].

The formula for converting an exchange rate differential into an interest rate differential is, in general terms,

$$\frac{\text{Swap rate} \times 100 \times \text{time}[3]}{\text{Spot rate} \times \text{time}}$$

or, for our example,

$$\frac{0.0180 \times 100 \times 12}{2.4000 \times 3} = 3 \text{ percent p.a.}$$

This formula converts the swap rate—the difference between the spot and forward rates—into a percentage of the spot rate. It also adjusts it for the number of months that the rate applies if that number of months is other than twelve, a year; i.e., if it is other than a per annum rate.

Money market or foreign exchange market

In the previous two sections we have described the relationships which must exist between the money market and the foreign exchange markets. If these relationships are present (in our example, a 3 percent p.a. interest differential in favor of the pound exists together with a 3 percent p.a. discount on the three-month forward pound), and if the only concern is profitability, both approaches would produce the same results, a 3 percent p.a. return.

---

[3] The swap rate (exchange rate differential) is derived by subtracting the forward rate from the spot rate in case of a discount, and by subtracting the spot rate from the forward rate in case of a premium. Thus, the formula to compute forward premiums or discounts is often expressed as:

$$\frac{\text{Forward rate} - \text{spot rate}}{\text{Spot rate}} \times \frac{12}{\text{no. of months forward}} \times 100$$

What would happen if the previous relationships do not prevail in the markets? Let's say the following rates exist:

Money Market, Three-Months Maturity

Pound sterling	13%
U.S. dollar	10%

Foreign Exchange Market

Three-month forward pound = 2.5% discount against U.S. dollar

That is, the discount in the foreign exchange market is less than the interest differential. In this case, the funds manager will do better to follow the money market route than the foreign exchange market approach. The exchange approach would still produce the desired cash flows, but the return would be only 2 ½ percent p.a. as compared with the 3 percent p.a. available via the money market approach.

How long is this situation likely to prevail? Briefly, as long as a competitive market exists. There are two reasons for the fast adjustment. First, funds managers and their colleagues will be borrowing U.S. dollars and investing in pounds more heavily than usual. This will tend to increase interest rates on the U.S. dollar and decrease them on pound sterling. These two forces combined will tend to narrow the interest differential between the pound and the U.S. dollar. Second, more important than the actions of our funds managers is the behavior of independent individuals who may want to profit from this situation of disequilibrium.

How does one profit from this situation of disequilibrium? Just by simple inspection, it makes sense to go ahead and borrow U.S. dollars and invest in pounds. The interest differentials alone provide a 3 percent return. The cash flow boxes for the individual who decides to take advantage of the interest differentials appear in Exhibit 3.6.

Three of the cash flow boxes meet the cash flow objectives. But Box D has an unknown net cash flow. The reason for this uncertainty is the fact that as of June 30 we do not know what the spot rate of pounds against U.S. dollars will be on September 30. If the spot rate continues at $2.40/£, the net cash flow for Box D will be zero, and the investor will realize a 3 percent p.a. return—the difference between borrowing dollars at 10 percent and investing in pounds at 13 percent. However, if the pound devalues between June 30 and September 30, we will receive less than the $2.4 million plus interest that we need to repay the dollar borrowing

Exhibit 3.6
CASH FLOWS ON INTEREST ARBITRAGE

RATE SCENARIO

Money Market, Three-Months Maturity

Pound sterling   13%

U.S. dollar   10%

Foreign Exchange Market

Three-month forward pound = 2.5% discount against U.S. dollar

CASH FLOWS

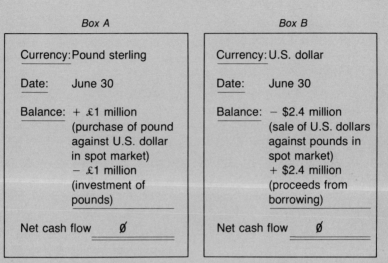

Box A

Currency: Pound sterling

Date: June 30

Balance: + £1 million
         (purchase of pound
         against U.S. dollar
         in spot market)
         − £1 million
         (investment of
         pounds)

Net cash flow   Ø

Box B

Currency: U.S. dollar

Date: June 30

Balance: − $2.4 million
          (sale of U.S. dollars
          against pounds in
          spot market)
          + $2.4 million
          (proceeds from
          borrowing)

Net cash flow   Ø

Box C

Currency: Pound sterling

Date: September 30

Balance: − £1 million
          (sale of pounds
          against U.S.
          dollars on Sept. 30
          in spot market)
          + £1 million plus
          13% interest
          (pound invest-
          ment matures)

Net cash flow   Ø

Box D

Currency: U.S. dollar

Date: September 30

Balance: + $2.4 (?) million
          (purchase of U.S.
          dollars against
          pound on Sept. 30
          spot market)
          − $2.4 million plus
          10% interest
          (borrowings are
          repaid)

Net cash flow   ?

which matures on that date. Under these conditions, the exchange loss which one may realize in reconverting the pounds into U.S. dollars at the end of the period will likely be large enough to more than compensate any interest differential in favor of the pound which existed as of June 30.

Notice that the foreign exchange risks in this last example were not present in the examples about the funds manager. The funds manager had a use already prepared for the proceeds from the pound investment (when following the money market approach) or the pounds purchased forward (when following the foreign exchange approach) for delivery on September 30: to repay the client's deposit. The funds manager also had a source of funds envisaged for the payment of the U.S. dollar borrowings (when following the money market approach) or the dollars sold forward (when following the foreign exchange approach) for delivery on September 30: the proceeds from the repayment of a loan granted to a customer. That is, the rate on the forward cash flows was locked in from the beginning on June 30. In the last example, where we are just taking advantage of the interest differentials, we have to wait until September 30 to find out what the prevailing spot rate of the pound against the U.S. dollar will be at the time to determine whether the dollar proceeds from the sale of pounds are sufficient to repay the loan.

In the earlier example, the funds manager had a *square position* in each currency for each date. From the beginning, June 30, the manager had arranged outflows to match the initial spot and forward inflows. In the last example, where we are trying to take advantage of a disparity between the money market and the foreign exchange market as of June 30, we have a *net exchange position*. We are *long in pounds* (net overbought) and *short in dollars* (net oversold) for September 30. We know that on that date there will be an inflow of pounds for which we have not yet contracted a matching outflow. We also know that we will have to repay dollar borrowings on September 30, and, as yet, we have not contracted a matching inflow of funds. Whenever a net exchange position exists, we are vulnerable to changes in the spot rate of the currencies involved. In this specific case, if the spot rate of the pound depreciates against the dollar (or the dollar appreciated against the pound), we shall lose money. On the other hand, were the pound to appreciate against the dollar, gains would materialize. We can say that a funds manager who allows net positions to develop has assessed to that extent, implicitly or explicitly, the future development of the spot rates. Any change in these rates will affect the profitability of the operation.

Since we shall be using the term *net exchange position* repeatedly, we want to provide a formal definition at this point. Net position in a given currency is the difference between all assets and liabilities plus the difference between all unliquidated exchange purchases and sales of that currency. The net of these numbers is the net position for that currency. If the spot rate for that currency appreciates, the position will generate profits if it was positive, i.e., a long position; the position will generate losses if it was negative, a short position.

Now, can one benefit from the situation of disequilibrium between the money market and the foreign exchange market *without* assuming a *net position*, i.e., without waiting until September 30 to find out what spot rates prevail on that date? Yes, by using the forward exchange market. That is, we use the same approach as the funds manager used when managing the cash flows: we arrange the precise size and timing of future cash flows beforehand so that the differentials in prices and interest rates will be profitable to us. The process is called "covered interest arbitrage."[4]

More specifically, on June 30 we fix the price at which pounds will be converted into U.S. dollars on September 30. This can be done by selling pounds against U.S. dollars for three-month delivery. We know from the data in the example that we shall have to take a 2.5 percent discount on the sale of the pound against the dollar, if we enter into a three-month forward contract on June 30. However, the 2.5 percent discount is less than the 3 percent interest differential which we will realize from the difference between borrowing and placing rates. That is, we are .5 percent ahead without incurring any foreign exchange risk. In other words, we borrow U.S. dollars at 10 percent and "swap them into pounds" (purchase spot pounds against dollars and sell three-month pounds against dollars) at a cost of 2½ percent. This generates fully covered pounds at 12½ percent (10 percent interest cost for borrowing dollars and 2½ percent exchange loss for the swap cost) which can be invested at 13 percent. This transaction is an example of covered interest arbitrage.

Covered interest arbitrage will contribute to making the disequilibrium situation short-lived. Individuals engaged in arbitraging the initial disequilibrium will not only do the same thing as the funds manager, that is, borrow U.S. dollars and invest in pounds; but, in addition, they will put additional pressures on the exchange markets. In the spot market the price of pounds will tend to appreciate against U.S. dollars because of the

---

[4] See also Chap. 7, pp. 125–134.

increased purchase of pounds, and in the forward market the price of pounds will tend to depreciate against the U.S. dollar because of the increased sales of pounds for three-month delivery. In terms of pounds, an upward pressure on the spot price and a downward pressure on the forward price combine to produce an increase in the discount (widening of the swap rate) of the forward pound against the U.S. dollar. These pressures will continue until the discount on the forward pound equals the interest differential, 3 percent.[5]

From the above discussion, we can derive a few rules of thumb.

1. The annualized premiums and discounts in the forward exchange market are equal to the *net accessible interest differential* between the two currencies involved. In the previous discussion we assumed that this was the case. Net accessible interest rates are usually only available in the external money markets. Domestic interest rates are usually either not net (they are subject to reserve requirements, interest withholding taxes, etc.) or not accessible (foreign capital inflow/outflow controls, banking regulations, etc.).[6]

2. a. The currency with the higher interest rate will sell at a discount in the forward market against the currency with the lower interest rate.

   b. The currency with the lower interest rate will sell at a premium in the forward market against the currency with the higher interest rate. (See Exhibit 3.7.)

3. If the interest differential in favor of a given currency is *higher* than the discount in the forward market on that currency, then there is an incentive to invest funds in the high interest rate currency and to cover the investment in the forward market. The gain from interest differential is larger than the discount on the high-interest currency. This is the case discussed earlier.

4. If the interest differential in favor of a given currency is *lower* than the discount in the forward market on that currency, then there is an incentive to invest funds in the low-interest currency and to cover the investment in the forward market. The loss in interest differentials is more than compensated for by the premium on the low-interest currency.

---

[5] See also Exhibit 7.4.

[6] Take, for example, the forward exchange rate of the pound against the U.S. dollar, which in the past was based on the interest differential between *Euro*sterling and *Euro*dollars rather than domestic pounds and domestic dollars. The reason is that domestic U.S. dollar rates were not *net* (there was an additional cost for reserve requirements), and domestic sterling rates were not *accessible* (there were capital outflow controls). For other influences on and adjustments of net rates, see also Chap. 5, pp. 97–99.

Exhibit 3.7
INTEREST DIFFERENTIALS A FOREIGN EXCHANGE MARKET

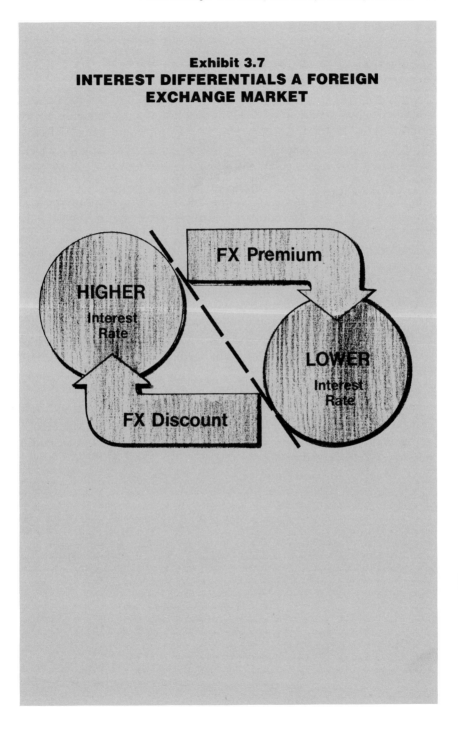

5. A forward exchange rate can move for two reasons:
   a. It may just be following the spot rate.
   b. Because of changes in interest rates, the swap rate may have changed.

Some economic developments may have a pronounced impact on a currency's spot exchange rate and almost no impact on that currency's interest rates. A good example would be an announcement of foreign trade figures which could be very much better or worse than market participants had expected. If the British trade figures are interpreted very positively in the marketplace, the spot rate for sterling might rise from 2.40 to 2.41. If there are no simultaneous changes in interest rates for Eurosterling and Eurodollars, then the swap rate of, for example, .0200 discount on sterling, will remain unchanged. This forces the forward rate also to move up from 2.38 to 2.39. This is an obvious example of a situation where the forward rate has followed a movement in the spot rate.

If the Bank of England were to reduce drastically the interest rate for sterling, which would probably also cause a reduction of the Eurosterling interest rate, then the assumed swap rate (discount on sterling) might be reduced from .0200 to .0100. A substantial decline in interest rates usually also puts pressure on a currency's spot exchange rate, which in our example might move from 2.4000 to 2.3950. As the swap rate is now .0100, the new forward rate will be 2.3850 (2.3950 minus .0100). In this case the forward rate clearly did not follow the spot rate. In fact, it moved in the opposite direction because the reduction in the discount on sterling was stronger than the decline of the spot rate. This situation led to an increase in the forward rate.

CHAPTER 4
Two-way markets: bid and offer rates

Now that we have established the intrinsic nature of quotations in the money market and the foreign exchange markets, and since we have seen the relationships among these markets, let's introduce the subject of two-way rates. With the exception of retail stores, such as supermarkets, which maintain fixed prices, the price which an individual pays in a market depends quite a bit on whether this person is on the buying or the selling side. One example of this situation is the person who is building a house with a two-car garage. The possibility of a teenage daughter having her own car in the near future looms almost as a certainty. As a consequence, the future house owner starts considering the possibility of enlarging the garage to hold three cars, since there is plenty of land for this. The following morning the prospective house owner calls the contractor.

House owner: I have been thinking that we might want to have a garage large enough for three cars. How much do you think that will cost?

Contractor: Oh gosh! That's the type of thing that really creates a lot of trouble. I cannot see how we can change to a three-car garage for less than $3000.

House owner: Golly, I never realized that a garage was so expensive! Perhaps, then, I should be thinking in the other direction. Usually, one of our cars is rather old, and we would not mind so much leaving it outdoors. How much do you think I could save if we built only a one-car garage?

Contractor: Well, once you have built a garage for two cars, you really do not save that much by cutting down on the two-car job. I don't think we could reduce the price by more than $2000 if you decided to eliminate the second-car space.

Anybody who makes a market for any good has to buy at a cost lower than its expected selling price in order to stay in business for any length of time. In the financial markets which we are discussing, the buying rate is referred to as the "bid rate"; the selling rate is referred to as the "offer rate" or "ask rate."

The money market

When we talk about the money market, we must distinguish between marketable securities, such as commercial paper, and the interbank money market. In the first instance, individuals and corporations, as well as banks, participate in the buying and selling. In the interbank market, as the name indicates, the transactions are restricted to members of the banking community.

Since our eventual purpose is to discuss the foreign exchange market, we shall restrict ourselves in this section to discussing the interbank rates. From the bank's point of view, these are the rates which are relevant for comparison with rates in the foreign exchange market. And, the banks are the ones who "make a market" in foreign exchange.

When a bank quotes 7 to 7¼ percent for one-month money to a calling bank, the implications are the following: First, the rates are on a per annum basis. If one should wish to compute the amount of interest payments involved on a monthly basis, one would have to multiply the 7 percent figure by 1/12 and apply the resulting interest rate figure to the amount borrowed or lent. Second, the first number, 7 percent, indicates the rate at which the quoting bank is willing to accept or borrow funds. The second rate, 7¼ percent, indicates the rate at which the quoting bank is willing to "place" or lend funds. The ¼ percent spread between the two rates represents the quoting bank's profit if the two parts of the transaction (borrowing and placement) take place at these rates. (See Exhibit 4.1.)

As explained in the previous section, when individuals and corporations deal with banks, they are only one side of the transaction. That is, they are either depositors (lenders to the bank) or borrowers. In both these cases, the rate is either predetermined or subject to negotiation.

The foreign exchange market

As in the money market, when a foreign exchange trader is asked for a quotation for a given foreign currency, the individual will answer with two numbers. The first number indicates the price at which the trader is

Exhibit 4.1
A TWO-WAY QUOTE IN THE MONEY MARKET
7.00%/7.25%

Quoting Bank	*Calling Customer*
Take 7.00%	Lend 7.00%
Lend 7.25%	Take 7.25%

willing to purchase the foreign currency in terms of local currency; the second number indicates the price at which the trader is willing to sell the foreign currency in terms of local currency.

For example, an American trader, when asked for a "two-way" quotation for the German mark against the U.S. dollar in American terms, might answer "36-37." This is a sort of shorthand expression for the quotation. When this quotation is expressed in full, it can be read as follows: Willing to purchase German marks against U.S. dollars (to sell U.S. dollars against German marks) at $0.36/DM; willing to sell German marks against U.S. dollars (to purchase U.S. dollars against German marks) at $0.37/DM. The trader has complied with the request asking for a two-way quote for German marks against U.S. dollars. By expressing the prices of German marks in terms of U.S. dollars, the trader has conformed with the request for American terms. The quotes also include the trader's desire to maintain a "spread" of $0.01/DM on the transaction.

Now let's introduce another actor: yourself. If you have listened to the quotation just given, what does it mean to you? If the *trader* is willing to *purchase* at a certain price, *you* must be willing to *sell* at that price. In the previous example, where the trader is willing to purchase German marks against U.S. dollars at $0.36/DM, you must be willing to sell German marks against U.S. dollars at that U.S. dollar price. In the same fashion, if the *trader* is willing to *sell* German marks against U.S. dollars at $0.37/DM, *you* must be willing to *purchase* German marks against U.S. dollars at that U.S. price if the transaction is to be consummated. That is, if the trader is purchasing foreign exchange against dollars (is selling dollars), the other party in the transaction must be selling the foreign exchange against U.S. dollars (purchasing U.S. dollars) and vice versa. And, since the spread is in favor of the trader, it is, by definition, against the party dealing with the trader. (See Exhibit 4.2.)

What if we had asked for the same information, a two-way quotation for the German mark against U.S. dollars, from a German trader? This individual would likely respond with numbers close to 2.70–2.77. Now we must be aware that the terms have changed[1]; the German trader will quote the price of foreign exchange (in this case, U.S. dollars) in terms of the domestic currency, German marks. Therefore, the shorthand quotation given abroad can be expanded to say: Willing to purchase U.S. dollars against German marks at DM2.70/$; willing to sell U.S. dollars against German marks at DM2.77/$. If you (the customer) wanted to sell U.S.

[1] See also Chapter 2, pp. 29–34.

Exhibit 4.2
DM QUOTE IN THE UNITED STATES:
$0.36 – $0.37

Quoting Bank

Purchase DM @ $0.36/DM

Sell DM @ $0.37/DM

Calling Customer

Sell DM @ $0.36/DM

Purchase DM @ $0.37/DM

Exhibit 4.3
U.S. DOLLAR QUOTE IN GERMANY:
DM2.70 - DM2.77

Quoting Bank	*Calling Customer*
Purchase US$ @ DM2.70/$ (sell DM)	Sell US$ @ DM2.70/$ (purchase DM)
Sell US$ @ DM2.77/$ (purchase DM)	Purchase US$ @ DM2.77/$ (sell DM)

dollars and to purchase German marks, the exchange rate would be DM2.70/$ (the price at which the trader is willing to purchase the foreign currency, US$). If you wanted to purchase U.S. dollars and sell German marks, you would have to do so at the rate of DM2.77/$ (the price at which the trader is willing to sell the foreign currency, US$). Again, you notice that the spread is always in favor of the party quoting the rate and against the party listening and dealing at a rate quoted by someone else. (See Exhibit 4.3.)

Regardless of the terms used in the quote, to arrange a match with the trader's quotation someone must do exactly the opposite of what the trader is quoting. If the trader's quote refers to purchasing dollars with German marks, then the closing of the transaction requires a party willing to sell dollars and to acquire German marks at that price. If the trader's quote refers to purchasing German marks with dollars, then the closing of the transaction requires a party willing to sell German marks and to acquire dollars at that price. And, the price will be expressed in different forms depending upon the terms in which the quote is given.

Reciprocal rates

At this point it is useful to note the relationship between the quotes given by the American trader and the German trader. When a trader says, "Willing to purchase German marks against U.S. dollars," this is equivalent to saying, "Willing to sell U.S. dollars against German marks." The American trader will use the number $0.36/DM; the German trader will use the number DM2.77/$. A summary of these relationships in the example used here is presented in Exhibit 4.4.

The relationship between the numbers used by the American and the German traders is one of reciprocity; 2.77 is approximately the reciprocal of 0.36 (1 ÷ 0.36 ≈ 2.77), and 2.70 is approximately the reciprocal of 0.37. The figures 0.36 and 2.77 are known as the *reciprocal rates* between the German mark and the U.S. dollar for the quoting trader to purchase DM and sell US$. The figures 0.37 and 2.70 are the reciprocal rates between the German mark and the U.S. dollar for the quoting trader to sell DM and purchase US$.

Cross rates

So far, we have dealt with only two currencies. Let's go back to a German trader and ask for the price of dollars against German marks. Also, let's ask a French trader for the price of dollars against French francs.

Exhibit 4.4
EXCHANGE RATES: RECIPROCAL
RELATIONSHIPS IN TWO-WAY QUOTES

QUOTES:		
In U.S.		$0.36 – $0.37
In Germany		DM2.70 – DM2.77

Quoting Bank	Calling Customer
Purchase DM @ $0.36/DM (Sell US$)	Sell DM @ $0.36/DM (Purchase US$)

or

Purchase DM @ DM2.77/$ (Sell US$)	Sell DM @ DM2.77/$ (Purchase US$)

where $\dfrac{1}{0.36} \simeq 2.77$

Sell DM @ $0.37/DM (Purchase US$)	Purchase DM @ $0.37/DM (Sell US$)

or

Sell DM @ DM2.70/$ (Purchase US$)	Purchase DM @ DM2.70/$ (Sell US$)

where $\dfrac{1}{0.37} \simeq 2.70$

German trader: DM/$ 2.8285–2.8295

French trader: FF/$ 4.5525–4.5575

However, we are actually interested in purchasing French francs against German marks. How can we carry out the desired transaction, given the above rates?

We have to find out at which rate we may sell marks, and at which rate we may purchase French francs. Each trader has quoted us rates in German and French terms respectively. Therefore, the bid and offer rates quoted give the price of a unit of foreign currency, the U.S. dollar, in these countries. Thus, if we are to use these rates, we must translate what we want to do with marks and French francs into what we would have to do with U.S. dollars against each of the two currencies in these quotes in order to accomplish our ends. If we want to sell marks against dollars, we mean that we want to purchase dollars against marks. As the German trader is offering dollars at 2.8295, that must be the rate we want to use for our calculations. If we want to purchase French francs against dollars, we mean that we want to sell dollars against French francs. As the French trader is willing to purchase dollars at 4.5525, that is the other rate to be used for our calculation.

What, then, is the effective exchange rate of DM versus FF? We know the following:

$$DM2.8295 = \$1 = FF4.5525$$

If we want the quotation in German terms, we must ask, "How many marks equal 1 French franc?" We know that FF4.5525 equals DM2.8295. Then, what is the value of 1 FF? The answer is:

$$FF = DM\frac{2.8295}{4.5525} = DM.621527/FF$$

If we want the quotation in French terms, we must ask, "How many French francs equal 1 mark?" The rate would be the reciprocal of .621527:

$$DM = FF\frac{4.5525}{2.8295} = FF1.608942/DM$$

The quotations for DM/FF and FF/DM *derived* from quotes of these two currencies against a third currency (U.S. dollars) are called *cross rates*.

As is the European custom, these quotes will be expressed as DM62.1527/FF100 and FF160.8942/DM100. Quotes are given for 100 units of foreign currency. This practice reduces the number of decimal places used in the quotation.

The chain. The previous paragraph may appear somewhat complex. An alternative way is to develop a mechanical approach to such a calculation. The mechanical approach presented here we call "the chain." This "chain" is developed in four steps, each one involving two columns. As an example, we use the same situation as in the previous paragraph. At what rate can we purchase French francs against marks expressed in German terms? The four steps are as follows:

1. Establish the question that you want answered, starting with the currency of the terms you desire (DM): How many DM/FF?
   1. How many DM   FF1

2. The second statement begins with the same currency that ended the initial equation (FF) and provides whatever information we have on that currency relevant to the type of transaction we wish to execute. Here, we want to purchase FF, which means we must use the rate at which the trader sells FF, that is, purchases US$.
   1. How many DM   FF1
   2. FF4.5525 $1

3. The third equation begins with the same currency that ended the second equation ($) and provides whatever information we have on that currency regarding the type of transaction we wish to execute. Here, we want to sell DM, which means we must use the rate at which the trader purchases DM, that is, sells US$. The last equation must finish with the same currency whose terms you desired in the first question; in this example, DM.
   1. How many DM   FF1
   2. FF4.5525 $1
   3. $1   DM2.8295

4. The product of the numbers in the right column of step 3 is the numerator. The product of the numbers in the left column is the denominator. The result of the division is the answer.

$$\frac{1 \times 1 \times 2.8295}{4.5525 \times 1} = DM\frac{2.8295}{4.5525} = DM0.621527/FF$$

(DM62.1527/FF100, in European terms)

This is the same answer that was obtained earlier.

Application of cross rates computations. Are cross rates just a nice convenience to express a price in terms of something that one understands? No. The importance of cross rates is that they do not always provide the same prices. The reason is that, on the one hand, the spreads in quotations for currencies traded continuously are much narrower than those for currencies traded in smaller volume. For example, the spreads in quotations for French francs or German marks against U.S. dollars or pounds sterling are much narrower than for quotations of French francs against German marks or vice versa. On the other hand, the particular position of a bank can explain quotations which are not in exact parity with the market. Therefore, when making a transfer of funds from one currency to another, it is important to check the various cross rates or alternative ways of performing the transaction. In addition, one must consider that the spread between buy and sell is always in favor of the trader.

As a practical example, let's take the case of a French subsidiary of a U.S. multinational company declaring a dividend. At the same time, the parent company decides to increase the capital of its subsidiary in Germany. The American finance officer then starts obtaining quotations.

	Bid	*Offer*
American bank	$/DM0.3660	0.3662
(American terms)	$/FF0.1877	0.1879
French bank	FF/$ 5.3250	5.3260
(French terms)	FF/DM1.9495	1.9499
German bank	DM/$ 2.7310	2.7320
(German terms)	DM/FF0.5128	0.5130

The problem from the American company's point of view is, what is the cheapest way to sell FF and purchase DM? Using DM as the currency to compute costs, and using German terms, the company has the following alternatives. It may:

1. Deal directly with the French trader who is selling foreign currency (DM) at FF1.9499/DM. The reciprocal cross rate in terms of DM is $\dfrac{1}{1.9499}$ = DM0.51285/FF.

2. Deal directly with the German trader who is purchasing foreign currency (FF) at DM0.5128/FF.

3. Deal indirectly, using dollars as an intermediary. In the United States, the American trader is willing to purchase FF at $0.1877/FF, and also to sell DM at $0.3662/DM. Applying the chain,

How many DM	FF1
FF1	$0.1877
$.3662	DM1

The cost of exchange is $\dfrac{1 \times .1877 \times 1}{1 \times 1 \times .3662}$ = DM0.51256/FF

In summary, the options for converting FF into DM include (in multiples of 100):

1. Directly through the French trader   DM51.285/FF

2. Directly through the German trader   DM51.280/FF

3. Indirectly through the American trader   DM51.256/FF

American financial officers are often tempted to use an American bank because of geographical convenience. However, the calculations show that in this case the direct quotation of the French bank is the best rate to use to accomplish the desired goal of transferring funds from French francs into German marks. For every FF100 the company can save DM0.029 by using the French bank instead of the American one. So, in a $10 million transaction, a saving of $5655 could be achieved.[2] Given the volume of funds moved across borders by multinational companies, it would not take many of these savings to pay the salary of the assistant treasurer who engages in these calculations.

Whether or not the use of a direct quote (DM/FF) is more advantageous than going through a third currency (usually US$) depends on the size of the spreads quoted by the various sources. Generally, it is true that having

---

[2] DM0.029 equals 0.05655% of DM51.28. That is, $\dfrac{0.029 \times 100}{51.28}$ = 0.05655, and 0.05655% of $10 million equals $5655.

only one spread against you is better than having two spreads. Rates between currencies other than US$ are less frequently quoted by banks, however; they are slightly more exotic quotations; and, therefore, it is possible that one spread may be larger than the total of two narrow spreads in the quotations of the two respective currencies against U.S. dollars. There is no rule as to which approach is better. But, there is certainly justification for the rule that it always pays at least to check the cross rate alternative.

This recommended continuous examination of cross rates and direct quotations brings up the additional disadvantage which treasurers usually inflict upon themselves. It is not at all uncommon for a financial officer to omit checking alternative cross rates. The opportunity gains lost by this omission have been expressed previously. However, in addition to this self-inflicted deprivation of information, the financial officer usually is not at all reluctant to give all sorts of information to the bank regarding the company's position. A practical example will show the result: A treasurer calls the bank and announces that the company has to make a payment in Swiss francs within a couple of months, and that it wishes to purchase the currency in advance. That is, the treasurer is providing the bank with information as to what side of the transaction the company will be on. It does not require much imagination to anticipate that the quoted rate will take this piece of information into account! The customer is clearly a buyer of Swiss francs against U.S. dollars; so, it is not very hard to conclude that the sell rate for Swiss francs offered by the bank is going to be somewhat biased upward.

From the previous paragraph, it is clear that one should not disclose whether one wishes to buy or sell a given currency. Instead, one should insist on receiving a two-way rate. This approach will not only reduce any anticipatory "trending" of the rate by the quoting party, but it will also permit judgment about the relative quality of the rate, the spread between bid and offer. This evaluation is discussed in the following section.

Some comments on quotations

How can you evaluate the quality of a quotation?

Since most of the rates that we have discussed in this chapter are in the foreign exchange market, let's restrict our comments in this area to that market.

A good quotation by a foreign exchange trader should possess three major qualities:

1. Fast reply to the request for the quotation

2. A narrow spread between bid and offer rates

3. Willingness to deal a "reasonable amount" at the rates quoted. What constitutes a "reasonable amount" depends on the marketability of a given currency and varies between the equivalent of US$500,000 and US$5 million.

Information content of quotations

The quotation given by a bank when compared with the market, or the quotations that most other people are making can yield information on the type of transaction that the bank wishes to perform, i.e., whether it prefers to buy or sell. Such a comparison may also convey some information as to the opinion of the bank about the future trends in that currency. For example,

	Bid	*Offer*
Standard market quotation	10	15
Specific bank's quotation	9	13

This difference in numbers can be explained in either of two ways: (1) The bank wishes to sell, or (2) it thinks that the market price will come down.

For the customer dealing with the bank, the 9–13 quote is better than the market if the customer wants to purchase the currency. The bank's quote makes it possible for the customer to purchase at 13, instead of at the standard rate of 15. If the customer wishes to sell the currency, then the market offers a better alternative than the specific bank. Thus, the quotation from the bank is designed to give an incentive to people to purchase from this specific bank. This incentive is justified either if the bank has excess funds in that currency, or if it expects the price of the currency to drop. As to the other side of the quotation, if any ill-informed market participant sells to the bank at 9, the bank still has the opportunity to resell the acquired funds at the market rate of 10. In other words, although the bank basically does not want to buy, it still does so happily at

9. The market is bidding 10, and the bank can sell immediately at 10. The degree of departure of the bank's rate from the prevailing rate will indicate the extent to which one of the explanations presented above holds true for the particular bank. Thus, in this case, if the bank were really pressured to sell the currency, it might go so far as to quote 9–12.

If the bank's quotation were 12–16, it would clearly show that either the bank wants to be a buyer of the currency or that it expects its value to increase. Again, if the bank were very eager to maintain this posture, the quotations would likely go as far as 13–16.[3]

It is obvious from this discussion that the party quoting the rate is in an advantageous position, provided the quoter knows what the market rate is. The trader can choose the bid and offer rates to quote in such a way that nothing can go wrong. The trader either accomplishes the objective pursued with a quote at odds with the market or makes a profit in an involuntary transaction suggested by an ill-informed trading partner.

One should be forewarned, however, that one danger of taking the previous paragraphs literally is that the techniques of using bid and offer rates intelligently are well known by the market. Therefore, one potential problem is that of second-guessing the motivation of the bank. Given that the bank knows that variations in quoted rates will be interpreted in a certain fashion, it may choose to use this conduit to convey special information which may not coincide with what the bank actually wishes to do.

There is one additional advantage in favor of the trader. Every time that someone else responds to the trader's quote, information is gained. For example, the calling party may answer by bidding in between the prices quoted by the trader. This procedure is not uncommon. If the quoted rate is 10 bid and 14 offer, the calling party may state a wish to sell at 11. The trader, the quoting party, may or may not improve the bid rate from 10 to 11. Even if the trader chooses not to buy at 11, information has been acquired about one market participant. If, during the next seconds or minutes, other callers also offer to sell at 11, then the quoting party should get the message that the market rate has probably changed. The party will probably quote something like 9 bid, 13 offered, next time.

The final advantage for the trader is this: Most of the activity takes place at the calling party's telephone or telex expense. In a global business, such as foreign exchange, this expense can be very high, sometimes amounting to as much as US$1 million a year.

---

[3] See also Chap. 7, p. 142, and Exhibit 7.8.

CHAPTER 5
Funds management in a two-way market

In Chapter 3, we presented the essentials of managing flows of funds in the money market and the foreign exchange market. For simplicity's sake, we talked in terms of "the rate." However, we know that in actuality a trader in funds, domestic or foreign, will usually quote two rates: bid and offer. This practice was discussed in Chapter 4.

In the preceding chapters, we were also careful to give examples in which all the cash flow maturities matched. In real life, one is not always presented with cash flows that match, for example, a three-month deposit together with a three-month loan. Actually, the mismatch of maturities of various cash flows becomes one of the variables to be handled by the funds manager.

Swap rates

What are swap rates?

When we introduced the relationship between the money market and the foreign exchange market in Chapter 3, we did so by making use of a new term: "swap rate." Here we wish to explain the meaning of this term in more detail. The swap rate is to the foreign exchange market what the interest differential is to the money market.

The swap rate is not an exchange rate; it is an exchange rate differential. In Chapter 3 we showed that when the interest differential between the U.S. dollar and the pound sterling was 3 percent in favor of the pound, the swap rate for three-month delivery was .0180 below the spot rate of $2.4000/£. This .0180 swap rate is equivalent to a 3 percent per annum discount of the forward pound rate relative to the spot pound rate.

In the foreign exchange market, a rate is the price at which individuals are willing to exchange currencies. At the swap rate of .0180, nobody is willing to exchange any currency. However, the swap rate of .0180 is related to the *spot rate* of $2.40/£ at which pounds are traded against dollars for two business days' delivery. The swap rate is also related to the *outright forward rate* of $2.3820/£ for three-month pound delivery (2.40 − .0180). The *rates* at which transactions are carried out in the foreign exchange market are either the spot or the various forward rates. The swap rate is the link between the spot rate and the forward rate, or the link between two forward rates for two different maturity dates. This link is directly related to the net accessible interest differential between the two relevant currencies.

The fact that a swap rate is *not* an exchange rate becomes particularly clear when one wants to find reciprocal rates. For example, the exchange rate for German marks against U.S. dollars may be US$0.40/DM in U.S. terms or DM2.50/US$ in German terms. One rate can be derived from the other by simply finding the reciprocal of one of the rates; in other words, $2.50 = \dfrac{1}{0.40}$. This calculation can be done with spot rates as well as forward outright rates, but it cannot be done with swap rates. If we have the following rates in U.S. terms:

Spot rate	$0.40/DM
Three-month forward outright rate	$0.41/DM
Three-month swap rate	$0.01/DM

and if we would like the same rate in German terms, we can get what we want by finding the reciprocal of the spot rate and the forward outright rate. The reciprocal of the swap rate would be meaningless.

To obtain the swap rate in German terms we have to find the difference between the spot and forward outright rates expressed in German terms. Accordingly,

Spot rate (1 ÷ 0.40)	DM2.5000/$
Three-month forward outright rate (1 ÷ 0.41)	DM2.4390/$
Three-month swap rate (2.50 − 2.4390)	DM0.0610/$

Swap rates are not true exchange rates and may not be reciprocated to change the terms in which they are expressed.

Bid and offer in the swap rate

The importance of the swap rate is partially derived from the customs which traders follow. Usually, when a bank's foreign exchange trader is asked for quotes on foreign currency for future delivery, say, in three months, the answer will be expressed in terms of swap rates, *not* outright forward rates. For example, a trader, when asked for the price of pounds against dollars for three-month delivery, might answer, "190–180." What does this mean?

1. We continue to assume that the spot rate is $2.4000/£, ignoring bid-offer prices. Since the swap rate is added to or subtracted from the spot rate to get the outright forward rate, one must conclude that the numbers 190–180 must ignore the appropriate place of the decimal point in relation to the spot rate. In general, the last digit of a swap rate corresponds to the last decimal place in the spot rates. Thus, if the spot rate is $2.4000/£ and the swap rate is 180, the 0 in 180 represents the fourth decimal place, the 8 is in the third, and the 1 is in the second decimal place. The entire swap rate, then, is actually 0.0180. In the trader's two-way quote of 190–180, the swap rates must be interpreted as $0.0190/£–$0.0180/£ when relating the swap rate to the spot rate.

2. We also know from the preceding chapters that the first number quoted is always related to the bid price, and the second number is related to the offer price.

3. Finally, we know that traders must deal with a spread in their favor. The trader's quotes always reflect the need to purchase at a price lower than the expected price of the currency when selling it. That is where the trader's profit lies, in the absence of other transactions. A bid-offer swap rate, when added to or subtracted from the spot rate, will produce the forward outright rate.

Now we have to decide whether the swap rate is to be added to (constituting a premium) the spot rate of $2.4000/£ or subtracted from it (constituting a discount). If we were to add the swap rate to the spot rate, we would end up with the following forward rates: $2.4190/£–$2.4180/£. That does not make any sense! It would indicate that the trader is willing to purchase pounds against dollars at a price higher than the one at which the trader is willing to sell pounds against dollars. Then, by elimination, the swap rate in this case must refer to a discount. If we subtract the swap

Exhibit 5.1
PREMIUM OR DISCOUNT IMPLIED BY SWAP RATE

SWAP RATE 190-180

Buy forward @ 190 points *below* spot

Sell forward @ 180 points *below* spot

SWAP RATE 180-190

Buy forward @ 180 points *above* spot

Sell forward @ 190 points *above* spot

rate from the spot rate, we have the following quotes: $2.3810/£ – $2.3820/£. This outright forward quote can be translated as "willing to purchase pounds against U.S. dollars at $2.3810 [to sell U.S. dollars against pounds]; willing to sell pounds against U.S. dollars at 2.3820 [to buy U.S. dollars against pounds]." Thus, the party which is quoting the swap rate 190–180 is willing to *buy forward* at 190 *below spot* and *sell forward* at 180 *below spot*. (See Exhibit 5.1.) Had the swap rate been 180–190, it would have indicated a premium of the forward rate over the spot rate. It would have shown that the quoting party was willing to *buy forward* at 180 *above spot* and *sell forward* at 190 *above spot* (as in Exhibit 5.1).

A rule of thumb when deciding whether the swap rate indicates a discount below or a premium above the spot rate is this: Look at the relationship between the numbers in the swap rate. If the first number (bid) is larger than the second number (offer), that is, if it looks "wrong" in terms of usual bid-offer relationships, it is a discount on the currency being quoted (pounds, in our example). Conversely, if the first number is smaller than the second number, we know that the forward price of the currency being quoted is at a premium over its spot price.

Swap transactions

A swap transaction is one where a currency is bought and sold simultaneously, but where the delivery dates for the purchase and sale are different. An example is a purchase of pounds against U.S. dollars for three-month delivery at the same time that one sells pounds against U.S. dollars in the spot markets for delivery two days later.

In a swap position, the amount of "buys" of a currency always equals the amount of "sells." Therefore, a swap transaction never changes the net exchange position. If there is a change in the spot rate of the currencies, there will not be a foreign exchange gain or loss as a result of a swap transaction. If there is an upvaluation, the amount of extra local currency lost on the sell part of the transaction is made up on the buy part of the transaction.

The nature of a swap transaction helps us to understand the meaning of the term "swap rate." The swap rate indicates the number of points at which the quoting party is willing to swap a currency spot against a future maturity of the same currency. For example, the three-month swap rate 190–180 for the pound gives the number of points at which the quoting party is willing to conduct two different swap transactions of spot versus three-month delivery. These swap transactions are:

1. Willing to sell spot pounds against dollars at the going spot rate and to buy three-month pounds against dollars at 190 points below that spot rate.

2. Willing to buy spot pounds against dollars at the going spot rate and sell three-month pounds against dollars at 180 points below that spot rate.

If the quoting party engages in either of these transactions, the impact on the net exchange position will be zero. For each currency involved, there is a buy and a sell. However, the maturity of each leg of the transaction is different; one part is spot, and the other is for three-month delivery. This point will be discussed more fully later in this chapter.

This interpretation of the swap rate also serves to highlight the significance of this rate. In a swap transaction, the important number is the swap rate. This rate is the difference between the price at which a currency is bought and the price at which it is sold in a swap transaction. The spot rate is an element common to both sides of the transaction. For example, the trader is willing to sell pounds at the spot rate and purchase pounds at the spot rate less 190 points. The 190 is the element which distinguishes the price of each part of the swap. We can go so far as to conclude that *in a swap transaction, the level of the spot rate is immaterial; what matters is the swap rate.*

We can distinguish between two types of swap transactions:

1. Pure swap transactions

2. Engineered swap transactions

In a pure swap, both the buy and the sell parts of the transaction are closed with the same party. The swap rate is negotiated, and, after agreement has been reached, it is reflected through two exchange rates.

The engineered swap consists of two transactions, each of which is closed with a different party. For example, a trader may negotiate with one party to purchase a specific currency forward at a forward outright rate. Shortly thereafter, the trader may negotiate a spot sale of that very same currency with another party. If we look at the two transactions separately, we find a forward purchase from one party and a spot sale to another party. Effectively, however, we find a swap position, not a pure one but, rather, an engineered (pieced together) swap position at a swap rate which we can determine by looking at the difference between the outright forward exchange rate at which the trader bought from one party and the spot exchange rate at which the trader sold to another party.

Why engage in a pure swap transaction? People engage in pure swaps for the following reasons:

1. To convert one currency into another temporarily without developing a net exchange position.[1] (This is done in the case of covered interest arbitrage.)

2. To build up a swap position forward against forward, e.g., sell pounds against dollars for three-months delivery and purchase pounds against dollars for one month delivery, with the expectation that the premium or discount reflecting net accessible interest differentials will change favorably

3. To reverse the position developed under (2) after the expected changes take place and a profit can be realized

The following sections illustrate these swap transactions. Further examples are presented in Chapter 7.

Swap transactions with matched cash flows: covered interest arbitrage

We have already discussed a case of a swap transaction conducted in search of profit—the individual who conducted the covered interest arbitrage transaction in Chapter 3. Let's expand on the example presented in that chapter by introducing bid and offer rates.

Assume the following market conditions prevail on December 31:

Money market, three-months maturity

U.S. dollar	10%	
		2¾% interest differential
pound	12¾%	

Foreign exchange market

Spot rate	$2.40/£
Three-month swap rate (pounds against U.S. dollars)	190–180

---

[1] See also "Swaps and Nonbanks," in Chap. 8, p. 188.

Notice first that we are using U.S. terms; in other words, the prices are quoted in terms of U.S. dollars, and the currency which is being bought or sold is the pound. The swap rate indicates that the pound is selling at a discount against the U.S. dollar. Actually, the *outright forward rate* for the pound against the dollar is:

$$\$2.3810/£-\$2.3820/£$$

To compare the swap rate with the interest differential, we have to express the swap rate in percentage terms:

1. Find the relevant bid or offer rate in the swap rate. If we wish to purchase pounds forward, the relevant number to discount from the spot rate is 180 (the rate at which the quoting trader is *selling* forward and we are *buying* forward).

2. Convert the swap rate to the same time basis as the interest rates. A discount of 180 for three months is equivalent to a discount of 720 for twelve months ($180 \times 4 = 720$). We have to put all rates on the same basis, in this case, on a per annum basis.

3. Convert the annualized swap rate to dollars and cents. When we express it in terms of dollars and cents, 720 really means $\$0.0720/£$.

4. Express the swap rate as a percentage of the spot rate. The 0.0720 represents a 3 percent discount on the three-month pound $[(0.0720 \div 2.4000) \times 100 = 3]$.

Therefore, the discount on the forward pound is larger than the interest differential in favor of the pound. So, there is an incentive to engage in covered interest arbitrage, which is a swap transaction.

The covered interest arbitrage indicates that one should borrow pounds at 12¾ percent, exchange them into U.S. dollars, invest the proceeds in the dollar money market at 10 percent, and purchase pounds for three-month delivery against U.S. dollars at a 3 percent discount on the pound, a 3 percent premium on the U.S. dollar. The profit is the difference between the 3 percent premium on U.S. dollars sold against pounds (pounds purchased at a discount against U.S. dollars) in the forward market, less the interest differential in favor of the pound, 2¾ percent. It is a profit of ¼ percent.

The swap transaction in this arbitrage is:

Spot: *Sell* pounds against U.S. dollars

Three-month: *Purchase* pounds against U.S. dollars

In this transaction, sterling was borrowed at 12¾ percent for three months and then swapped into dollars by selling spot sterling and purchasing three-month forward sterling at 3 percent in our favor. As a result, the dollars purchased spot are available for three months on a fully hedged basis, without incurring any foreign exchange risk, at an "all-in" cost of 9¾ percent, that is, 12¾ percent interest paid for the pounds borrowed less the exchange profit of 3 percent, or 180 points. These dollars can be placed at 10 percent, thus generating a ¼ percent net profit. This is a case where the swap transaction allowed the funds manager to move from one currency into another (from pounds into dollars) while keeping a zero *net* exposure.

Because the pounds sold in the spot market were raised out of borrowings, and the dollars sold in the forward market are the proceeds from the maturing investment in dollars, the "cash flows are square." At each maturity the inflows match the outflows. Because the buys in each currency equal the sells in each currency, there is a *square exchange position* or no *net exchange position*. Also, there is no *swap position*, or mismatched maturities.

Swap transactions with mismatched cash flows

A swap transaction, by definition, guarantees that no net exchange position will be created by the swap. However, the maturity of the various cash flows may not be properly matched. Actually, the cash flows in a swap transaction will be matched as to maturity only when imperfections in the market give rise to opportunities for covered interest arbitrage, as in the previous example.

If the market is in equilibrium (if interest differentials match the discounts or premiums on the respective currencies), a swap transaction with squared cash flows from the beginning will generate no profit; the buying and selling prices will be the same. If the markets are in equilibrium, the profits in a swap transaction are derived from establishing unmatched cash flow positions which can be squared after market rates change in the direction initially expected.

Let's take an example. On June 30 the following rates are quoted to us:

Money Market, Three-months Maturity	*Bid*	*Offer*
U.S. dollar	10.00%	10.25%
Pound sterling	13.16%	13.25%

Foreign Exchange Market		
Spot rate	$2.4010/£	$2.4015/£
Three-month swap rate	190	180
Outright forward rate	$2.3820/£	$2.3835/£
Discount on three-month pound	3.16%	3.00%

The market is in equilibrium. On both sides, bid and offer, interest differentials in favor of the pound equal the discount of the three-month pound.

Given these rates, if we should wish to sell pounds spot, the market would be willing to purchase them at $2.4010/£. If we should wish to purchase three-month forward pounds, the market would be willing to sell them to us at $2.3835. However, if we should wish to sell spot pounds and purchase three-month pounds simultaneously with the same party— a swap transaction—the relevant rate is the swap rate. In this case the relevant number is 180. The market is willing to sell three-month pounds to us at 180 points below the spot rate. As we discussed in a previous section, the level of the spot rate is immaterial in a swap transaction.

In practice, after we decide to accept the quoting party's swap rate of 180, we will establish the actual spot and forward rates at which the transaction will be booked. Let's assume that we agree to book the transaction at $2.4012 for the spot rate and at $2.3832 for the forward rate. The difference is still 180 points, or $0.0180 discount per pound. The cash flow boxes will then look like the ones in Exhibit 5.2.

The swap transaction has not affected our *net* foreign exchange position. For each currency every outflow is accompanied by an inflow. The difference in the size of the flows in U.S. dollars is the point at which part of the profit is expected to lie. However, as mentioned before, the cash flows are not matched by maturity. For example, for pounds the £1 million outflow (Box A) will take place on June 30, while no inflow is yet planned until September 30 (Box C). How can the cash flow imbalances be solved?

Exhibit 5.2
CASH FLOW IMPACT OF SWAP TRANSACTION

RATE SCENARIO

Money Market, Three-Months Maturity	Bid	Offer
U.S. dollar	10.00%	10.25%
Pound sterling	13.16%	13.25%

Foreign Exchange Market

Spot rate	$2.4010/£	$2.4015/£
Three-month swap rate	190	180
Outright forward rate	$2.3820/£	$2.3835/£
Discount on three-month pound	3.16%	3.00%

CASH FLOWS

Box A

```
Currency: Pound sterling

Date:     June 30

Balance:  − £1 million
          (spot transaction)
```

Box B

```
Currency: U.S. dollar

Date:     June 30

Balance:  + $2,401,200
          (spot transaction)
```

Box C

```
Currency: Pound sterling

Date:     September 30

Balance:  + £1 million
          (forward trans-
          action)
```

Box D

```
Currency: U.S. dollar

Date:     September 30

Balance:  − $2,383,200
          (forward trans-
          action)
```

Exhibit 5.3
SQUARING OF CASH FLOWS GENERATED BY SWAP TRANSACTIONS: THE FOREIGN EXCHANGE MARKET APPROACH

RATE SCENARIO

Money Market, Three-Months Maturity	Bid	Offer	
		Before	*After*
U.S. dollar	10.00%	10.25%	10.25%
Pound sterling	13.16%	13.25%	12.83%
Foreign Exchange Market			
Spot rate	$2.4010/£	$2.4015/£	$2.4015/£
Three-month swap rate	190	180	170
Outright forward rate	$2.3820/£	$2.3835/£	$2.3845/£
Discount on three-month pounds	3.16%	3.00%	2.83%

CASH FLOWS

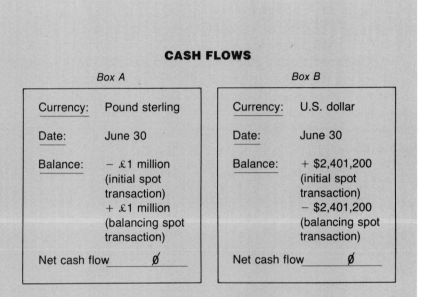

Box A

Currency:	Pound sterling
Date:	June 30
Balance:	− £1 million (initial spot transaction) + £1 million (balancing spot transaction)
Net cash flow	∅

Box B

Currency:	U.S. dollar
Date:	June 30
Balance:	+ $2,401,200 (initial spot transaction) − $2,401,200 (balancing spot transaction)
Net cash flow	∅

Box C

Currency:	Pound sterling
Date:	September 30
Balance:	+ £1 million (initial forward transaction) − £1 million (balancing forward transaction)
Net cash flow	∅

Box D

Currency:	U.S. dollar
Date:	September 30
Balance:	− $2,383,200 (initial forward transaction) + $2,384,200 (balancing forward transaction)
Net cash flow	$1,000

Solution through the foreign exchange market. One solution might be to do the reverse of the previous transaction: to purchase pounds in the spot market and sell pounds in the forward market. However, if we do this at the prevailing rates, we are assured of a loss. The three-month swap rate for sterling against U.S. dollars is 190 bid and 180 offer below spot. As we would have to sell forward pounds (and purchase spot), we would have to accept a rate of 190 discount against us. Since, in the initial swap transaction, we purchased forward pounds at a discount of 180 in our favor, we would lose 10 points if we sold them at a discount of 190 points. Expressed in actual rates, the price of buying spot sterling could be $2.4012/£ and of selling forward at a discount of 190 points would be $2.3822/£. As a result, we would have a "wash" (zero profit or loss) in spot and a 10-point loss in three-month forward because we purchased at $2.3832/£ and sold at $2.3822/£. If we did that, we would just be proving that the spreads are in favor of the trader who has been quoting rates.

If we want to solve the cash flow problem at a profit, we shall have to do the transaction just described at a loss smaller than the profit of $0.0180/£ (or a discount for the pound of less than 180) locked in by the initial swap transaction; for example, at a swap rate of 170 discount against us.

Purchase £ spot at	$2.4012/£
Sell £ forward at 170 points discount	$2.3842
Loss	$0.0170/£

In this case we would satisfy the cash flow requirements while providing a profit of $0.0010/£ (0.0180 − 0.0170). The cash flow boxes are balanced now, as shown in Exhibit 5.3. The small imbalance in Box D provides the net profit of $1000, or $0.0010/£ on £1 million in this transaction.

If we had chosen a spot rate different from $2.4012 to settle the second swap transaction at a swap rate of 170, the net profit would still be $1000. Depending on whether we chose a higher or lower spot rate than 2.4012, we would have had a profit or loss in Box B and a respectively smaller or larger profit or loss in Box D. For example, if the spot rate chosen for the second swap transaction had been 2.5000, we would have had the following rates:

Spot rate	$2.5000/£
Swap rate	170
Forward rate	$2.4830/£

As a result, the balances in Boxes B and D would be:

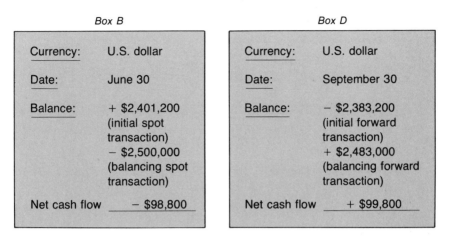

Box B	
Currency:	U.S. dollar
Date:	June 30
Balance:	+ $2,401,200 (initial spot transaction) − $2,500,000 (balancing spot transaction)
Net cash flow	− $98,800

Box D	
Currency:	U.S. dollar
Date:	September 30
Balance:	− $2,383,200 (initial forward transaction) + $2,483,000 (balancing forward transaction)
Net cash flow	+ $99,800

The net of the two boxes is a profit of $1000 composed of a loss of $98,800 in Box B and a gain of $99,800 in Box D. As long as the swap rate in the second transaction is 170, the net profit of the two transactions will always be $1000, regardless of the actual spot and forward rates used to book the transaction.

The profits in these swap transactions are based on the fact that we are locking in one swap rate which we expect to change, in this case one we expect to decrease. This decrease will occur when the net accessible interest differential in the money market changes, that is, if dollar rates increase and/or pound rates decrease. Whether the spot rate remains constant or not is immaterial as long as the swap rate decreases.

Solution through the money market. The cash flows generated by the initial swap transaction were shown in Exhibit 5.2.

If we want to square these cash flows in the money market, we have to do the following:

1. In pounds, we must have an inflow for June 30 and an outflow for September 30. We can accomplish this by borrowing pounds to be delivered on June 30 which mature on September 30.

2. In dollars, we must have an outflow for June 30 and an inflow for September 30. We can achieve this by investing the dollars in the money market on June 30 with a maturity for September 30.

Exhibit 5.4
SQUARING OF CASH FLOWS GENERATED BY SWAP TRANSACTIONS: THE MONEY MARKET APPROACH

RATE SCENARIO

Money Market, Three-Months Maturity	**Bid**		**Offer**	
	Before	*After*	*Before*	*After*
U.S. dollar	10.00%	10.00%	10.25%	10.25%
Pound sterling	13.16%	12.73%	13.25%	12.83%
Foreign Exchange Market				
Spot rate	$2.4010/£		$2.4015/£	$2.4015/£
Three-month swap rate	190		180	170
Outright forward rate	$2.3820/£		$2.3835/£	$2.3845/£
Discount on three-month pounds	3.16%		3.00%	2.83%

CASH FLOWS

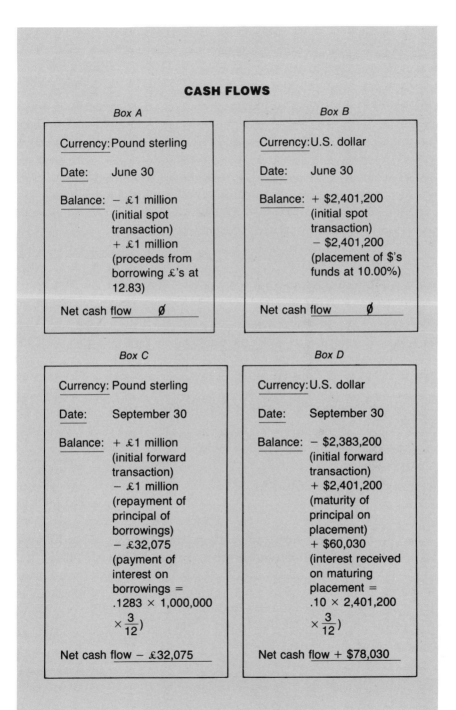

Box A

Currency: Pound sterling

Date: June 30

Balance: − £1 million
          (initial spot
          transaction)
          + £1 million
          (proceeds from
          borrowing £'s at
          12.83)

Net cash flow   ∅

Box B

Currency: U.S. dollar

Date: June 30

Balance: + $2,401,200
          (initial spot
          transaction)
          − $2,401,200
          (placement of $'s
          funds at 10.00%)

Net cash flow   ∅

Box C

Currency: Pound sterling

Date: September 30

Balance: + £1 million
          (initial forward
          transaction)
          − £1 million
          (repayment of
          principal of
          borrowings)
          − £32,075
          (payment of
          interest on
          borrowings =
          .1283 × 1,000,000
          $\times \frac{3}{12}$)

Net cash flow − £32,075

Box D

Currency: U.S. dollar

Date: September 30

Balance: − $2,383,200
          (initial forward
          transaction)
          + $2,401,200
          (maturity of
          principal on
          placement)
          + $60,030
          (interest received
          on maturing
          placement =
          .10 × 2,401,200
          $\times \frac{3}{12}$)

Net cash flow + $78,030

The initial swap transaction where pounds were sold spot and purchased for three-month delivery was done at a swap rate of 180. In previous calculations we showed that this swap rate is equivalent to a 3 percent p.a. discount on the pound. We have also proven in the preceding section that if one tries to square the cash flows at the initial swap rates, one will only be providing spread profits to the quoting trader. Then, given that we are trying to square the position through the money markets, what interest rate differentials will have to prevail to square the initial swap at a profit? The differentials will have to be less than 3 percent p.a. That is, the differential between the rate at which pounds are borrowed and the rate at which dollars are placed will have to be less than 3 percent p.a.

Let's assume that on June 30 the money market rates given in the rate scenario of Exhibit 5.4 come to prevail.

	Bid	*Offer*
U.S. dollar	10.00%	10.25%
Pound sterling	12.73%	12.83%

The cash flow boxes will then be balanced as shown in Exhibit 5.4.

The net gain from the transaction is:

Gain in forward transaction in dollars plus interest (Box D)	$78,030
Interest payment on pound borrowing (Box C)	
£32,075 at $2.4015/£	−$77,028
Net gain	$ 1,002

The profit realized in this transaction is made up of the difference between the 3 percent interest differential which prevailed initially (and which was adequately reflected in the exchange market in terms of the swap rate of 180) and the 2.83 percent interest differential at which the cash flows were squared in the money market. This provides a profit of 0.17 percent p.a. (3.00 − 2.83). In terms of dollars, this is approximately the $1002 calculated above ($.0017 \times 2,401,200 \times \dfrac{3}{12} = 1,020$).[2]

[2] The small discrepancy is due to rounding.

Notice that the profit of $1002 generated when using money market transactions to square our position is approximately the same as the $1000 profit achieved when using the foreign exchange market. This is not an accident. The change in interest differentials which we assumed when using the money market was from 3.00 percent to 2.83 percent. This is equivalent to the decrease in the discount on the three-month forward pound from 180 to 170 points; that is, the swap rate of 170 is equivalent to the 2.83 percent discount on the pound [(170 × 4) ÷ 2.4012].

Swap transactions and the spot rate. In this last example, we started with a swap transaction which, although not generating a net exchange position, did produce a mismatch of cash flow maturities. The cash flow problem was solved at a profit in the foreign exchange market when the swap rate changed, in this case decreased. In the money market, the cash flow problem was solved by borrowing and investing at an interest differential lower than the one reflected in the initial swap transaction. In none of these cases was there a concern for the level of the spot rate because the net exchange position, at every step, was always zero. However, there are two areas where the level of the spot rate is of interest.

In the foreign exchange market example, it is true that the only determinant of profits was the reduction of the swap rate from 180 to 170 points. This reduction by itself does not involve the spot rate. However, we have established earlier that the swap rate is a function of interest differentials. We proved that the three-month swap rate of 180, when the spot rate was $2.4000/£, meant a 3 percent discount on the pound against the dollar. This 3 percent discount coincided with the interest differential between the two currencies. At a spot rate in the neighborhood of $2.4000/£, a decrease in interest differentials from 3 percent to 2.83 percent will be associated with a change in the swap rate from 180 to 170. However, if the spot rate were to change drastically, say from $2.4000 to $2.5000, a 3 percent interest differential would be equivalent to a three-month swap rate of 188 and a 2.83 percent interest differential to a three-month swap rate of 177. In our example the swap rate of 177 will drastically reduce the $1000 profit based on a swap rate of 170. Thus, to the extent that time elapses between the initial swap and the one generated to square the cash flows, the level of the spot rate may influence the level of the swap rate.

The other area where the level of the spot rate may become important is in the case of the solution through the money market. If we look back, we shall see that the interest expenses accumulate in pounds (Box C); however, the interest earnings accumulate in dollars (Box D). To the extent that a large change in the spot rate of pounds against dollars takes place before September 30, the profits may be reduced and even converted into losses. In our example, this would happen if the pound upvalued against the U.S. dollar. That is, the interest earned on the dollar investment and the interest payable on the borrowings generate a small net exchange exposure. To avoid this situation, the funds manager may wish to lock in the going rate by engaging in an additional foreign exchange transaction. In our example the manager would sell sufficient dollar forwards to purchase the £32,075 necessary to pay the interest in pounds. Since, in this case, the three-month pound is selling at a discount against the dollar, an additional small profit will be realized in covering the interest payments.

Thus, the foreign exchange risk involved in the £32,075 interest payable could be covered by purchasing pounds against U.S. dollars, value September 30, at the discount of $0.0170/£. This transaction would produce a profit in the amount of $545.28 (£32,075 × $0.0170/£). This additional profit is equivalent to 0.09 percent p.a. on the principal capital of $2,401,200 $\left(\dfrac{545.28}{2,401,200} \times 100 \times \dfrac{12}{3} \right)$. In this case the larger the discount of the pound against the dollar, the larger the size of the additional profit involved in covering the interest payable.

If only one foreign currency is involved, covering that currency against local currency is necessary. If both currencies involved are foreign currencies, they must both be covered against local currency, with one forward purchase and one forward sale. The aggregate of the respective premiums and/or discounts on the forward transactions will then affect the total profit or loss.

We can summarize the steps one must take to cover the exposure to foreign exchange risk involved in interest payments and receivables involved in swap transactions as follows:

1. Determine the amount of interest payable and/or receivable in foreign currency. (In the previous example, we assumed that the local currency was the U.S. dollar; therefore, the exposure to changes in the spot rate occurred only in the interest payable in pounds, £32,075. The interest receivable in U.S. dollars was not considered to be exposed.)

2. Purchase forward outright the amount of any foreign currency payable against local currency. Sell forward outright the amount of any foreign currency receivable against local currency.

To calculate the additional costs/returns involved in the covering transaction, we do the following:

1. Multiply the amount of premium/discount by the amount which must be covered. The result is the absolute amount of additional costs/returns involved in the covering transaction. (In the previous example, this amount was a profit of $545.28, computed by multiplying the discount of $0.0170/£ by the amount to be covered, £32,075.)

2. To express the amount of profits/costs involved in the covering transaction in terms of percentage per annum, we compute first the percentage which the profit/cost represents of the amount of principal involved in the swap transaction, and then annualize this percentage. In the previous example, the **profit of $545.28 is 0.023 percent of the principal amount in** the swap transaction, $2,401,200. Since this profit is realized over three months, the annual rate is 4 times the quarterly rate of 0.023 percent, or 0.09 percent.

This additional cost/return should then be added to the interest differential in the swap transaction in the money market to obtain the *net* cost/return of the swap transaction. This is particularly important when one of the currencies involved in the swap transaction carries extremely high interest rates relative to the other. This is usually the case in swap transactions involving the currency of a developing country. (In our example, the net profit of the swap transaction is 0.26 percent, composed of the 0.17 percent calculated initially plus the 0.09 percent profit involved in covering the interest payable in pounds.)[3]

---

[3] For further discussion see p. 179.

CHAPTER 6
Factors affecting spot exchange rates

For any party who assumes net exchange positions, an assessment of future prices of currencies is imperative. However, this assessment is hard to make. It can take the form of only a forecast, and forecasting remains more of an art than a science. Nevertheless, these limitations do not excuse the funds manager who must operate in these markets from making an educated estimate of the future movements of the values of relevant currencies. In this chapter, we shall examine the major fundamental forces which shape the destiny of exchange rates.

The underlying force which determines changes in exchange rates (as well as any other price) is the relationship between the amounts of currency supplied and demanded at a given price. If, at a certain price, the amount supplied exceeds the amount demanded, that price will show a tendency to decline. If, at a certain price, the amount demanded exceeds the amount supplied, that price will tend to increase. As discussed in Chapter 2, the price of a currency is expressed in terms of other currencies—the exchange rates.

What are the forces which determine the amounts of currency demanded and supplied at a given exchange rate? To answer this question, it is best to introduce the report required to measure the various sources of supply of and demand for a given currency; that report is the so-called balance of payments.

The balance of payments

Despite the implications of its name, the balance of payments *does not* measure the levels of anything. The balance of payments measures *changes, flows*. If we have to compare the balance of payments with one of the traditional statements used to report the financial condition of a company, the balance of payments is most similar to a statement of sources and uses of funds. The balance of payments measures the sources and uses of foreign exchange during the period indicated by the statement. Of course, the only transactions reflected in the balance of payments are those between the citizens of the given country and the residents of other countries. Transactions among citizens of the same country do not enter the balance of payments. They are not a source or a use of foreign exchange for the country as a whole.

In the balance of payments, the sources of foreign exchange, or the supply of foreign exchange, are indicated by positive numbers. The uses of foreign exchange, or the demand for foreign exchange, are indicated by a minus sign. Exhibit 6.1 shows a summary of the balance of payments for the United States in 1975. In this exhibit, we can see that the figure for merchandise exports has a positive sign. (In many presentations the positive sign is not printed.) When a country exports merchandise, foreigners make payments in their currency. Foreigners' currency is a source of supply of foreign exchange to the country for which the balance of payments is being prepared. In Exhibit 6.1 the figure for merchandise imports is accompanied by a minus sign. As a country purchases merchandise, it offers its own currency, that is, it demands foreign exchange, to be able to pay for the imported merchandise.

Most of the accounts in the balance of payments can be classified into two major groups: trade accounts and capital accounts. For each group of accounts it is possible to compute a "balance." Thus, the net between exports and imports in goods and services is called the *trade balance*. In Exhibit 6.1 the trade balance is +$16,270 million. Here, the trade balance is a surplus; exports exceed imports. This surplus indicates that the supply of foreign currency exceeds the demand for foreign currency used to trade goods and services in the United States. In the absence of any other transaction in the balance of payments, this balance will tend to put downward pressure on the price of foreign currency against the domestic currency. In other words, there will be pressure for a devaluation of foreign currencies relative to the domestic currency, which is the same as an upvaluation of the local currency against the foreign currency.

News about developments in the trade balance usually have an immediate impact on the foreign exchange markets, and of all the accounts in the balance of payments, trade figures are available earliest. In addition, the trade balance constitutes the major portion of the balance of payments in most countries.

The capital accounts follow the same conventions as the trade accounts; so, entries preceded by a minus sign indicate an increase in the demand for foreign currency. This occurs when the citizens of the given country purchase foreign securities. In order to pay for these securities, the domestic citizens must purchase, i.e., demand, foreign currency. These purchases of foreign securities are often referred to in the balance of payments as "claims" on foreigners. In Exhibit 6.1, these entries appear under "U.S. assets abroad."

When the entries in the capital accounts are positive, they indicate an increase in the supply of foreign currency. This increase occurs when foreigners purchase securities issued by the country in question. In order to pay for their purchases, foreigners offer foreign exchange to the given country. The purchase of securities by foreigners is an increase in the country's liabilities. The financial asset purchased by the foreigner is a promise, a liability of the given country to pay in the future. These transactions are shown in Exhibit 6.1 under "Foreign assets in the U.S."

If all the accounts in the balance of payments are considered, we shall find that (as with the sources and uses of funds statements for a firm), the plus amounts equal the minus amounts. Adding all the balance entries in the right-hand column of Exhibit 6.1 will produce a zero balance. In this sense, the balance of payments always "balances." It is an historical report; after the fact, total sources are always equal to total uses of funds, or, quantity supplied is always equal to quantity demanded.

To use the balance of payments as a barometer of the forces of demand for and supply of foreign exchange in the market, it is necessary to isolate those entries which respond to relative economic conditions from those transactions which are made solely to fill the gap between the initial supply of and demand for foreign exchange. For example, to obtain a reading of the forces in the market, we shall want to exclude the entries which reflect government intervention in that market for the purpose of stabilizing exchange rate fluctuations. The exclusion of the government accounts which measure intervention will produce a balance for the remaining accounts.

In Exhibit 6.1, we can compute an approximate measure of the supply of and demand for foreign exchange in the United States, excluding the

Exhibit 6.1
UNITED STATES BALANCE OF PAYMENTS, 1975
(millions of dollars)

Trade Accounts
Merchandise trade

Exports	+107,133	
Imports	− 98,150	
Balance on merchandise trade		+ 8,983

Service trade

Travel	− 1,541	
Transportation	− 962	
Dividends and interest	+ 6,007	
Fees and royalties	+ 3,852	
Other	− 69	
Balance on services		+ 7,287
Trade balance		+16,270
Unilateral Transfers		− 4,620
Balance on Current Accounts		+11,650

Capital Accounts
U.S. assets abroad
   Official reserve assets   −   607
   U.S. government assets, other than
      official   −   3,463
   U.S. private assets
      Direct investments   −   6,307
      Foreign securities   −   6,206
      U.S. claims reported by banks
         and nonbanks
         Long-term   −   2,735
         Short-term   − 11,812
Net changes in U.S. assets abroad   −31,130

Foreign assets in the U.S.
   Foreign official assets in the U.S.   +   6,336
   Other foreign assets in the U.S.
      Direct investments   +   2,437
      Securities   +   5,376
      U.S. liabilities reported by banks
         and nonbanks
         Long-term   −   42
         Short-term   +   773
Net changes in foreign assets in the
United States   +14,879

Statistical Discrepancy   + 4,601

SOURCE: U.S. Department of Commerce, *Survey of Current Business*, June 1976, pp. 32–33.

government sector. Under "U.S. assets abroad," official reserve assets are entered in the amount of − $607 million. The U.S. monetary authorities purchased foreign assets in that amount, and U.S. foreign exchange reserves increased. Under "Foreign assets in the U.S.," foreign official assets in the United States appear in the amount of + $6,336 million. United States liabilities to foreign central banks increased in that amount. The net of these two figures is + $5,729 million, a *net* increase in liabilities. If we exclude these items from the balance of payments, we shall find that the net balance of the remaining accounts is − $5,729 million, a measure indicating a deficit in the U.S. balance of payments. We can say that this deficit of $5,729 million was "financed" by a net increase in liabilities of the United States to foreign official agencies.

The balance figure of − $5,729 million, which excludes only official transactions, is usually referred to as the "overall balance." In this balance, official reserves are considered to be the buffer account which bridges the gap created by discrepancies between the levels of supply of and demand for foreign exchange. When supply of foreign exchange exceeds demand for foreign exchange in the overall balance, foreign reserves increase. When demand for foreign currencies exceeds supply of these currencies, as in the computations above, official reserves decline, or the countries' liabilities increase to meet the gap. In our case, the increase in U.S. liabilities to foreign official agencies was the major factor compensating for the deficit in the overall balance. Of course, these differences between supply and demand and adjustments through changes in reserves and liabilities exist only to the extent that authorities insist on a fixed exchange rate. If exchange rates were allowed to float freely, official reserves would not be needed to bridge any gap. There would be no gap. The exchange rate would change, instead.

In many countries the overall balance is considered a good measure of the aggregate forces in the exchange market. In the case of the United States, this balance measure may not be adequate because of the special position of the U.S. dollar, which is a large component of the exchange reserves of many countries. The increase in U.S. liabilities held by foreign official agencies shown in Exhibit 6.1 may have been due to a desire of these authorities to maintain a larger proportion of their foreign exchange reserves in securities issued by the United States government. By contrast, official liabilities of other countries—particularly developing countries—usually grow in order to bridge the gap created by an excess demand for foreign exchange over the supply of that exchange.

What is behind each of the accounts in the balance of payments?

We have seen that in order to use the balance of payments as an instrument to measure pressures in the exchange market, we must understand the motivation behind different entries. Up to this point, the major distinction was between the accounts which should be included in computing the "balance" in the balance of payments and those which should be excluded because they represent actions directed toward "stabilizing" the tendencies of the market.

This emphasis helps explain historical pressures in the exchange markets. However, our major interest is in anticipating these pressures. In order to forecast the exchange rate movements, we must disaggregate the flows in the market, understand the forces that trigger them, and forecast the direction of these forces in the future. Only then can we obtain an overall picture of the net forces which are likely to be exerted in the exchange market in the future.

A thorough analysis of the economic forces at work in the various transactions in the exchange markets belongs to the domain of the economists. However, the funds manager must understand the major forces which shape these transactions. In the following discussion, we shall describe the major considerations which affect the different transactions in the exchange markets.

Merchandise trade

What are the economic variables which one must study to anticipate the behavior of the trade accounts? In a nutshell, there are three variables which largely determine the nature of the trade accounts:

1. Relative prices

2. Relative incomes

3. Degree of responsiveness on the part of the public to changes in the first two variables

Notice that the first two factors are prefaced by the word "relative." This points to two considerations one must keep in mind in analyzing these factors:

1. The level of prices in a given country, by itself, is devoid of meaning in this context unless it is compared with the levels of prices in the other countries that are major trading partners. The same consideration applies to the level of income.

2. Prices in each country which are relevant for comparison are only those of goods traded; changes in prices of nontraded goods affect prices of traded goods only indirectly.

Relative prices. We can think of changes in domestic prices as also being the result of the interaction of supply of and demand for those goods. Costs will determine the prices at which different amounts of goods are offered for sale. Growth in income will determine the amount demanded at different prices. We shall discuss relative incomes in the following section. Now let's concentrate on the forces which, independently of the amount demanded, affect the price of goods offered for sale.

Costs of goods can be segregated into the prices which must be paid to each factor of production: labor and capital. The prices paid to each of these factors are interrelated through productivity. The higher the amount of capital and degree of technology, the higher the productivity of a given labor-hour. The higher the skill of labor, the higher the productivity of capital. In assessing future developments in the costs of production, we should look at (1) wage levels and (2) output per labor-hour, or productivity.

Relative income. As income expands, consumption and investment also tend to expand. Domestically, this increase in demand will put an upward pressure on prices unless there is some unutilized capacity in the economy. The impact on the trade account depends on how the increased demand is channeled. An increased demand completely channeled into consumption will surely increase the amount of goods imported. On the other hand, an increased demand completely channeled into greater levels of investment, particularly in the export industries, will make these industries more competitive and will increase exports.

In the context of increases in demand, we must analyze the role which the government plays in stirring up demand. Government has two major sets of tools at its disposal: fiscal policy and monetary policy. When the government's objective is to increase aggregate demand, the national budget will be in deficit through lower taxation or higher government expenditures. In the area of monetary policy, to increase aggregate demand monetary authorities will act in such a way that money supply will increase faster than normal, and interest rates will tend to decline. The role of government in aggregate demand is discussed in more detail later in this chapter.

Responsiveness of the public to changes in relative prices and income. To understand fully the impact which a change in one of the variables just discussed would have on the trade account, it is necessary to study the commodity composition of the trade account. There are certain goods whose purchase is highly sensitive to changes in prices. As the price of beef, for example, increases, in many cases there is more than a proportional reduction in quantity purchased. On the other hand, there are some products where changes in prices have little, if any, impact on the amount purchased. For example, when the price of Mercedes Benz cars began to soar because of the upvaluation of the German mark against the U.S. dollar, people in the United States continued to buy them.

In evaluating the responsiveness of quantity purchased to changes in prices, one must bear in mind the magnitude of the price changes. In general, statements about how responsive purchases of a certain good are to changes in prices refer to relatively small price shifts. If large changes are perceived to be permanent, the changes in amount purchased relative to the change in price may be proportionally very different from what they would have been if the change in price had been relatively small. Historically, it has been thought that the consumption of oil in developed countries was very insensitive to changes in the price of oil. However, the quadrupling of prices of that product in 1973 resulted in large reductions in the purchases of oil.

The impact of changes in income on quantities purchased, like the impact of changes in prices, also depends on the magnitude of the income change as well as on the general level of income in the given country. A change in income in a developed country is likely to have less impact on the amount of beef purchased than when the change in income takes place in a less wealthy country.

The last paragraph points to the need also to disaggregate the trade account according to the major trading partners of the country of interest. This disaggregation is also useful in assessing the impact of changes in income on the amount consumed at a given price level. The purchase of all goods is not affected equally when income changes. There are some goods whose purchase is rather independent of the level of income, for example, bread. On the other hand, there are goods where a change in the income level may imply very different levels of purchases of those goods, e.g., cars.

Trade in services

The most important items in the service trade account are travel, transportation, and interest and dividends. Fees for various services, such as commissions on insurance, are also included in this account.

Travel and transportation are closely related to relative levels of income, relative prices of vacations in various lands, and transportation to those lands. Interest and dividends are the result of investments that the given country has made abroad, or that foreigners have made in the country for which the balance of payments is being prepared. When dividends and interest are received, they are a source of foreign exchange; when they are paid to foreigners, they represent a use of foreign exchange. In countries with sophisticated financial centers, fees and commissions usually represent a source of foreign exchange as financial services are rendered to foreigners. For example, Great Britain earned £742 million from such services in 1975.

Unilateral transfers

The importance of the unilateral transfers account in the balance of payments varies from country to country. This account is a mirror image of the migration profile of the country. In countries like Turkey, where citizens migrate to work abroad, this account is a source of foreign exchange as the migrants send funds to their relatives at home. On the other hand, countries such as West Germany and Switzerland, which have large numbers of immigrants coming in to work, find a large outflow in this account in the balance of payments.

Capital account

In describing the capital account, we must first distinguish among the various types of capital flows: direct investment, portfolio investment, and short-term investment.

Direct investment. This is the type of long-term investment where the investor controls a substantial portion of the management of the foreign operation. (For balance of payments purposes, substantial management control has often been defined as 10 percent or more of the ownership of the foreign unit.)

The reasons for extending business operations into foreign lands in the form of direct investment are many. On the cost side, investment abroad may be due to better accessibility to raw materials or to lower labor costs. On the marketing side, it may be a defensive move to preserve a market that was previously supplied by exports.

In addition to the economic considerations which motivate starting a new business in a foreign country, there are also considerations of a political nature. These considerations can be translated into economic terms; however, the triggering force is usually political. For example, investments may be made in one country rather than a neighboring one because of the relative political stability of the two countries. Also, one country may encourage direct investment more than another by giving special concessions, such as tariff protection, to the foreign investor.

Portfolio investment. For balance of payments purposes, portfolio investment involves investments with a maturity longer than one year. This investment can be in bonds or stocks. Thus, the expected returns on these investments in one country relative to the others are the determinants of the flows in this account. Given the scope of financial markets in most countries, the comparisons of expected returns are limited to the handful of countries with developed financial markets, such as the United States and the United Kingdom.

In assessing the relative returns on these securities, the element of foreign exchange risk must be introduced. It is not sufficient to compare the respective yields of ten-year bonds issued by the governments of the United States and the United Kingdom; rather, one must also assess the expected performance of the pound against the U.S. dollar to obtain the effective yields of the two securities.

Short-term capital. There are two major types of short-term capital flows:

1. Those made in connection with other entries in the balance of payments, such as a bank deposit received in payment for merchandise exported

2. Those made in search of profit

The short-term capital flows in search of profit are the flows considered in a comparison of relative returns. Again, as in the case of portfolio investments, the effective returns on short-term investments are a composite of the relative interest rates and the expected fluctuations of the exchange rate. In many cases, one of these two elements is the dominant one. For example, investments are made because of the relatively high interest rate paid in a given currency. The implicit assumption is that the given currency will remain relatively stable. In other cases, investors are willing to forgo high interest rates and invest in a currency with a very low interest rate in expectation of an upvaluation in the exchange rate of that currency.

Official reserves

We can call the official reserves account the short-term capital account for the government of the country in question. Government's motivations to operate in the exchange markets differ substantially from those considered in our discussion of short-term capital flows. The profit motive is not the triggering force in the change in official reserves. Changes in these reserves are actually the buffer for the net of all the transactions discussed above. In other words, the changes in official reserves are dictated by the government's policy toward fluctuations in the exchange rate of its currency together with the net of supply and demand in the market for the currency.

If the government follows a policy of fixed exchange rates, official reserves will increase whenever the demand for the country's currency exceeds its supply. The extra foreign currency which foreigners are offering in exchange for the country's currency will be reflected in increased official reserves. On the other hand, if the supply of domestic currency exceeds the demand for this currency, foreign reserves will decrease. The excess of foreign currency demanded in exchange for domestic currency will have to be contributed from official reserves.

In a system of truly floating rates, the government does not need to maintain reserves. Any disequilibrium between supply of and demand for foreign exchange will be settled through changes in the relative values of currencies. Under these conditions, official reserves are not called for to fill the gap between the market forces of supply and demand.

The bibliography in this book provides, for various countries, sources of the types of information discussed in this chapter.

Government economic policy

In order to understand the role of governments in the foreign exchange markets, it is necessary to grasp the complexity of the multiple objectives which these authorities pursue. In this discussion we shall concentrate on the most general of these objectives.

The broad objectives to which all governments are committed are full employment, price stability, and stability or improvement in the balance of payments. At times, different objectives appear to have a higher priority; at other times, particularly in election periods, it is hard to tell which objective is most important. The politician always promises eternal economic bliss in all areas! As we shall show, recognizing the priorities open to governments in choosing among these objectives is very important. Often, following one objective can be accomplished only at the expense of another. The measures used to attain the desired objectives, either domestic or international, all have repercussions in the external market.

Governments have a battery of tools at their disposal to attain their desired objectives. For simplicity's sake, we can group these tools into three major groups:

1. Monetary policy

2. Fiscal policy

3. Other policies, such as price controls

In this discussion we shall concentrate on the first two, monetary policy and fiscal policy.

Exhibit 6.2 shows in a simplified manner the actions which are called for to tackle individual problems. It also shows the impact of such actions on other economic objectives. For example, if obtaining high employment is the major concern of the government, we can expect that an undesirable level of unemployment in the economy will be met by a combination of expansionary monetary policy and fiscal deficit. Both these measures will tend to stimulate aggregate demand and, therefore, to create more jobs. Regardless of how successful the economic measures are in decreasing unemployment, they will have an impact on the level of inflation and on the external balance of payments. Depending on how fully industrial capacity is being utilized at the moment, an increase in demand will tend to increase prices, that is, to accelerate inflation. If there is a high degree of capacity utilization, the impact on inflation will be high. If, on the other hand, there is a good deal of slack capacity in the economy, prices will not be affected much by the increase in demand. However, in this context, one must differentiate among industries. Although there may be excess capacity in some industries, other industries may already be working at full capacity. The price increases will tend to affect different industries at different rates. In our context, we are particularly interested in analyzing the inflationary impact on the export industries.

Exhibit 6.2
INTERACTIONS BETWEEN GOVERNMENT POLICY AND ECONOMIC OBJECTIVES

Problem	Prescription to Attack Problem	Impact on Other Economic Objectives
1. High unemployment	Expansionary monetary and fiscal policy	*Price Levels:* Inflationary trends mitigated by extent of excess capacity *External Balance:* Deterioration; import increase, mitigated by extent to which new investment improves exports' competitiveness
2. High inflation	Contractionary monetary and fiscal policy	*Employment:* Tendency to decrease as aggregate demand declines *External Balance:* Improvement; imports decrease, mitigated by any loss in export competitiveness
3. Balance of payments deficit	Contractionary monetary and fiscal policy	*Employment:* Tendency to decrease as aggregate demand declines *Inflation:* Tendency to decrease as aggregate demand declines
4. Balance of payments surplus	Expansionary monetary and fiscal policy	*Employment:* Tendency to increase as aggregate demand increases *Inflation:* Tendency to increase as aggregate demand increases

In terms of external balance, expansionary measures taken by the government in response to high unemployment will tend to increase demand for imports. As aggregate demand increases, so will the demand for imports. We must also consider the impact of aggregate demand on the export industries. To the extent that the increased demand is channeled into new investment in the export industries, the increased competitiveness of these industries may generate incremental growth in exports. Thus, the increase in aggregate demand tends to increase imports, but it may also affect export competitiveness.

If the problem on which the government chooses to focus is a balance of payments deficit, the economic measures called for are a contractionary monetary policy and a fiscal surplus. In contrast to the previous example, these measures will tend to increase unemployment and decrease the inflation rate. The desired objective will be achieved to the extent that the dampened aggregate demand translates itself into lower imports, and the lower inflation rate is reflected in more competitive exports.

These two examples point to the dilemma which policymakers must face constantly in choosing among various objectives. In these examples, if the high level of unemployment coincides with the problem of a persisting balance of payments deficit, the government must make a conscious decision as to which objective is most important. The outcome of such a decision will affect the foreign exchange markets in diametrically opposite ways. Attention to the domestic problem of unemployment will tend to aggravate the problem of balance of payments deficits. Attention to the balance of payments deficits will tend to aggravate the domestic problem of unemployment.

A similar dilemma between the external position of the country and its domestic objectives is encountered when a persisting balance of payments surplus appears in conjunction with a high rate of domestic inflation. The more the government combats domestic inflation, the more competitive its goods become internationally, and the larger the balance of payments surplus. The more the government attempts to control the balance of payments surplus, the larger the inflation rate in the domestic economy.

From this discussion, it is obvious that an assessment of the relative importance which a government places on the solution of its economic problems is essential in anticipating the behavior of the exchange markets. Attention to the utilization of the tools at the command of the government can indicate how the government is ranking its various priorities at the time. A study of the changes in money supply, interest rates, government expenditures, and government revenues is of the utmost importance to an understanding of which policies the government is following as demonstrated by its actions. This understanding will then contribute to the overall perception of the relative weight that different goals are receiving and, therefore, the impact of government in the exchange markets.

Before leaving this topic, it may be useful to point to the association of economic philosophy with different parties in a country and with different governments. Traditionally, in the United States the Democratic Party has placed more emphasis on the problem of unemployment and less on the problem of inflation than the Republican Party. At the international level, countries such as the United Kingdom have been known to place a much larger emphasis on full employment while West Germany has been most concerned with the problem of inflation.

A major factor affecting the choice between external equilibrium and domestic objectives is the nature of international agreements among nations. The dilemma in policy, discussed earlier, assumes that restoring external equilibrium has to be done at a given exchange rate. This is true under a system of fixed exchange rates. An alternative system is to allow exchange rates to fluctuate in order to settle the imbalances in the external balances. A brief history of the systems of adjustment which have prevailed since World War II and the considerations behind these agreements are presented in the final section of this chapter.

Technical and psychological factors

Movements in the trade figures and capital account figures certainly determine the behavior of a currency over a long period of time. In addition to these long-term forces, operators in the exchange and money markets are also sensitive to psychological and technical reactions which may reverse temporarily the basic longer-term trend of exchange rates.

It is not uncommon for professional market participants to have two opinions at the same time regarding the trend of a specific currency in the exchange market. One opinion may relate to the long-term trend which is based on the fundamental economic forces discussed above. The other opinion may be concerned with the very short-term trend of a currency which is based on the technical and psychological conditions of the market. We shall present some examples of how these temporary discrepancies may develop.

Whenever there is a discrepancy between the previously held expectation of a given economic event and the actual outcome of that event, exchange rates will usually be affected. For example, the market may expect trade figures for a specific month for a country like West Germany to be a surplus of US$1.5 billion. However, when the actual figures are announced, they report a surplus of "only" US$1.0 billion. This surplus still represents an historically positive impact on the balance of payments—an increase in the demand for marks. Furthermore, to the extent that this trade surplus will continue in the long term, the mark will tend to continue to increase in value relative to other currencies. However, the immediate reaction of the market to the announcement will probably be negative. The exchange rate before the report of the real surplus was based on the expectation of a demand for marks, that is, of a trade surplus even larger than the one actually reported. The adjustment of expectations to reality will tend to depress the price of the mark temporarily.

The behavior of a major participant in the market can affect the exchange rate in the short term, regardless of the long-term economic forces. Just the fact that a major market operator is either buying or selling a specific currency for some unknown reason is enough motivation for some other participants to do the same. Over a short period of time, this type of activity can have the effect of a self-fulfilling prophecy.

Another influence on the exchange rate is any knowledge of agreements among central banks. For example, the central banks of two countries may agree to keep their two currencies at approximately the same exchange rate level against each other. Over the last few years the Swiss franc and the mark have frequently maintained such a relationship. Obviously, the assumption that the relative levels of these two currencies will be kept stable has not held true all the time, but it has prevailed often enough to be used as an example. Traders could be fairly confident that a rise in the rate of the U.S. dollar against the Swiss franc would soon be followed by a similar rise in the rate of the U.S. dollar against the mark, and vice versa. Thus, when one rate moved, traders acted in such a way that changes in the other rate tended to follow promptly.

Another example of how the knowledge of the behavior of a large market participant affects the market is the case of a country with large exchange reserves in sterling which decides to switch some of its reserves from pounds into marks. The market for sterling against marks is not nearly so well developed as the markets for sterling against U.S. dollars and for marks against U.S. dollars. Therefore, the country chooses to sell sterling against U.S. dollars and then sell the U.S. dollar proceeds against marks. The net of these two transactions is a sterling sale and a mark purchase. Professional market participants soon learn during this period that whenever large blocks of sterling are sold against U.S. dollars (putting downward pressure on the sterling rate), there will shortly be a similar upward pressure on the mark against the U.S. dollar.

Considerations of a psychological or technical nature do not always cause short-term rate movements which are opposite to those movements supported by an analysis of long-term forces. It is just as likely and possible that psychological and technical factors will accelerate and reinforce an already existing long-term basic trend. The challenge for the professional operator in the exchange market is to determine whether a movement contrary to the basic trend is of a temporary nature, or whether this movement is the beginning of a change in the basic long-term trend. In this endeavor, we must note the way in which psychological factors can have their greatest impact on the exchange markets. The "gut feeling" fueled by these factors can be very important in subconsciously arriving at decisions which are thought to be solely the result of a rational evaluation of anticipated movements in the trade and capital accounts.

International monetary system

Before closing this chapter, it may be useful to introduce a bit of historical perspective in the development of the present monetary system. Let's begin with the contemporary period after World War II. With the economic disaster of the Great Depression of the 1930s and the devastation of the war as a background, representatives of the noncommunist world gathered at Bretton Woods, New Hampshire, in 1944 to define the characteristics of a new international monetary system. The highlights of the agreements reached at the Bretton Woods Conference are the following:

1. *Unit of account.* The value of the U.S. dollar was expressed in gold; the value of other currencies was expressed mostly in terms of U.S. dollars although the participating nations had the option of defining the value of their currencies in terms of gold.

2. *Adjustment mechanism.* Exchange rates were to remain fixed except in the case of "fundamental disequilibrium," when a devaluation or an

upvaluation was called for. To maintain the fixed rate, the participating governments agreed to intervene in the foreign exchange markets to counteract forces which threatened the agreed-upon exchange rates. An alternative to intervention in the exchange markets was to adjust the domestic economy in such a manner as to compensate for the imbalance between the supply of and demand for the country's currency. For example, when the market supply of a currency exceeded the demand for it—a tendency for devaluation of the currency—the government of the country in question was expected to intervene in the foreign exchange market by offering foreign exchange from its official reserves and purchasing its own currency. Concurrently, particularly if the crisis was severe, the government was also expected to install domestic austerity measures designed to curb aggregate demand.

3. Sources of liquidity. Two major items constituted the reserves which countries were expected to maintain to balance any temporary disequilibrium between supply of and demand for its currency: gold and U.S. dollars. For most countries, international reserves were composed chiefly of U.S. dollars.

4. Supervision. A new institution was created to "supervise" the system and to serve as lender to countries in temporary balance of payments deficit—the International Monetary Fund.

This system served the world well through the 1950s and early 1960s. By the mid-1960s, two weak points of the agreement started to become increasingly burdensome. In the adjustment mechanism, deficit countries appeared to carry the burden of adjustment while surplus countries could endure the rage of the rest of the world while accumulating foreign reserves. Deficit countries, such as the United Kingdom, had to revert periodically to tough economic measures designed to dampen economic growth in demand. As these crises persisted, the burden of deflating domestic economies appeared heavier and heavier. In the case of the United Kingdom, the pound sterling was finally devalued in 1967.

One other weak point of the Bretton Woods system was that it relied heavily on the United States to provide U.S. dollars to give liquidity to the system. This could be accomplished in only one fashion: by continued deficits in the U.S. balance of payments, i.e., a continuous increase in the liabilities of the United States. On the one hand, this provision appeared to put the United States in a privileged position relative to other countries;

it could run deficits continuously without being forced to curb its domestic economy. On the other hand, the foreign exchange markets started raising questions as to the reasonableness of the increased amount of U.S. dollars in foreign hands. Now the crises of confidence turned away from deficit countries, such as the United Kingdom and France, to the surplus countries. Actually, turning funds into the currencies of the surplus nations was the same as getting rid of unwanted U.S. dollars. The difference was that now the pressure was felt most directly by the surplus countries that saw themselves flooded with speculative funds attracted by the possibility of an upvaluation of these currencies against the U.S. dollar—a devaluation of the U.S. dollar against these currencies.

These crises continued through the late 1960s until August 1971, when the United States cut the link between the value of its currency and gold, let the U.S. dollar's value float in the market, and stopped convertibility of its currency into gold. By the end of that year, with the Smithsonian Agreement, a new value for the U.S. dollar in terms of gold had been established, and the developed world returned to a system of fixed rates at the newly revised parities. However, the U.S. dollar remained unconvertible into gold at the official rate.

The country which had resisted monetary crises the longest in the past, the United Kingdom, was the first now to allow the value of its currency to float in the exchange markets in June 1972. Early 1973 was to put the final seal on the new economic reality that fixed rates are very hard to maintain in a market where currencies are freely convertible into one another, and where a large amount of liquid funds can move from one currency into another. After a second devaluation of the U.S. dollar in February 1973, the turmoil of the foreign exchange markets forced the major European currencies to declare that they would allow the value of their currencies to float against the U.S. dollar. However, the exchange rate of the currencies participating in this bloc, the European Monetary Union—also referred to as "the snake"—was to remain relatively stable through intervention of the participating countries.

Floating rates as an accepted general adjustment mechanism in the international monetary system had come of age. The remaining part of 1973 and 1974 witnessed wide fluctuations in the exchange markets. Forces that had been clamped down in previous periods were now free to operate. In addition, the quadrupling of oil prices at the end of 1973 was to bring the world into the largest downswing since the Great Depression. Some individuals say that under such conditions, exchange rates fluctuated within reasonable bounds; a system of fixed exchange rates would not have survived the economic instability of those years.

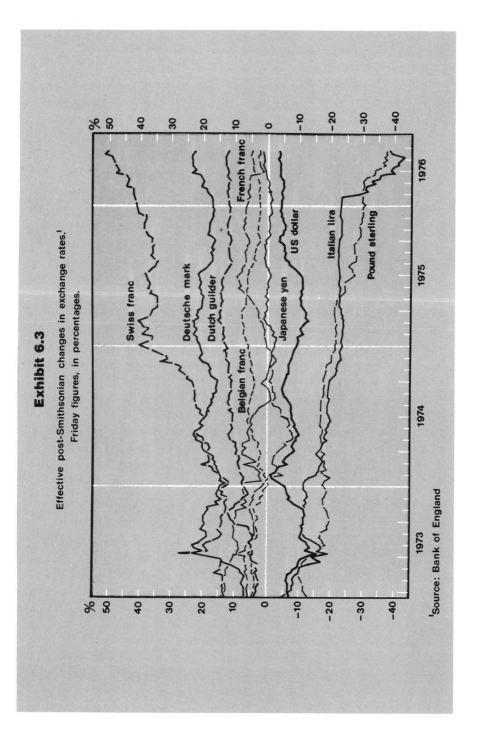

Exhibit 6.3

Effective post-Smithsonian changes in exchange rates.[1]
Friday figures, in percentages.

[1]Source: Bank of England

In spite of the limitations attributed to the system of fixed rates, now that the world had had a taste of widely fluctuating exchange rates, there was a desire for some stability. By the end of 1975 and in early 1976 governments were signing agreements in support of a greater stability in the exchange markets. The mechanism to achieve this goal, while maintaining the freedom of floating exchange rates, was to encourage better coordination among the economic policies of the various countries.

Anybody who has witnessed the difficulties of reaching compromises among different parties within the domestic economy can imagine the problems of coordinating economic policies among countries. Thus, 1976 saw some of the largest fluctuations in the values of currencies in the postwar period. Again, the pound sterling was to lead the world into this new pattern of behavior. The value of the pound sterling moved from \$2.00/£ to \$1.60/£. The lira also experienced a large devaluation. The mark upvalued toward the end of the year. Floating exchange rates so far had proven to be highly volatile.

For a picture of the nature of fluctuations in exchange rates for the period 1973–1976, see Exhibit 6.3. Of course, flexible rates were used only by the major currencies of developed countries. Most of the countries in the world continued in a system of fixed rates with their currencies' values usually pegged to one of the major currencies.

It is true that the social, economic, and political pressures in the countries undergoing the large fluctuations in their exchange rates during the 1970s were unprecedented in the postwar era. Perhaps the exchange markets were just reflecting the instability of the economic conditions of those countries. However, it was clear that governments had become much less willing to try to oppose the prevailing forces in the foreign exchange market. Forecasting the intervention of governments in the exchange markets was much more difficult. Some would argue that even the direction in which the governments would intervene was less predictable. Some even said that governments had, on occasion, joined the market forces in precipitating impending changes in the value of their currencies.

PART II

A few days in the life of a funds manager

The groundwork has now been covered. We understand the pricing system in the foreign exchange market and the money market; we have mastered the nature of the relationship between the money market and the foreign exchange market; and, we have been introduced to the problems of the funds manager who must operate in these markets.

What we need now is further practice in these basic concepts. To provide this, the following chapters will discuss a series of problems which funds managers must deal with. These problems are found in real life with relative frequency. Thus, these examples will serve to analyze specific problems as well as to develop our further understanding of the functioning of these markets.

We have divided this section into three chapters. In Chapter 7 we focus on the problems encountered in the trading room. This trading room may be a full-fledged operation in a commercial bank, or it may be thought of as only one of the many functions which must be performed in the treasurer's office. In Chapter 8 we address some of the problems which nonfinancial businesses must confront in the exchange markets. Nonfinancial businesses look at financial markets as one among many resources which must be marshaled to accomplish their primary business goal—something other than profiting from dealing in the financial markets. Finally, in Chapter 9 we have gathered several cases which illustrate some of the considerations which must be taken into account in order to calculate properly the yield or cost of funds in the money and foreign exchange markets.

CHAPTER 7
Problems and opportunities in the trading room

Most of the discussion in this chapter refers to the funds manager who operates in the financial markets, trying to make a profit, given risk constraints. However, this manager must also accommodate to the demands imposed by the rest of the organization; for example, the need to offer services to one of the organization's customers. In the last section of the chapter, we shall talk about the problems confronted by central banks, which have objectives other than making a profit.

Cases about business enterprises

With the exception of the last case, we shall assume in this section that we do not wish to maintain any exchange position. The net exchange position at each point must be zero. However, the maturity of the cash flows in each currency does not need to match every time.

In the earlier examples, we shall abstract from the complications of bid and offer rates. The rates presented here can be assumed to be the mid-rates between the bid and offer. Alternatively, we may take these rates as being the market rates at which we must deal; that is, we are the rate takers. Later on, we shall introduce the impact of the existence of bid and offer rates on the trader's behavior.

How to take advantage of disequilibrium situations

In the previous chapters we have established the nature of the relationship between the foreign exchange market and the money market. The annualized swap rate expressed as a percentage of the spot rate must equal the difference between the net accessible interest rates in the two currencies in question. Whenever this relationship does not prevail, there is an incentive for the funds manager to profit without any foreign

Exhibit 7.1
ARBITRAGE WHERE SWAP RATE IS
LARGER THAN INTEREST DIFFERENTIAL

RATE SCENARIO

Money Market, Three-Months Maturity

Eurodollar rate	7%
Europound rate	10%

Foreign Exchange Market

Spot rate	$2.4000/£
Three-month swap rate	$0.0200/£ (discount on pound against dollar)

CASH FLOWS

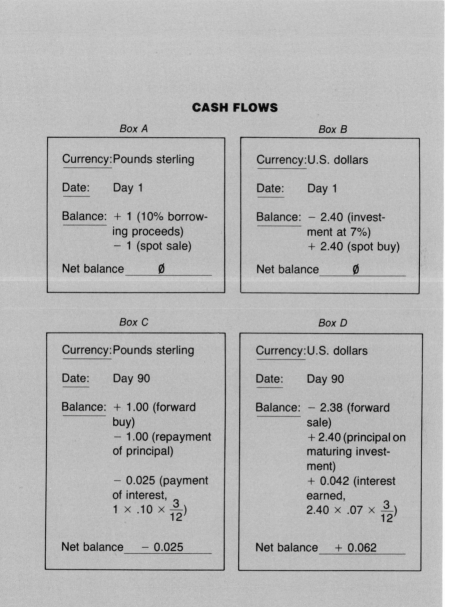

Box A

Currency: Pounds sterling

Date: Day 1

Balance: + 1 (10% borrow-
         ing proceeds)
         − 1 (spot sale)

Net balance _____Ø_____

Box B

Currency: U.S. dollars

Date: Day 1

Balance: − 2.40 (invest-
         ment at 7%)
         + 2.40 (spot buy)

Net balance _____Ø_____

Box C

Currency: Pounds sterling

Date: Day 90

Balance: + 1.00 (forward
         buy)
         − 1.00 (repayment
         of principal)

         − 0.025 (payment
         of interest,
         $1 \times .10 \times \frac{3}{12}$)

Net balance _____− 0.025_____

Box D

Currency: U.S. dollars

Date: Day 90

Balance: − 2.38 (forward
         sale)
         + 2.40 (principal on
         maturing invest-
         ment)
         + 0.042 (interest
         earned,
         $2.40 \times .07 \times \frac{3}{12}$)

Net balance _____+ 0.062_____

exchange risk; i.e., there is an opportunity to profit from *covered interest arbitrage*.

Swap rate is larger than interest differential. In the scenario presented in Exhibit 7.1, the interest differential is 3 percent in favor of the pound. The 200 points of swap rate for three months is equivalent to 800 points on an annual basis. These 800 points on an annual basis represent a 3.33 percent discount on the three-month pound against the dollar. Therefore, the discount implied by the swap rate is larger than the interest differential. How can we benefit from this situation?

The general rule of thumb is that we should prefer to invest in the higher interest rate currency on a covered basis unless the discount on that currency is larger than the advantage provided by the higher interest rate. If the discount is larger than the interest differential, we shall benefit by investing in currency with the lower interest rate.

In our specific example, the discount on the pound, the higher interest rate currency, exceeds the interest differentials. Therefore, we should benefit from investing on a covered basis in dollars, the lower interest rate currency. The funds to finance this investment will be raised in pounds. These pounds will be converted into dollars at the spot rate and swapped back into pounds at the forward rate. The net cost of these funds will be:

Interest rate on pound borrowing	10.00%
Swap rate in our favor (sell pounds against dollars spot; buy three-month pounds against dollars at a discount on pounds)	− 3.33
Net cost of dollar funds on a covered basis	6.67%

At this point we have dollars available to be invested at the going rate of 7 percent without incurring any foreign exchange risk. The net exchange position is zero, and the maturity of the cash flows are all matched. This is shown in the cash flow boxes in Exhibit 7.1. The net of the balances in Box C and Box D represents the net profit in the operation:

Interest earned in dollars plus favorable swap rate	$0.062
Less cost of borrowings (£0.025 × 2.40)	−0.060
	$0.002

A profit of \$0.002/£ represents a profit of .0833 percent $\left(\dfrac{0.002 \times 100}{2.40}\right)$ *for*

Exhibit 7.2
IMPACT OF INTEREST ARBITRAGE WHEN SWAP RATE IS LARGER THAN INTEREST DIFFERENTIAL

Trends of Rates

Borrow pounds at 10%   ↑

Sell pounds spot at $2.40   } 3.33%
Buy pounds forward at $2.38   } discount   ↓
                                   } on pounds

Invest dollars at 7%   ↓

Exhibit 7.3
ARBITRAGE WHERE SWAP RATE IS
SMALLER THAN INTEREST DIFFERENTIAL

RATE SCENARIO

Money Market, Three-Months Maturity

Eurodollar rate	7%
Europound rate	10%

Foreign Exchange Market

Spot rate	$2.4000/£
Three-month swap rate	$0.0150/£ (discount on pound)

CASH FLOWS

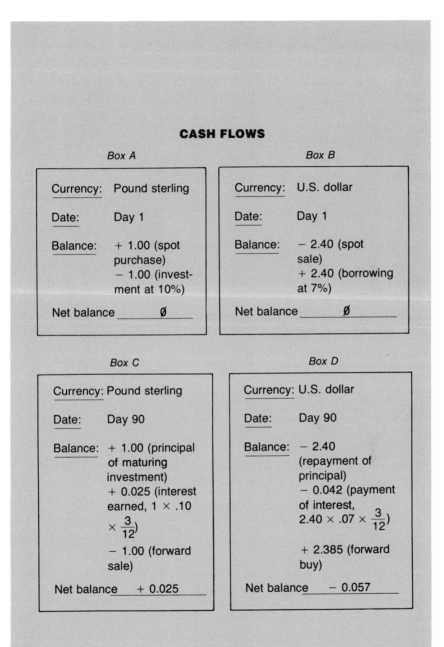

Box A

Currency: Pound sterling

Date: Day 1

Balance: + 1.00 (spot purchase)
− 1.00 (investment at 10%)

Net balance ___ Ø ___

Box B

Currency: U.S. dollar

Date: Day 1

Balance: − 2.40 (spot sale)
+ 2.40 (borrowing at 7%)

Net balance ___ Ø ___

Box C

Currency: Pound sterling

Date: Day 90

Balance: + 1.00 (principal of maturing investment)
+ 0.025 (interest earned, $1 \times .10 \times \frac{3}{12}$)
− 1.00 (forward sale)

Net balance ___ + 0.025 ___

Box D

Currency: U.S. dollar

Date: Day 90

Balance: − 2.40 (repayment of principal)
− 0.042 (payment of interest, $2.40 \times .07 \times \frac{3}{12}$)
+ 2.385 (forward buy)

Net balance ___ − 0.057 ___

three months, which is equivalent to 0.33 percent p.a., the difference between the swap rate and the interest differential.

This disparity or disequilibrium between net accessible interest rates and the forward discount for pounds against dollars cannot prevail in the marketplace for long. The constant demand for pounds will tend to increase the interest rate of 10 percent. Likewise, continuing swaps (selling spot pounds against dollars, buying forward pounds against dollars) will tend to reduce the 3.33 percent forward discount on the pound. Also, the placements of dollars at 7 percent will put downward pressure on the interest rate of 7 percent. These three pressures will continue until change in one, two, or all three of the above-mentioned rates will result in parity again. (See Exhibit 7.2.)

Swap rate is smaller than interest differentials. In this case, presented in Exhibit 7.3, the interest differential is also 3 percent. However, the swap rate of 150 points for three months indicates a discount of 2.50 percent p.a. on the three-month pound against the dollar.

The general rule is that in covered interest arbitrage, we shall want to invest in the higher interest currency except when the discount in that currency is higher than the interest differential. Thus, in this case we will want to invest in the pound, the higher interest rate currency.

To generate pounds which can be invested without assuming any foreign exchange risk, we should borrow dollars and swap them spot into pounds and back into dollars for three-month delivery. The cost of doing this will be:

Interest rate on dollar borrowings	7.00%
Swap rate against us (sell spot dollars against pounds; buy three-month dollars against pounds at a premium for dollars)	+ 2.50%
Net cost of funds on a covered basis	9.50%

The pounds obtained in the spot part of the swap transaction can be invested at 10 percent. The net result is a profit of 0.50 percent p.a.

Again, in this transaction all cash flows are matched: for every inflow in a given currency at a given date, there is an outflow, and vice versa. Also, the net exchange position is basically zero except for the net profit which can be covered in the forward exchange market. Profits will accumulate in pounds while the interest on the borrowings is payable in dollars. (See Exhibit 7.3.) To eliminate this risk, the interest earned in the pound

Exhibit 7.4
IMPACT OF INTEREST ARBITRAGE WHEN SWAP RATE IS SMALLER THAN INTEREST DIFFERENTIAL

		Trends of Rates
Borrow dollars at 7%		↑
Sell dollars spot at $2.40/£ Buy dollars forward at $2.385/£	} 2.50% discount on pound	↑
Invest pounds at 10%		↓

investment could be sold in the exchange market for three-month delivery at the initial 2.5 percent discount on the pound against the dollar.

This disequilibrium in the market will also tend to be short-lived. The arbitrage transaction described here will tend to move the various rates back into equilibrium, as shown in Exhibit 7.4.

How to take advantage of expected changes in interest rates

If we anticipate a change in interest rates, we are also anticipating a change in net accessible interest differentials and, therefore, in the swap rate. We can take advantage of the expected change in rates in either the money market or in the foreign exchange market. In the money market, we will simultaneously borrow and invest in the currency whose interest we are expecting to change. However, the maturity of the borrowing will be different from that of the investment. In the foreign exchange market, we have to deal with two currencies. To take advantage of the expected change in swap rates, we will buy and sell each currency simultaneously. However, the maturity of the buy and sell in each currency will be different. Let's illustrate the mechanics of this transaction.

Consider a case where the interest rate of a currency is expected to decrease. The rates in Exhibit 7.5 summarize the present situation and the forecast.[1] We expect interest rates on the pound will decline by 1 percent within a month, and so will the discount on the forward pound. How does one take advantage of this piece of intelligence?

Money market. In this market we want to lock in the present high return of 13 percent on placements in pounds. So, we make a placement for, say, six months. To finance this loan we need to raise funds; however, since we expect interest rates to decline in a month, we shall borrow the funds only for that period. Assuming that the pound interest rate changes as anticipated, the returns will be zero for the first month (lending and borrowing costs are the same) and 1 percent p.a. for the remaining five months (13 percent on the loan less 12 percent borrowing costs).

We can see this money transaction in terms of cash flow boxes in Exhibit 7.5. The net gain of the transaction when dealing with £1 million is

---

[1] Normally, we would not find such flat yield curves where interest rates are the same, regardless of maturity. In addition, the shape of the yield curve is likely to be different for each currency; so, interest differentials do not remain constant, regardless of maturity. However, these assumptions help to simplify the presentation.

£4,167 (£15,000 net inflow in Box C less £10,833 net outflow in Box B). At an exchange rate of $2.40, this amounts to $10,000 profit.

Foreign exchange market. The information from which we are trying to benefit is the expected decline in the discount in the forward pound. We expect that discount to decrease from the present 3 percent to 2 percent. (In our example, this decline is based on the prediction of a decrease of 1 percent in the pound interest rate from 13 percent to 12 percent.) If the discount of a given currency is going to decrease, then, as long as the spot rate remains unchanged, one can say that the forward outright price of that currency is going to increase. On the basis of basic economic principles, we want to buy when prices are low and sell when prices are high. In this case we will want to buy the forward pound now while the discount is large (the price is relatively low) and sell it later when the discount is smaller. When we deal in the foreign exchange market, we have to deal with two currencies. Therefore, the previous statement can also be read as "sell forward U.S. dollars now at the present high premium and buy them later when the premium against the pound has decreased."

If we do not wish to assume a net exchange position to take advantage of the expected change in rates, we have to operate through swap transactions. From the previous paragraph we know that we want to buy pounds against dollars for delivery, say, in six months after the change in rates has taken place. However, if we do only this transaction, we shall have a net exchange position. We will be overbought in pounds and oversold in dollars. To eliminate the exchange risks associated with this net exchange position, we have to produce the opposite cash flows for each currency. We have to sell pounds and buy dollars. However, we know that if we do the compensating transaction for six-month delivery as well, we will not profit from our forecast. We actually want to make the compensating transaction only for the period up to the rate change. After the rate change takes place, then we can square the cash flow position. Since we are expecting the change in rate to occur within a month, we shall enter the compensating transaction for only one month. During that month we will have a zero net exchange position with purchases equal to sales in each currency, but we will not realize any profit, and our cash flows will not be matched. At the end of the first month, after the rates have changed, we can redo the compensating transaction at the new rates and with a maturity to match the initial six-month purchase of pounds against dollars. In this second move we shall not only lock in the new rates, a lower discount on the pound, but we shall continue having a zero net exchange position—now with a "matched cash flow" position.

Exhibit 7.5
ACTING ON ANTICIPATED
CHANGES IN INTEREST RATES:
MONEY MARKET APPROACH

RATE SCENARIO

	Money Market (all maturities up to six months)	Foreign Exchange Market
Initial Situation:		
Pound sterling	13%	
		3% discount on pounds
U.S. dollar	10%	
Anticipated Situation in One Month:		
Pound sterling	12%	
		implies 2% discount on pounds
U.S. dollar	10%	

CASH FLOWS

Box A

Currency:	Pound sterling
Date:	January 1
Balance:	− 1,000,000 (placement at 13% for six months)
	+ 1,000,000 (borrowings at 13% for one month)
Net balance	Ø

Box B

Currency:	Pound sterling
Date:	February 1
Balance:	− 1,010,833 (repayment of one-month borrowings at 13%)
	+ 1,000,000 (borrowings at 12% for five months)
Net balance	− 10,833

Box C

Currency:	Pound sterling
Date:	July 1
Balance:	+ 1,065,000 (repayment of our placement at 13% on January 1)
	− 1,050,000 (repayment of five-month debt at 12% initiated on February 1)
Net balance	+ 15,000

In our example, the following rates will prevail:

Spot rate—$2.40/£
3 percent discount on the pound is equal to:

$.0720 per year[2]   so one-year outright rate is $2.3280
(.03 × 2.40)   (2.4000 − .0720)

$.0060 per one   so one month outright rate is $2.3940
month[2]   (2.4000 − .0060)
(.0720 ÷ 12)

$.0360 per six   so six-month outright rate is $2.3640
months[2]   (2.4000 − .0360)
(.0060 × 6)

2 percent discount on the pound is equal to:

$.0480 per year[2]   so one-year outright rate is $2.3520
(.02 × 2.40)   (2.4000 − .0480)

$.0040 per month[2] so one-month outright rate is $2.3960
(.0480 ÷ 12)   (2.4000 − .0040)

$.0200 per five   so five-month outright rate is $2.3800
months[2]   (2.4000 − .0200)
(.0040 × 5)

The sequence of events will then be as follows:

On January 1:

1. Purchase pounds against U.S. dollars at *3 percent discount* value date July 1. (Outright rate is $2.3640/£.)

2. Sell pounds against U.S. dollars at 3 percent discount for value date February 1. (Outright rate is $2.3940.) This second transaction guarantees a zero net exposure; however, the cash flow maturity is different from the first one. We have a swap position.

---

[2] These swap rates are for the pound against the dollar for the maturities indicated; i.e., when we anticipate a change in the forward outright rate, we are anticipating a change in the swap rate, provided the spot rate does not change.

On February 1:

1. Purchase pounds against U.S. dollars in the spot market to satisfy the original one-month forward contract entered into on January 1. (Spot rate is $2.4000/£.)

2. *Sell pounds* against U.S. dollars at *2 percent discount* against us, value date July 1. (Outright rate is $2.38/£.) This second transaction locks in the profit derived from the change in the forward discount. (The pounds value date July 1 were initially purchased at 3 percent discount in our favor; now we are selling them at 2 percent discount against us.) This leg of the transaction also guarantees that on July 1, cash flows are squared, which they were not throughout January.

We can visualize this transaction in the cash flow boxes in Exhibit 7.6. These boxes show a net profit of $10,000 ($16,000 in Box D less $6000 in Box B). This profit is the result of zero profits for the first months when purchases and sales of pounds against dollars were made at the same discount, 3 percent, plus 1 percent per annum profit on the spread realized during the remaining five months when pounds were purchased against dollars at 3 percent discount and sold at 2 percent. In terms of points, we know that the 3 percent discount for five months is $0.0300 (0.0060 × 5), and that 2 percent discount for five months is $0.0200 (0.0040 × 5). Therefore, we have realized $0.0100 profit per pound in the swap transaction for five months. Since we illustrated the example with £1 million, here we have realized $10,000, which is what the example shows.

Notice that the profit obtained by operating in the foreign exchange market is the same as that realized using the money market. In both cases the profit is $10,000 when dealing with £1 million[3]. If we convert this profit to percentage terms, we find that we have made a return of 0.417 percent in five months on the $2.4 million or £1 million we were dealing with. A return of 0.417 percent for five months is equivalent to 1 percent per annum. This is the amount of the change in interest differentials from which we profited.

Since the profit obtained by either route is the same, one must decide which one to use by evaluating the risks that each approach involves. This problem is discussed in Chapter 11.

[3] In Exhibit 7.5 the profit of £4167 equals $10,000 at the spot rate of $2.4000/£.

Exhibit 7.6
ACTING ON ANTICIPATED CHANGE IN INTEREST RATES: EXCHANGE MARKET SOLUTION

RATE SCENARIO

	Money Market (maturities up to six months)	Foreign Exchange Market
Initial Situation:		
Pounds sterling	13%	Spot rate: $2.40/£ 3% p.a. discount on pounds
U.S. dollars	10%	One-month swap rate: $0.0060/£
Anticipated Situation:		
Pounds sterling	12%	Spot rate: $2.40/£ 2% p.a. discount on pounds
U.S. dollars	10%	One-month swap rate: $0.0040/£

CASH FLOWS

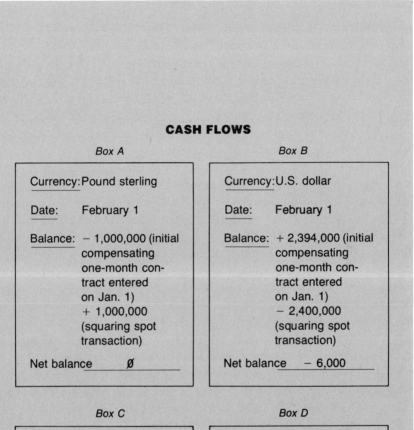

Box A

Currency: Pound sterling

Date: February 1

Balance: − 1,000,000 (initial compensating one-month con- tract entered on Jan. 1) + 1,000,000 (squaring spot transaction)

Net balance   ∅

Box B

Currency: U.S. dollar

Date: February 1

Balance: + 2,394,000 (initial compensating one-month con- tract entered on Jan. 1) − 2,400,000 (squaring spot transaction)

Net balance   − 6,000

Box C

Currency: Pound sterling

Date: July 1

Balance: + 1,000,000 (six-month con- tract entered on Jan. 1) − 1,000,000 (squaring five- month contract entered on Feb. 1)

Net balance   ∅

Box D

Currency: U.S. dollar

Date: July 1

Balance: − 2,364,000 (six-month con- tract entered on Jan. 1) + 2,380,000 (squaring five- month contract entered on Feb. 1)

Net balance   + 16,000

How to get out of an exchange position

The trading room often finds itself with net exchange positions which are imposed on the trader who has the function of providing services to the rest of the organization. This is quite common in a commercial bank where the foreign exchange department must provide services to the bank's customers. It also happens as a result of the normal cash flows generated by any business enterprise. Here we choose the example of a bank to illustrate the point. However, the initial position could be imposed by any unanticipated business transaction.

Let's take the case of an unanticipated purchase of forward foreign exchange. To provide a service to a customer, the bank purchases pounds against dollars value one month forward at $2.3930/£. The transaction occurs late in the afternoon in the United States when the foreign exchange market is about to close (Europe is already closed). For this reason the bank gives a quote 10 points lower than the general market rate of 2.3940. The bank knows that it cannot get out of the forward position today. It has to wait until tomorrow. The 10 points are not only profit margin but also a cushion for the overnight risk. The market rates are presented in Exhibit 7.7.

The first problem which our trader confronts is that of now having a net overbought position in pounds (and a net oversold position in dollars). To remedy this situation, our trader does the opposite in the spot market of what was just done with each currency in the forward market. That is, the trader will sell pounds against dollars spot. Now, for both pounds and dollars, buys equal sells. Our trader has created a swap position. Before, we called this situation "an engineered swap position." This is shown in the first entry in each box in Exhibit 7.7.

The engineered swap transaction (the spot sale of pounds) eliminated the risk of having a net overbought position in pounds overnight. Now our trader's profits are unaffected by any change in the spot rate of the pound. However, a problem of mismatched maturities remains, as Exhibit 7.7 shows. In other words, our trader has switched a *net* exchange position into a *swap* position, and is no longer vulnerable to movements in the spot rate for pounds against dollars. The trader's profits can now be affected only by a change in interest rate differentials and the corresponding change in the swap rate. Overnight interest rate differentials usually move less drastically than spot exchange rates; thus, the engineered swap position is a lesser overnight risk than a net exchange position.

On the following day, our trader has the choice between the money market approach and the exchange approach to get out of the swap

Exhibit 7.7

HOW TO GET OUT OF AN OUTRIGHT FORWARD POSITION

RATE SCENARIO

Money Market, One-Month Maturity

Eurodollar rate	7%
Europound rate	10%

Foreign Exchange Market

Spot rate	$2.4000/£
One-month swap rate	$0.0060/£ (discount on pounds)

CASH FLOWS

Box A

```
Currency: Pound sterling

Date:    Day 1

Balance: - 1.0000 (spot to
         compensate
         forward)
         + 1.0000 required
         matching flow
```

Box B

```
Currency: U.S. dollar

Date:    Day 1

Balance: + 2.4000 (spot to
         compensate
         forward)
         - 2.4000 required
         matching flow
```

Box C

```
Currency: Pound sterling

Date:    Day 31

Balance: + 1.000 (forward
         imposed by
         customer)
         - 1.000 required
         matching flow
```

Box D

```
Currency: U.S. dollar

Date:    Day 31

Balance: - 2.3930 (forward
         imposed by
         customer)
         + 2.3930 required
         matching flow
```

position. Assuming that interest rates for one-month pounds and dollars have not changed, the trader can either borrow the pounds at 10 percent and invest the dollars at 7 percent, or purchase spot pounds against dollars and sell one-month pounds against dollars at a .0060 discount against the trader. The economics of the two approaches are the same, because .0060 for one month below a spot rate of $2.40/£ equals the interest rate differential of 3 percent (10 percent for pounds and 7 percent for dollars). The cash flows produced by either approach are those required, as shown in Boxes A through D in Exhibit 7.7.

To make sure that the matching swap or money market transactions will be closed at the chosen rate, the trader will probably change the quotes to give an incentive to the market to do with him transactions which he wants to make. That is, if the trader wants to "buy," the quote must give an incentive for the market to "sell." Exhibit 7.7 shows that our trader will want to have the following cash flows:

Day 1: Inflow in pounds—outflow in dollars

Day 31: Outflow in pounds—inflow in dollars

As mentioned, these flows could be generated by operating in either the money market or the foreign exchange market.

If using the money market, our trader will have to:

1. Borrow pounds for delivery value spot and with maturity of thirty days

2. Invest dollars to be delivered value spot and with maturity of thirty days

These transactions square the cash boxes in Exhibit 7.7. If using the foreign exchange market, our trader will want to:

1. Purchase pounds against dollars spot

2. Sell pounds against dollars for one-month delivery

This swap transaction will also square the cash boxes in Exhibit 7.7.

Exhibit 7.8 shows the direction in which our trader will change all the various market quotes to make sure that the desired cash flows take place. Notice that in each case the trader is giving an incentive for other market

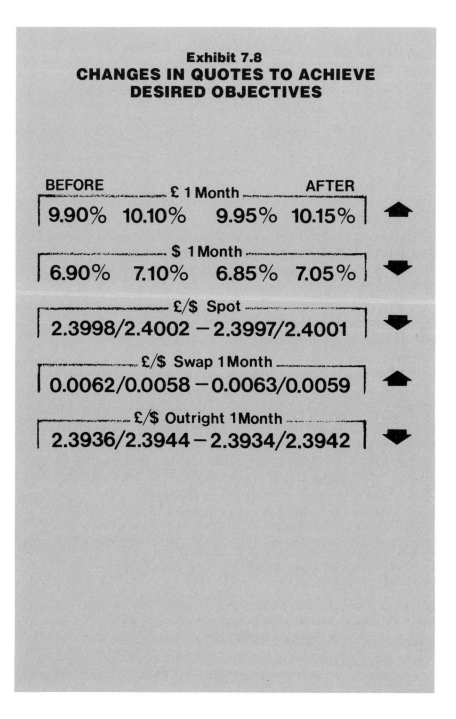

Exhibit 7.8
CHANGES IN QUOTES TO ACHIEVE DESIRED OBJECTIVES

BEFORE ———————— £ 1 Month ———————— AFTER

| 9.90% | 10.10% | 9.95% | 10.15% |

———————— $ 1 Month ————————

| 6.90% | 7.10% | 6.85% | 7.05% |

———————— £/$ Spot ————————

| 2.3998/2.4002 — 2.3997/2.4001 |

———————— £/$ Swap 1 Month ————————

| 0.0062/0.0058 — 0.0063/0.0059 |

———————— £/$ Outright 1 Month ————————

| 2.3936/2.3944 — 2.3934/2.3942 |

participants to deal at the trader's rate; however, our trader will still get a rate better than could be obtained if it were necessary to deal at the rates which these other participants are quoting.

For example, the trader would like to have an inflow of spot pounds. If this inflow takes place in the money market, the trader may change the quote for pounds as follows:

Before	After
9.90% – 10.10%	9.95% – 10.15%

At the market rates existing in the initial situation, the trader has to pay 10.10 percent to borrow pounds from another trader. At the new rates, the trader obtains pounds if somebody places pounds with him or her at 9.95 percent. This is clearly advantageous to the trader when compared with the alternative of dealing at somebody else's rate of 10.10 percent. The new rate is also attractive to the other market participants. The market has the alternative of either placing the pounds at the market rate of 9.90 percent or placing them with our trader at 9.95 percent. This is the incentive given to influence the market to do what the trader wants.

Here is another example. If, dealing in the foreign exchange market, the trader wants to swap pounds against dollars by (1) purchasing pounds against dollars spot, and (2) selling pounds against dollars for one-month delivery, we know that the swap rate indicates a discount on the forward rate relative to the spot rate. Since the trader wants to sell pounds forward against dollars, the other party will have to purchase pounds forward against dollars. To make it worthwhile for the other party to purchase pounds from our trader rather than anywhere else, the trader will have to offer a larger discount on pounds than the one the market is offering. Therefore, the swap rate goes up as follows:

Before	After
0.0062 – 0.0058	0.0063 – 0.0059

In this way the other party can get a better discount, 59 points, from our trader than from the market, which offers a 58-point discount. The trader also gets a better deal than would have been obtained by dealing at other traders' rates. At other traders' rates, our trader would have had to accept a discount of 62 points as compared with the 59 that are allowed for at the rates the trader is now quoting.

How to create a forward exchange market

The creation of a forward exchange market can be a major business goal of the manager to initiate a source for developing new business, or it may be a necessity generated by the desire to service a customer in a market where a forward exchange market does not exist. In any event, this situation appears often in the case of currencies with very thin exchange markets, currencies which are not traded actively. To find what the quote for forward rates should be, the funds manager can use the money market rates for the two currencies involved. We know that the forward market should reflect the net accessible interest differential between the two currencies.

Let's assume we have received a request for a quote of forward rates in a currency where a forward market does not exist at the time, say, the Mexican peso. The rate scenario is presented in Exhibit 7.9. A trader who is asked to quote forward rates must be willing to deal at the quoted rates. Our assumption is that the trader does not wish to assume a net exchange position. Therefore, if a transaction takes place at the quoted prices, the trader will want to get out of the outright forward net exchange position, as in the situation described earlier in the subsection "How to get out of an exchange position." Knowing the steps which the trader must take to get out of the outright forward position, we can estimate the costs or earnings involved in escaping from that position. These costs or earnings can then be used to calculate the forward rate.

In the previous case, we saw that to get out of an outright forward position, a swap position is created by dealing in the spot market after the net forward position develops. Then, to square the cash flows in the swap position, we could act in either the foreign exchange market or the money market. Since, in this case, there is not a forward market in existence, we are forced to use the money market to square the cash flow position.

More specifically, the steps to estimate the rates which the trader would be willing to quote in the forward market are these:

1. Do in the spot market the opposite of what is done in the forward market. If a transaction takes place at the quoted price, a net outright forward position will be created. By doing the opposite in the spot market, the net exchange position is brought down to zero, and, instead, a swap position is created. The spot transaction in this case will be done at the market's rate.

Exhibit 7.9
CREATING A FORWARD EXCHANGE MARKET

RATE SCENARIO

Money Market, Three-Months Maturity

	Bid	Offer
Dollar	7.00%	7.25%
Peso	10.00%	12.00%

Foreign Exchange Market

Spot rate	P12.4900/$	P12.4915/$

CASH FLOWS

Box A

Currency: Mexican peso

Date: Spot

Balance: + 12.49 (spot purchase)
         − 12.49 (investment at 10%)

Net balance   Ø

Box B

Currency: U.S. dollar

Date: Spot

Balance: − 1.00 (spot sale)
         + 1.00 (borrowings at 7.25%)

Net balance   Ø

Box C

Currency: Mexican peso

Date: 90 Days

Balance: + 12.49 (principal on maturing investment)
         + 0.3122 (interest on investment)
         − 12.5759 (expected forward)

Net balance   + 0.2263

Box D

Currency: U.S. dollar

Date: 90 Days

Balance: − 1.00 (payment of principal on borrowings)
         − 0.0180 (interest on borrowings)
         + 1.00 (expected forward)

Net balance   − 0.0181

2. Square the cash flow position (swap position) created by the spot transaction by using the money market (i.e., borrowing the currency sold spot, investing the currency purchased spot) for a maturity to match the value date of the forward transaction.

3. Compute the interest differential resulting from the two money market transactions and convert it into a swap rate.

4. Obtain the desired forward quote by adding or subtracting the swap rate from the spot rate used in the initial spot transaction.

To determine the three-month forward bid rate of dollars against Mexican pesos, using Mexican terms, we follow the steps indicated above:

1. We want a quote that gives the rate at which we are willing to buy forward dollars against pesos. Doing the opposite in the spot market means selling dollars against pesos. Since we are dealing at market rates, this is done at P12.4900/$—the rate at which the market purchases dollars against pesos.

2. Now we have an outflow in dollars and an inflow in pesos spot. To square the cash flow position, we:
   Borrow dollars at 7.25 percent for three months
   Invest pesos at 10 percent for three months
   Again, we use the market's rates.

3. The money market transactions produce an interest gain of 2.75 percent p.a. To convert this to a three-month swap rate, we use the spot rate from the initial spot transaction, P12.4900/$. The 2.75 percent p.a. on P12.49 equals P0.3435/$, which is thus the one-year swap rate. Therefore, the three-month swap rate is P0.0859/$ (0.3435 × 3/12). It is a premium on the dollar against the peso because it indicates how much we can afford to lose in the purchase of dollars against pesos without having a net loss.[4]

4. Therefore, the three-month forward bid rate is P12.5759/$ (12.49 + 0.0859).

The cash boxes in Exhibit 7.9 show that if we follow the steps just described and a transaction is closed at the estimated bid rate, the net

---

[4] We know, in any event, that the dollar must have a premium against the peso because the dollar has the lower interest rate. See also Exhibit 3.7.

exchange position is zero at all times, and profits equal zero. Boxes C and D show small balances due to the interest paid and received. At the spot rate of P12.49/$, these balances roughly equal one another.

What is the three-month forward offer rate of dollars against pesos? We follow the same steps as above:

1. The forward quote requires the rate at which the trader is willing to sell forward dollars against pesos. Doing the opposite in the spot market means purchasing dollars against pesos. The market spot rate for this transaction is P12.4915/$, the rate at which the market is willing to sell dollars against pesos.

2. The spot transaction has created an inflow of dollars and an outflow of pesos. To square the cash flow position we:
   Invest dollars at 7 percent for three months
   Borrow pesos at 12 percent for three months
   These are the market's rates.

3. The money market transactions produce an interest loss of 5 percent p.a. To convert this to a three-month swap rate, we use the spot rate used in the initial spot transaction, P12.4915/$. The 5 percent p.a. on 12.4915 equals P0.6246/$, which is the one-year swap rate. Therefore, the three-month swap rate is P0.1561/$ (0.6246 × 3/12). This is a premium; it indicates the minimum profit that must be obtained in the forward sale of dollars against pesos to compensate for the interest loss.

4. Therefore, the three-month offer rate is P12.6476/$ (12.4915 + 0.1561).

This case shows once more the relationship between the foreign exchange market and the money markets. Forward rates can be quoted on the basis of the spot exchange rate and the interest rates for the two currencies involved. More specifically, in a quote expressed in Mexican terms, the forward rates can be calculated as follows:

1. The bid rate is a function of
   a. The market's spot exchange bid rate
   b. The interest rate on dollar borrowings at the market's offer rate
   c. The bid rate for pesos in the money market

2. The offer rate is a function of
   a. The market's spot exchange offer rate
   b. The interest rate on dollar placements at the market's bid rate
   c. The offer rate for pesos in the money market

In practice, the spot rates and the rates at which funds can be placed or borrowed in the *Eurodollar* market can be estimated by just looking at the latest quotes in the market. However, to estimate the rates at which funds are placed or borrowed in the *local* market requires some further attention. Because of the nature of the money markets in currencies where no forward market exists, a deep interbank market is usually not readily available in these currencies. Thus, the trader who is generating funds in local currency must think carefully about the rate at which the bank is willing to lend those funds. For the same reason, the trader who requires borrowings in the local currency must think carefully about the rate which the bank would be willing to pay for deposits in the local currency.

We have seen that the trader who engages in purchasing forward dollars against local currency (pesos) will be generating funds in local currency. This is the result of the spot sale of dollars required to cover the forward purchase. Likewise, the trader engaging in sales of forward dollars against local currency will need to borrow funds in the local currency. This is the result of the spot purchase of dollars required to cover the forward sale. In this situation, where a forward exchange market does not exist and where the local money market is not fully developed, the trader will be making decisions constantly about loans and deposits in the local currency. We can think of the purchase of forward dollars as a source of loanable funds in the local currency—a "printing press" for local currency. On the other hand, the sale of forward dollars will produce a demand for local funds—a "vacuum cleaner" absorbing local currency. (See Exhibit 7.10.)

How to raise needed funds in a given currency

Let's assume that a need for German marks has appeared; for example, a subsidiary requires German marks temporarily. Our objective is to raise German marks at the lowest possible cost without incurring any exchange position. There are two ways of obtaining German marks. One can

Borrow German marks directly in the money market

or

Borrow dollars (or another currency) and swap them into German marks (with the full forward cover provided by the swap)

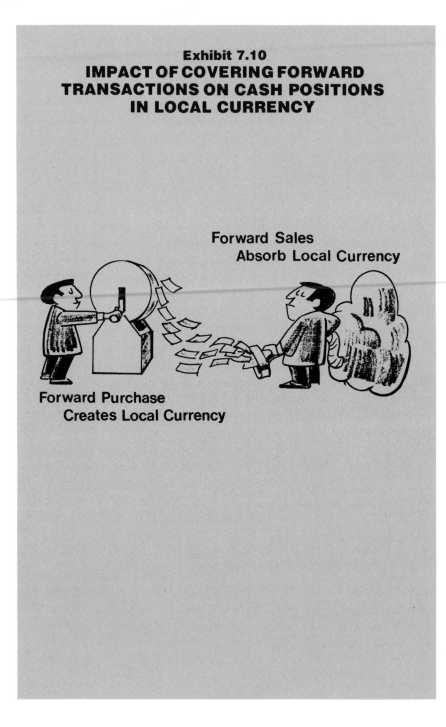

Exhibit 7.10
IMPACT OF COVERING FORWARD TRANSACTIONS ON CASH POSITIONS IN LOCAL CURRENCY

Forward Sales
Absorb Local Currency

Forward Purchase
Creates Local Currency

Either of these approaches can be carried out by dealing at the market's rates with the spreads against us, or at our own rates with the spreads in our favor. For simplicity's sake, suppose that we and the market are quoting the same rates; in other words, if we want to borrow marks, the offer rate is the market's rate, and the bid rate is our rate. The costs of funds under the two alternatives, priced at the market's rates and at our rates, are shown in Exhibit 7.11.

The costs of borrowing marks in either alternative are lower when dealing at our rates than when dealing at the market's rates. Borrowing marks directly costs 4.25 percent when dealing at the market's rate, but only 4 percent when dealing at our rate. In the swap transaction, marks cost 4.35 percent when dealing at the market's rates, but only 3.91 percent when dealing at our rates. *If we are able to deal at our own rates, we will prefer to obtain the marks from a swap transaction* at a cost of 3.91 percent. This is in contrast to the cost of 4 percent of borrowing marks directly. When we deal at our own rates, we have the benefit of spreads in our favor. In the swap approach, we have the benefit of two spreads. When borrowing the marks directly, however, we benefit from only one spread. For the same reasons, if we must give the benefit of the spread to the market, it is better to reduce the number of spreads for which we pay. Thus, *when dealing at the market's rates, it is cheaper to borrow marks directly* at 4.25 percent than to borrow indirectly by swapping dollars into marks at a total cost of 4.35 percent.

How to invest available funds in a given currency

Let's assume that U.S. dollars are available for temporary investment—for a buildup of cash to pay a maturing debt in U.S. dollars. Our objective is to invest the U.S. dollars at the maximum possible return without incurring any exchange position. Again, there are two ways in which we can accomplish this goal. We can:

Invest U.S. dollars directly in the Eurodollar market

Swap the U.S. dollars into Canadian dollars (or another currency) and invest this currency (with the full forward cover provided by the swap)

There are two ways in which each of these approaches can be carried out: We can deal at the market's rates, or the market can deal at our rates. The

Exhibit 7.11
COSTS OF RAISING NEEDED FUNDS
IN A GIVEN CURRENCY

OBJECTIVE: To borrow German marks

RATE SCENARIO

Money Market, Three-Months Maturity

	Bid	Offer
Eurodollar	6½%	6⅝%
Euromark	4%	4¼%

Foreign Exchange Market

Spot rate	DM2.5500/$	
Three-month swap rate	165	145

CASH FLOWS

Alternative 1—Borrow German marks directly:

Dealing at Market's Rate	Dealing at Our Rate
4.25%	4.00%

Alternative 2—Borrow dollars and swap them into marks:

Dealing at Market's Rates		Dealing at Our Rates	
Dollar borrowings	6.625%	Dollar borrowings	6.50%
Swap rate at 145* (buy forward dollars at discount)	− 2.27 %	Swap rate at 165† (buy forward dollars at discount)	− 2.59%
Total cost	4.35 %	Total cost	3.91%

---

* A three-month swap rate of 145 is equivalent to a one-year swap rate of 580. DM0.0580/$ below a spot rate of DM2.5500/$ indicates a 2.27 percent p.a. discount on the dollar against the German mark.

† A three-month swap rate of 165 is equivalent to a one-year swap rate of 660. DM0.0660/$ below a spot rate of DM2.5500/$ indicates a 2.59 percent p.a. discount on the dollar against the German mark.

net yield on the investment under the two approaches is presented in Exhibit 7.12.

In this case we come to the same conclusion as in the previous case. To achieve our goal, it is better to deal at our rates than at the market's rates. If dealing at our rates, we can benefit from an additional spread if we achieve the desired objective of investing the dollar funds through a swap transaction instead of investing directly in the dollar money market. The returns are 6.82 percent when going through Canadian dollars and dealing at our own rates, compared with 6.62 percent when placing the U.S. dollars directly. At the market's rates, a direct placement of U.S. dollars yields 6.50 percent, compared with 6.33 percent when the additional spread involved in the swap transaction must also be paid.

How to roll over a net exchange position

Let's assume that today is Monday, and we have a net overbought position in spot pounds, value Wednesday. On Wednesday we shall have to accept delivery of the pounds and pay for them with dollars. However, we wish to maintain the net overbought position for one more day—until value Thursday. We may want this position because we expect the spot pound to appreciate against the dollar.

Exhibit 7.13 shows the market rates and the cash flow boxes associated with this case. The first balance lines for Wednesday delivery show the picture as seen on Monday, that is, an inflow in pounds and an outflow in dollars. We have two problems: (1) how to obtain an inflow in dollars that day, and (2) what to do with the pounds received that day. To solve these problems and still maintain the net overbought position in pounds until Thursday, we must produce an outflow in pounds and an inflow in dollars for Wednesday and the opposite flows for Thursday. This is shown in Exhibit 7.13 as the second balance line in the boxes for Wednesday and the balance line for Thursday.

To accomplish our objectives, we have two options open to us:

1. In the foreign exchange market, to sell pounds against dollars, value Wednesday; to purchase pounds against dollars, value Thursday

2. In the money market, to invest pounds from Wednesday until Thursday; to borrow dollars from Wednesday until Thursday

Exhibit 7.12
RETURNS FROM INVESTING AVAILABLE FUNDS IN A GIVEN CURRENCY

OBJECTIVE: To place U.S. dollars

RATE SCENARIO

Money Market, Three-Months Maturity

	Bid	Offer
Eurodollar	6.50%	6.62%
Canadian dollar	9.25%	9.50%

Foreign Exchange Market

Spot rate		US$0.9850/C$
Three-month swap rate	72	66

CASH FLOWS

Alternative 1: Place U.S. dollars directly

Dealing at Market's Rate	Dealing at Our Rate
6.50%	6.62%

Alternative 2: Swap U.S. dollars into Canadian dollars and invest Canadian dollars

Dealing at Market's Rates		Dealing at Our Rates	
Place Canadian dollars	9.25%	Place Canadian dollars	9.50%
Swap rate at 72* (sell Canadian dollars forward at a discount)	− 2.92	Swap rate at 66† (sell Canadian dollars forward at a discount)	− 2.68
Total profit	6.33%	Total profit	6.82%

---

* A three-month swap rate of 72 is equivalent to a one-year swap rate of 288. US$0.0288 below a spot rate of US$0.9850/C$ indicates a discount of 2.92 percent p.a. on the Canadian dollar against the U.S. dollar.

† A three-month swap rate of 66 is equivalent to a one-year swap rate of 264. US$0.0264 below a spot rate of US$0.9850/C$ indicates a discount of 2.68 percent p.a. on the Canadian dollar against the U.S. dollar.

Exhibit 7.13 shows the net yield of the position rollover computed for each alternative for both the assumption that the market deals at our rates and the assumption that we deal at the market's rates. (Again, we assume that we are quoting the same rates as the market. If we want to sell pounds against dollars, the bid rate is the market's rate, and the offer rate is our rate.) It is clear that we are better off dealing at our rates than at the market's rates. When we deal at our rates, the spread is in our favor. Also, at our rates the foreign exchange approach is better than the money market approach. However, if we must deal at the market's rates, it would be better to follow the money market approach than the foreign exchange market approach. The reason is that the spreads for very short periods tend to be smaller in the money market than in the exchange market.

In the exchange market, the swap rate of 125 implies a discount of 1.875 percent; a swap rate of 225 means a discount of 3.375 percent on the pound. The spread in the swap rate is 1½ percent. This spread will be in our favor if the market deals at our rates. It will be against us if we deal at the market's rate. On the other hand, the spreads in the money market in this case are 0.20 percent for each currency. When we deal in the money market at our rates, we have two spreads in our favor of 0.20 percent each for a total of only 0.40 percent. This spread is much narrower than the 1½ percent for the swap rate. So, if the spread is in our favor, we prefer the exchange market approach; if the spread is against us, however, we prefer the money market approach where the spreads are narrower.

We shall often find this situation to prevail for these very short maturities. The reason is that the swap rate for very brief periods tends to exaggerate the implied percentage discount or premium on the spot rate when converted to an annual basis. For example, the overnight swap rate has to be multiplied by 360 days to obtain the annual swap rate on which the percentages are based. Any small discrepancy between the swap rate and the interest differential for very short maturities tends to be distorted enormously when annualized.

Central banks' interventions in foreign exchange markets

In all our discussions in this book, we have assumed that the goal of the funds manager is to run a profitable operation, subject to risk constraints. However, there is a large market participant whose goals are different. This participant is the central bank.

Exhibit 7.13
ROLLING OVER A SPOT POSITION

RATE SCENARIO

Money Market, Overnight

	Bid	Offer
Europound	9.85%	10.05%
Eurodollar	6.95%	7.15%

Foreign Exchange Market

Spot rate		$2.4000/£	
Overnight swap rate	0.000225		0.000125

CASH FLOWS

Box A

Currency:	Pound sterling
Date:	Wednesday
Balance:	+ 1
	− 1

Box B

Currency:	U.S. dollar
Date:	Wednesday
Balance:	− 1
	+ 1

Box C

Currency:	Pound sterling
Date:	Thursday
Balance:	+ 1

Box D

Currency:	U.S. dollar
Date:	Thursday
Balance:	− 1

COSTS

Dealing at Market's Rates		**Dealing at Our Rates**	
Foreign Exchange Approach:			
Swap rate of 125* (sell pounds Wednesday; buy pounds Thursday)	1.875%	Swap rate of 225† (sell pounds Wednesday; buy pounds Thursday)	3.375%
Money Market Approach:			
Place pounds	9.85%	Place pounds	10.05%
Borrow dollars	− 7.15%	Borrow dollars	− 6.95%
	2.70%		3.10%

---

* An overnight swap rate of $0.000125/£ is equivalent to an annual swap rate of $0.0450/£; $0.0450/£ below a spot pound rate of $2.40/£ is a discount of 1.875 percent.

† An overnight swap rate of $0.000225/£ is equivalent to an annual swap rate of $0.0810/£; $0.0810/£ below a spot pound rate of $2.40/£ is a discount of 3.375 percent.

It is the function of the central bank of a country to maintain orderly exchange markets and to try to achieve the exchange rate goals that economic policy and international arrangements dictate. Making a profit is not an objective of central banks. In this section we present some examples of the impact which the actions of central banks can have on exchange markets.

How *not* to do it

To understand the impact that unilateral action by the central bank, or any other market participant, can have on the financial markets, let's look at the market situation as illustrated in Exhibit 7.14. Let's assume that the monetary authorities of some country have decided to create a forward exchange market for their currency against the dollar. They have a feeling that the dollar is relatively weak; therefore, they conclude that the dollar should be selling at a discount against the local currency. After some discussion, a consensus emerges that the central bank should enter the market by offering dollars against the local currency (LC) at LC3.96/$ for three-month delivery. Since the spot rate is LC4.00/$, the offered forward rate represents a discount of 4 percent p.a. on the dollar against the local currency. What will be the reaction of the other market participants?

It is clear that the discount of 4 percent on the dollar against the local currency is out of line with the interest differential of 2 percent. The central bank has provided an incentive for the market to engage in covered interest arbitrage. The discount on the dollar is more than the interest differential in favor of this currency. The incentive is to convert funds spot from dollars into local currency and cover forward. The relevant rates are the following:

Borrow dollars	7%
Swap dollars into local currency (sell dollars spot; purchase three-month dollars at a discount)	− 4%
Net cost to generate fully covered local currency	3%

The local currency generated in the spot part of the swap transaction is now available to be invested at 5 percent, i.e., a net profit of 2 percent.

Exhibit 7.14
CENTRAL BANK INTERVENTION IN EXCHANGE MARKETS: THE INCORRECT WAY

RATE SCENARIO

Money Market, Three-Months Maturity

Local currency (LC)	5%
U.S. dollars	7%

Foreign Exchange Market

Spot rate	LC4.00/$

CENTRAL BANK INTERVENTION

Central bank action:	Offer three-month forward dollars at Three-month swap rate is LC.04/$ 4% p.a. discount on three-month dollars against local currency	LC3.96/$
Reaction:	Market borrows dollars at	7%
	Swaps dollars into local currency (sells dollars spot; purchases dollars forward at 4% discount)	− 4
	Net cost of fully covered local currency	3%
Central bank action:	Buy three-month forward dollars at Three-month swap rate is LC0.01/$ 1% p.a. discount on three-month dollars against local currency	LC3.99/$
Reaction:	Market borrows local currency at	5%
	Swaps local currency into dollars (sells local currency spot; purchases local currency forward at 1% premium)	+ 1
	Net cost of fully covered dollars	6%

With a large number of market participants taking advantage of the situation, the country sees its financial markets flooded with investible funds.

Realizing that a discount of 4 percent p.a. on the dollar may be too much, the central bank decides to change the quoted three-month forward rate to LC3.99/$. This implies a discount of 1 percent on the dollar against the local currency. Again, the central bank has set a forward rate which is out of line with the interest differentials between the dollar and the local currency. The forward discount on the dollar is less than the interest differential in favor of that currency. There is an incentive to move funds from local currency into dollars on a covered basis. The costs of obtaining covered dollars are:

To borrow local currency	5%
To swap local currency into dollars (to sell local currency spot; to purchase it forward at a premium)	+ 1%
Net cost to generate fully covered dollars	6%

The dollars obtained in the spot transaction are now available to be invested at the market rate of 7 percent, providing a net profit of 1 percent. With a large number of market participants taking advantage of the situation that the central bank has created, the local financial markets will witness a substantial outflow of funds. Local funds are more valuable when invested via dollars than when invested in the local market.

Given that the objective of the central bank in this case was merely to provide a forward exchange market for its currency, the foreign capital flows produced by the central bank's intervention were undesirable in each instance. The central bank ignored the natural relationship between interest differentials and the forward exchange markets. In such a situation, large foreign capital flows in search of arbitrage profits are inevitable.

Intervention to accomplish desired objectives

Let's look at a country whose currency is considered by the market to be a candidate for upvaluation against the dollar. This has often been the case with the German mark in the past. Market participants who wish to benefit from the expected upvaluation would like to have a net over-bought exchange position in marks. To achieve this position, they will transfer funds from weaker currencies into marks. In both the spot market and the forward market, they will purchase marks against, let's say, the dollar.

As foreign capital flows move from the dollar into the mark, West Germany will see its foreign exchange reserves increase. Most likely, the increase in reserves will be accompanied by an increase in domestic money supply and a decrease in local interest rates. Of course, the pressures on the exchange markets will be toward a realization of the expected appreciation in the spot rate of the mark against the dollar.

What are the options open to the central bank to cope with this situation?

Intervention in the spot market. In this market the central bank has two options. It either accepts the pressures of the market and lets the spot price of the mark increase without active intervention, or, alternatively, it acts as a banker of last resort, maintaining the spot price at the desired level. To do the latter, the central bank must be willing to sell marks in exchange for dollars to the extent that the market wishes to engage in this transaction. A strong posture on the part of the central bank may discourage the foreign capital flows. If the market perceives the central bank as willing to support the spot price of the mark at any cost, the market may conclude that the expected upvaluation will not take place after all. If the upvaluation does not materialize, the low interest rates received in the so-called appreciating currency will make investors move funds away from that currency. This, of course, is exactly what the central bank would like to see.

Intervention in the forward market. In the market scenario presented in Exhibit 7.15, the central bank can advise the market that it is willing to purchase outright three-month dollars against marks at DM2.59/$. This price for dollars is higher than what the market is offering, DM2.5870/$. Therefore, there is an incentive for market participants to benefit from this intended disparity and to sell dollars against marks for three-month delivery. However, this transaction would create a net oversold exchange position for sellers of dollars, who would also be overbought in marks. To square this exchange position, it is necessary to purchase dollars and sell

Exhibit 7.15
CENTRAL BANK INTERVENTION IN EXCHANGE MARKETS: THE CORRECT WAY

RATE SCENARIO

Money Market, Three-Months Maturity

German mark   4%

Eurodollar   6%

Foreign Exchange Market

Spot rate	DM2.6000/$	
Three-month swap rate	DM0.0130/$	} 2% p.a. discount on
Three-month forward rate	DM2.5870/$	} dollars against marks

PROBLEM: Pressures for appreciation of mark against dollar

ALTERNATIVE SOLUTIONS

Spot Market: a. Deal only at DM2.6000/$
        b. Let the mark appreciate against the dollar

Outright Forward: Quote three-months   DM2.59/$

Swap Rate: Quote three-months   DM0.0100/$

marks. This can be done in the spot market at the rate of DM2.60/$. Since the central bank is not selling dollars against marks for spot delivery, the spot transaction will have to be carried out with other parties in the market. In this fashion the parties which dealt with the central bank are the ones who are supporting the spot rate of dollars against marks because they are buying spot dollars. This may change the psychology of the market. People with short positions in dollars and/or long positions in marks may decide to cover—to purchase dollars and sell marks—which will further strengthen the spot rate. At this point the central bank may want to start selling carefully the dollars it acquired earlier.

When successful, the transactions just described show how the German central bank can support the dollar without increasing its foreign exchange reserves or the local money supply. It bought forward dollars, broke the speculative trend, even reversed the trend, and sold the previously purchased dollars prior to maturity.

Intervention in the swap rate. Instead of offering to purchase outright forward dollars at a price higher than the market, the central bank may choose to quote a swap rate below the market rate. With the market rates in Exhibit 7.15, the central bank may quote a swap rate of DM0.0100/$. This implies a discount on dollars against marks of 1.5 percent p.a. in contrast with the market discount of 2.0 percent p.a. Again, the central bank rate provides an incentive for market participants to profit from this deviation from parity rates. Market participants will have an incentive to swap marks into dollars. More precisely, there are an incentive and an advantage to deal with the central bank when purchasing dollars against marks spot, and selling dollars against marks for three-month delivery. This will make dollars available on a covered basis at a swap rate of 0.0100 against the other party. The central bank can then stipulate that the dollars acquired spot through this swap must be invested outside Germany. The yield for these dollars in the market is 6 percent. This provides a net profit of 0.5 percent for the other party:

Cost of borrowed marks	4.0%
Cost of swap (selling marks spot; purchasing three-month marks at a premium)	1.5%
Cost of fully covered dollars	5.5%
Return on invested dollars	6.0%
Net profit	0.5%

In the three approaches presented here, the central bank will be supporting the spot price of its currency. In the spot market, this is done directly. In the forward market, it is done indirectly. The advantage of the two methods involving the forward market is that, in addition to supporting the spot rate, the central bank also accomplishes the domestic objectives of reducing domestic money supply and increasing interest rates. The level of foreign exchange reserves is also reduced. However, these measures can be seen only as stopgap measures. When the forward part of the transaction matures, the domestic markets will be affected negatively again; that is, money supply will increase and interest rates will decrease.

To eliminate the pressures on the exchange rates on a more permanent basis, it is necessary to change the fundamental economic factors on which exchange rates are based. This requires a package of economic policies which addresses the basic problems. Operations in the exchange markets cannot be relied upon to change the underlying economic forces which determine rates (see Chapter 6). Intervention in the exchange market against basic economic forces can succeed only on a temporary basis.

CHAPTER 8

Problems and opportunities of the nonfinancial business

Funds managers in nonfinancial businesses work in an environment different from that of the trader. They may choose to conduct active trading operations. But, most likely, the relatively small size of this operation will force the manager to deal at rates quoted by professional traders in banks. With the exception of large multinational companies with huge volumes of liquid assets, most of these businesses have neither the resources nor the inclination to participate in active trading. However, as shown in the preceding chapter, there are a number of opportunities which develop in the market from which one can benefit by simply being attentive to market movements. Such opportunities, which are open to all participants in the market, include covered interest arbitrage and the discovery of the most economical way to obtain a desired exchange position.

The typical world of the funds manager in the nonfinancial business involves two major problems: (1) balancing cash flows which are triggered elsewhere in the organization, and (2) protecting against undesirable moves in exchange rates. We shall look at each of these problems in the major sections of this chapter. In the last section, we shall present an example of how nonfinancial businesses can also benefit from operating through swap transactions.

Funds management

An introductory example

As a bridge from the problems of the trading room into the more general problems of funds management in the nonbank business, let's look at the financial problems of an industrial corporation, the case of Mansona

Corp. Mansona is a U.S. multinational corporation which, in the early 1970s, had US$15 million deposited in the Eurodollar market in London. The money was earmarked to finance the company's expansion abroad. At the time, however, it was not known in what countries and currencies these funds would ultimately be needed. The major worry at the time was that the dollar had already devalued at the end of 1971 and still appeared weak against other major currencies. Finally, it was decided that the $15 million should be switched into a stronger currency if a reasonable opportunity appeared.

This opportunity developed in mid-October 1972. At that time, the company was offered bonds denominated in German marks and maturing in 1977 (an acceptable maturity) at a 7½ percent yield. This was the same interest rate that Mansona's U.S. dollar deposits were then earning. Therefore, the company decided to go ahead with the purchase of the bonds. However, the Eurodollar deposits would not mature until the end of October 1972 while the bond offer was good at the current rate only for a few days. In addition, Mansona was afraid that the German mark might appreciate against the dollar before the end of the month.

To summarize the problem, Mansona's dollars did not mature until the end of October, and the company did not want to break the deposit, i.e., to ask the bank to advance the maturity date. However, Mansona could not delay purchasing the mark bonds until the end of the month because it feared that by then the mark exchange rate would have gone up and the mark bond interest rate might have gone down. Taking into account the maturity of the Eurodollar deposit and the intended purchase of the bonds in mid-October, Mansona's cash flow boxes looked like Boxes A and D in the first part of Exhibit 8.1. On October 15 there would be an outflow in marks to purchase the bonds. On October 31 there would be an inflow in dollars from the maturing Eurodollar deposits. Clearly, a solution to the mismatch situation required an inflow of marks on October 15 and an outflow of dollars on October 31. Given the market scenario outlined in Exhibit 8.1, how was Mansona to provide these cash flows without incurring additional exchange risk? The options were the following:

1. Borrow dollars on October 15 at 7 percent p.a. with maturity for October 31. On October 15, the dollar borrowings would be converted into marks in the spot market, and the bonds would be purchased. On October 31, the dollar borrowings could be repaid with the proceeds from the maturing Eurodollar deposit.

Exhibit 8.1
MANAGING CASH FLOWS: THE MANSONA CASE

RATE SCENARIO

Money Market, Half-Month Maturity	Bid	Offer
Eurodollar	6½%	7%
Euromark	5%	5½%

Foreign Exchange Market

Spot rate	DM3.1850/$	DM3.1900/$
Half-month swap rate	DM0.0025/$	DM0.0015/$
Half-month forward rate	DM3.1825/$	DM3.1885/$

CASH FLOWS

Initial Situation

Box A

Currency:	mark
Date:	October 15, 1972
Balance:	− (purchase of bonds)

Box D

Currency:	U.S. dollar
Date:	October 31, 1972
Balance:	+ (proceeds from maturing deposit)

Exhibit 8.1 (continued)

A. BALANCING BY BORROWING DOLLARS

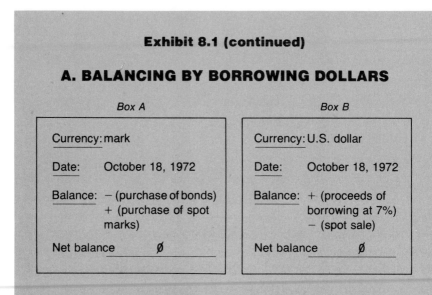

Box A

Currency: mark

Date: October 18, 1972

Balance: − (purchase of bonds)
         + (purchase of spot marks)

Net balance   ∅

Box B

Currency: U.S. dollar

Date: October 18, 1972

Balance: + (proceeds of borrowing at 7%)
         − (spot sale)

Net balance   ∅

Box D

Currency: U.S. dollar

Date: October 31, 1972

Balance: + (proceeds from maturing deposit)
         − (repayment of borrowing)

Net balance   ∅

B. BALANCING BY BORROWING MARKS

Box A

Currency: mark

Date: October 18, 1972

Balance: − (purchase of bonds)
          + (proceeds from
          borrowings at 5½%)

Net balance   Ø

Box C

Currency: mark

Date: October 31, 1972

Balance: − (repayment of
          borrowings)
          + (forward purchase
          @ DM3.1825/$
          [1.88% premium
          on mark])

Net balance   Ø

Box D

Currency: U.S. dollar

Date: October 31, 1972

Balance: + (proceeds from
          maturing deposit)
          − (forward sale
          @ DM3.1825/$
          [1.88% discount
          on dollar])

Net balance   Ø

2. Borrow German marks on October 15 at 5½ percent p.a. with maturity for October 31. Purchase the bonds. To fix the exchange rate between dollars and marks at the time when the borrowings matured, dollars would be sold forward against marks (marks would be purchased against dollars) for delivery on October 31 at the forward rate of DM3.1825/$. This forward rate was a 1.88 percent p.a. discount on the dollar against the mark based on the spot rate of DM3.1850/$.

As illustrated in Exhibit 8.1, both approaches would accomplish the objective of squaring Box A, the need for marks resulting from the purchase of bonds on October 15, and Box D, the inflow from the maturing Eurodollar deposit on October 31. The specific measure taken under the first approach, borrowing dollars, is shown in Box B. The dollar proceeds from the borrowings in Box B are converted into marks in the spot market. This balances both Boxes A and B. The repayment of the Eurodollar borrowing is funded with the Eurodollar deposit maturing October 31 in Box D.

In the second approach, borrowing marks, the proceeds from the borrowings are used to purchase the bonds in Box A. This balances Box A. The repayment of the marks is shown in Box C. To lock in the exchange rate between dollars and marks, the company sells dollars against marks on October 15 for delivery on October 31. This transaction balances Boxes C and D. The inflow of dollars from the maturing deposit in Box D is used to repay the mark borrowings in Box C after converting dollars into marks at the delivery time of the forward contract.

In terms of costs, it is clear in this case that borrowing dollars at 7 percent would be cheaper than borrowing marks on a covered basis at 5½ percent. A premium of 1.88 percent must be paid in the latter case to establish the rate at which dollars will be converted into marks on October 31, and this produces a total cost of 7.38 percent for this alternative.

Uncovered borrowing and investing— net effective interest rates

We have shown in preceding discussions that any premium or discount on the forward exchange rate (the swap rate) is a function of the net accessible interest differential between the two currencies. If the market is in equilibrium, which it will be if arbitrageurs are allowed to operate, the net yield on borrowings and investments on a covered basis is the same for all currencies. The currency with high interest rates will be selling at a discount in the forward market; the currency with low interest rates will be selling at a premium in the forward market.[1] What is gained by investing in the high interest rate currency is lost through the discount in the forward market when the investment is covered. What is lost in interest income when investing in the low interest rate currency is gained as exchange income in the forward market when the investment is covered.

With a market that is in equilibrium, the financial officer can obtain a lower cost for borrowings or a higher return on investments only if the borrowings and investments are not covered in the forward market. Of course, the opportunity of reducing borrowing costs or increasing returns on excess funds is achieved only at the risk of experiencing losses which would not occur if the operation were done on a covered basis. The effective yield of a transaction on an uncovered basis is not known until the transaction is ended and the final spot rate is taken into account.

Let's look at the case illustrated in Exhibit 8.2. The interest differential is 4 percent in favor of the dollar. In the forward market, the six-month swap rate of SF0.0520/$ represents a 4 percent p.a. discount on the dollar against the Swiss franc. The market is in equilibrium. Under these conditions, the financial manager is indifferent as to which currency to borrow or invest in on a covered basis. Converting Swiss francs into dollars to take advantage of the 7 percent interest rate on dollars yields only 3 percent when the 4 percent discount on the forward dollars against Swiss francs is taken into account. Likewise, borrowing in Swiss francs to benefit from the low 3 percent interest rate on that currency will cost as much as 7 percent when the 4 percent premium on the forward Swiss franc against the dollar is taken into account.

At times, the funds manager may be willing to take calculated risks to reduce the cost of borrowings or increase the return on investments. For example, in the scenario of Exhibit 8.2, the funds manager may choose to borrow Swiss francs for six months at 3 percent, even though the funds are needed in U.S. dollars. To have a chance of benefiting from the lower interest rate, the transaction is not covered; that is, Swiss francs are not purchased in the forward market. If the transaction were covered, the 4 percent premium on Swiss francs would make the cost of francs equal to the cost of U.S. dollars at 7 percent. If the spot rate of the Swiss franc against the dollar remains at SF2.60/$, the manager would have saved 4 percent p.a. on the borrowings. On the other hand, if the Swiss franc

---

[1] See Exhibit 3.7, p. 61.

Exhibit 8.2
COMPUTATION OF EFFECTIVE
INTEREST RATES: BORROWING

RATE SCENARIO

Money Market, Three-Month Maturity

Swiss franc	3%
U.S. dollar	7%

Foreign Exchange Market

Spot rate	
Initial	SF2.6000/$
After three months	SF2.5700/$
After six months	SF2.5600/$
Swap rate	a 4% p.a. discount on the dollar against the Swiss franc
Three-month	SF0.0260/$

appreciates substantially against the dollar, the total cost of the borrowing, including the exchange loss, may be more than the alternative cost of 7 percent p.a. on dollars.

If, at the end of three months, the Swiss franc has appreciated to SF2.5700/$, the total cost of funds for those three months is roughly 7.62 percent p.a., computed as follows:

Initial spot conversion rate	SF2.6000/$
Spot rate after three months	2.5700
Exchange loss	SF0.0300/$ = 4.62% p.a.
Interest cost for borrowing Swiss francs	3.00% p.a.
Total cost of U.S. dollars via Swiss francs	7.62%

Although the interest rate is only 3 percent p.a., the Swiss franc has appreciated at a rate of 4.62 percent p.a. Since the alternative for the funds manager was to borrow U.S. dollars at 7.00 percent, borrowing Swiss francs and running an exchange risk cost the officer an extra 0.62 percent p.a.

Let's now assume that the funds manager, in spite of the Swiss franc upvaluation during the first three months, continues to have confidence in the U.S. dollar and does not expect the Swiss franc to appreciate further. Therefore, the manager rolls over the Swiss franc borrowing for another three months at, let's say, the same three-month interest rate. Exhibit 8.2 shows that the dollar does drop further—from SF2.57/$ to SF2.56/$. At first, we may think that if we already have a loss on the basis of a spot rate of SF2.57/$, we should certainly have a loss at a spot rate of 2.56. However, the total cost of Swiss francs for the six months is only 6.08 percent p.a., compared with a cost of 7 percent for U.S. dollar borrowings:

Initial spot conversion rate	SF2.6000/$
Spot rate after additional three months (total of six months)	2.5600
Exchange loss	SF0.0400/$ = 3.08% p.a.
Interest cost of borrowing Swiss francs	3.00% p.a.
Total cost of U.S. dollars via Swiss francs	6.08% p.a.
Cost of borrowing U.S. dollars	7.00% p.a.
Net saving	0.92% p.a.

The exchange loss of SF0.0400/$ materialized over a six-month period represents only a 3.08 percent p.a. upvaluation of the Swiss franc against the U.S. dollar. Adding this exchange loss to the borrowing cost for Swiss francs of 3 percent, we arrive at an "all-in" borrowing cost of 6.08 percent, a net saving of 0.92 percent p.a. over the alternative of borrowing U.S. dollars directly.

This example shows that exchange losses are flat losses and that their annualized impact is stronger as the period of time over which the exchange loss occurs is shorter. Expressed differently, the longer the period of time over which an interest saving occurs, the more money is made or saved to absorb a flat exchange loss.

When engaging in uncovered borrowing or investing, the funds manager always should first determine the break-even exchange rate. The break-even exchange rate is that spot rate, at the end of the borrowing period, at which the interest differential equals the currency revaluation. In the previous example, the funds manager borrowed Swiss francs at 3 percent. The manager could thus afford up to a 4 percent p.a. upvaluation of the Swiss franc against the U.S. dollar and still break even with the alternative of borrowing U.S. dollars. Thus, the break-even rate is a function of the currency spot rate, the interest differential, and the period of time over which the interest differential will exist. In our example, the break-even rate for the initial three-month borrowing is SF2.5740/$, computed as follows:

$$\text{Current spot rate} - (\text{current spot rate} \times \text{annualized interest differential} \times \frac{3}{12})$$

or

$$2.6000 - (2.6000 \times .04 \times \frac{3}{12}) = \text{SF2.5740/\$}$$

This means that if the spot exchange rate drops from SF2.6000/$ to SF2.5740/$ at the end of the initial three-month period, the Swiss franc borrowing costs of 3 percent p.a. plus the annualized exchange loss of 4 percent p.a. will equal the cost of U.S. dollar borrowings at 7 percent p.a. The funds manager could look at this uncovered foreign currency borrowing as if it had been an outright forward purchase of U.S. dollars against Swiss francs at SF2.5740/$. Computed by the same approach, the break-even exchange rate for the six-month borrowing period is SF2.5480/$.

The problem of choosing the proper currency in which to invest excess funds is similar to the case of Swiss franc borrowings just described.

Assume the market scenario presented in Exhibit 8.3. Let's say the funds manager has Saudi riyals and must decide whether to keep them in riyals at 4 percent p.a. or whether to invest them in dollars at 7 percent p.a. The interest rate earned on dollars is clearly higher than the rate on riyals. However, if the riyal appreciates against the dollar, there is a risk of earning even less than 4 percent if the appreciation is substantial.

After three months, the rate for U.S. dollars against Saudi riyals drops from SR3.55/$ to SR3.52/$. The net return at this point is roughly 3.62 percent or an opportunity loss of .38 percent p.a. in comparison with an investment in Saudi riyals at 4 percent.

Initial spot conversion rate	SR3.5500/$
Spot rate after three months	3.5200
Exchange loss	SR0.0300/$ = 3.38% p.a.
Interest earned on U.S. dollar investment	7.00% p.a.
Net return on U.S. dollars via Saudi riyals	3.62% p.a.
Alternative return on direct Saudi riyal investment	4.00% p.a.
Opportunity loss	0.38% p.a.

Here again, we assume that the funds manager extends the investment for another three months, during which time the exchange rate continues to appreciate to SR3.5100/$. The net return now is 4.75 percent, or 0.75 percent better than the alternative of keeping the funds invested in riyals.

Initial spot conversion rate	SR3.5500/$
Spot rate after additional three months (total of six months)	3.5100
Exchange loss	SR0.0400/$ = 2.25% p.a.
Interest earned on U.S. dollar investment	7.00% p.a.
Net return on U.S. dollars via Saudi riyals	4.75% p.a.
Alternative return on direct Saudi riyal investment	4.00% p.a.
Net gain	0.75% p.a.

The enlarged exchange loss of SR0.0400 equals only 2.25 percent p.a. over the entire six-month period. We find again that interest gains over a longer period are better suited to absorb exchange losses. Put differently, exchange losses have a more devastating effect on annualized earnings when they occur over a relatively short period.

Exhibit 8.3
COMPUTATION OF EFFECTIVE
INTEREST RATES: INVESTMENTS

RATE SCENARIO

Money Market, Three-Month Maturity

U.S. dollar	7%
Saudi riyal	4%

Foreign Exchange Market

Spot rate

Initial	SR3.5500/$
After three months	SR3.5200/$
After six months	SR3.5100/$

Before engaging in any uncovered foreign currency borrowing or investing, the funds manager must calculate the break-even exchange rate and consider how the spot rate is expected to compare with that break-even rate at the end of the borrowing or investing period. Uncovered foreign currency borrowings and investments generate interest receivable or interest payable, both of which, together with the principal, are also exposed to changes in the spot rate. If the funds manager expects the spot rate for these two currencies to move drastically, or if there is a very large interest differential between the two currencies, the impact of change in the spot rate on the interest payable or receivable must also be taken explicitly into account.[2]

A formula to compute accurately the break-even exchange rate for borrowings in the Swiss franc example is the following:

$$\frac{\text{Swiss franc interest payment} + \text{Swiss franc principal}}{\text{New exchange rate}}$$
$$= \text{dollar interest payment} + \text{dollar principal}$$

where "new exchange rate" is the exchange rate, expressed in terms of SF/\$, which would make the cash flows in each currency equal. If the alternatives are to borrow SF2.60 or \$1, the break-even rate for three months is:

$$\frac{(2.60 \times .03 \times 3/12) + 2.60}{\text{New exchange rate}} = 1(.07 \times 3/12) + 1$$

$$\text{New exchange rate} = \frac{.0195 + 2.60}{.0175 + 1} = \text{SF2.5744/\$[3]}$$

Using the same formula for six months, we find that the break-even rate is SF2.5498/\$.

$$\frac{(2.60 \times .03 \times 6/12) + 2.60}{\text{New exchange rate}} = 1(.07 \times 6/12) + 1$$

$$\text{New exchange rate} = \frac{0.039 + 2.60}{0.035 + 1} = \frac{2.639}{1.035} = \text{SF2.5498/\$[3]}$$

A generalized formula to estimate accurately the break-even exchange rate required to equalize the returns between the two currencies in the Saudi riyal example is as follows:

---

[2] See Chapter 5, pp. 98–99.

[3] The break-even rates without considering interest payments are SF2.5740/\$ and SF2.5480/\$ for three and six months respectively. See p. 176.

(Dollar interest + dollar principal earned) × new exchange rate
$$= \text{riyal interest} + \text{riyal principal}$$

where "new exchange rate" is the exchange rate of dollars against riyals that would make the returns in dollars and riyals equal.

Assuming we can invest either SR3.55 or $1, for the period of three months the break-even exchange rate is SR3.5238/$.

$$[(1 \times .07 \times 3/12) + 1] \times \text{new exchange rate} = (3.55 \times .04 \times 3/12) + 3.55$$

$$\text{New exchange rate} = \frac{3.5855}{1.0175} = \text{SR3.5238/\$}$$

For the period of six months the break-even exchange rate is SR3.4986/$.

$$[(1 \times .07 \times 6/12) + 1] \times \text{new exchange rate} = (3.55 \times .04 \times 6/12) + 3.55$$

$$\text{New exchange rate} = \frac{3.6210}{1.0350} = \text{SR3.4986/\$}.$$

Notice that in the two cases just discussed, we have been dealing with periods of less than a year. In these conditions, the flat percentage change in the spot value of the currencies had to be annualized before we could add it to or subtract it from the interest rate figures, which are on an annual basis. If we were talking of periods of time longer than a year, it would be an error to add the expected percentage appreciation to the interest rate. This procedure would be valid only if we were talking of the same percentage appreciation for *every* year involved in the transaction. If this assumption is not valid, then estimates of how much revaluation and in what year or years the revaluation will take place will have to be made.

Hedging exposure to foreign exchange risk

The foreign exchange risks which multinational companies face can be divided into two major types:

1. Foreign currency cash flows whose timing, amount, and currency can be identified specifically; for example, an account receivable maturing in ninety days in the amount of £100

2. Value of an investment that will continue generating profits in the future; for example, the net investment in a subsidiary in the United Kingdom

The risks in these situations are comparable with those of having a net exchange position. If the spot exchange rate changes against the holder of the position, losses will occur; on the other hand, if the exchange rate changes in favor of the position holder, gains will result. In the first type of risk exposure, the size and time characteristics of the exchange position can be estimated precisely. In the second type, however, this problem is much more difficult. The problems in the second type are complicated by the fact that the cash flows associated with an investment tend to be of a long-term nature and difficult to estimate. In addition, corporations are required to consolidate financial statements and report them on a regular basis. Accounting conventions as to how to define the exposure to foreign exchange risk often do not coincide with an educated assessment of what future cash flows will be.

Dealing with the problems of measuring exposure to foreign exchange risk is outside the scope of this book.[4] In this section, we shall assume that an exposure has been identified and measured. In addition, we shall assume that a decision has been made to cover or hedge the exposure. The issue is, then, what is the most efficient way to do the hedging. The rate scenario is presented in Exhibit 8.4.

For simplicity's sake, the scenario presented in Exhibit 8.4 does not include bid and offer rates; we shall talk only about mid-rates. The Eurodollar rate of 6½ percent is assumed to be the interbank rate. The domestic dollar base rate of 7 percent is a combination of the domestic market cost of funds to the bank, plus a markup to cover reserve requirements and insurance costs, plus a profit margin. The market cost of certificates of deposits (CDs) is assumed to be 1¼ percent below the base rate. In this case, their market cost would be 5¾ percent. The aggregate cost of reserve requirements and insurance required by the Federal Deposit Insurance Corporation (FDIC) is about ½ percent. Thus, the true cost of domestic dollars on an "interbank" basis in the domestic market is

---

[4] See R. Ankrom, "Top Level Approach to the Foreign Exchange Problem," *Harvard Business Review*, July–August 1974, pp. 79–90; A. Prindl, *Foreign Exchange Risk*. London: John Wiley & Sons, 1976; R. M. Rodriguez and E. E. Carter, *International Financial Management*. Englewood Cliffs, N.J.: Prentice-Hall, Inc., 1976.

Exhibit 8.4
HEDGING A FUTURE POUND CASH INFLOW

RATE SCENARIO

Money Market, Three-Month Maturity

Eurodollars, interbank	6.50%
Domestic dollars, base rate	7.00%
Europound, interbank	12.00%
Domestic pound, interbank	10.00%

Foreign Exchange Market

Spot rate	$2.02/£
Three-month swap rate	$0.0278/£ (5.5% p.a. discount on the pound)
Three-month forward rate	$1.9922/£

PROBLEM: Cover a three-month receivable in pounds

OPTIONS:

1. Cover in the forward market; sell pounds against dollars forward at $1.9922/£.

2. Cover in the spot exchange and Euro-currency money market:
   a. using interbank rates, borrow pounds at 12.00%, exchange into dollars, invest dollars at 6.50%.
   b. using nonbank borrowers rates, borrow pounds at 13.50%, exchange into dollars, invest dollars at 6.50%.

3. Cover in the domestic money market. Using nonbank borrowers' rates, borrow pounds at 11.50%, exchange into dollars, and invest dollars at 6.50%.

6¼ percent. This is ¼ percent below the interbank Eurodollar rate. This difference is not uncommon, although the disparity usually does not exceed 25 basis points, as here. It is attributed to the difference in political risk (sovereign risk) between a deposit located in the United States and one located in the United Kingdom. Finally, ¾ percent is added to the domestic "interbank" rate to obtain the domestic dollar base rate. The Eurodollar rate does not include either of the last two markups. For this reason, the rate appears to be lower in our example. On an *interbank* basis, the Eurodollar rate is about 0.5 percent higher.

The interest rates in Europounds and domestic pounds are both inter-bank rates. The difference between them is due to the foreign exchange controls imposed by Great Britain. These controls limit the local funds which can be converted into foreign currency. They also restrict the amount of borrowing by nonresidents in the British market. The result is an excess demand for pound borrowings in the Euromarkets, which raises the interest rates in that market above the domestic rates.

The three-month swap rate of dollars against pounds of $0.0278/£ reflects a 5.5 percent p.a. discount on the pound against the dollar on the basis of a spot rate of $2.02/£. This figure of 5.5 percent p.a. is also the difference between the Eurodollar and the Europound rates, the net accessible interest rates.

We shall now review several alternative ways of hedging a receivable in pounds sterling which is expected to mature in three months.

Hedging in the forward exchange market

The simplest form of hedging an expected future receipt of foreign currency is the forward outright sale of that currency. In our example, the three-month outright rate for pounds against dollars is $1.9922/£, which is a $0.0278/£ discount from the spot rate of $2.0200/£. This equals an annual discount rate of 5½ percent. In other words, although the present spot exchange rate is $2.02/£, the company locks in a firm forward rate for the sale of pounds against dollars at $1.9922/£. As we are talking about £1 million, the company will not get US$2,020,000, which it would if it should sell the pounds now for spot delivery, but, instead, it will receive only US$1,992,200. The exchange loss equals 5½ percent p.a. Three months from now the company will receive £1 million from the British customer, give them to the bank to whom the pounds were sold forward, and receive $1,992,200 from the bank.

Hedging in the spot exchange market and money market

Another form of hedging consists of borrowing pounds now, converting them into dollars, and investing the dollars. When the payment in pounds due to the company is received, it can be used to repay the pound borrowings.

Using the Euro-market. We assume first that domestic pounds are not available for borrowing; so, they have to be borrowed at 12 percent in the Euro-markets. The dollars can be invested at 6½ percent. The cost of this hedge is the difference between the 12 percent borrowing cost for Europounds and the 6½ percent income from the invested Eurodollars. This difference equals 5½ percent. In this case, the cost of hedging in the money market is the same as the cost of hedging in the forward market— 5½ percent. In the forward market approach, the cost shows up as an exchange rate differential or an exchange loss; in the money market approach, the cost shows up as a negative interest differential or an interest loss.

We have shown the procedure of hedging in the money market on the assumption that Europounds can be borrowed at 12 percent. However, this is an interbank rate to which only banks have access. Nonbanks, such as our assumed multinational corporation, have to pay a premium over the interbank rates. We shall assume this premium to be 1½ percent. Therefore, our company will have to pay 13½ percent for borrowing Europounds, sell the pounds spot at $2.02/£, and invest the resulting dollars at 6½ percent. Under these circumstances, the hedging cost is 7 percent (13½ percent borrowing cost less 6½% income from the investment).

The hedging cost of 7 percent is 1½ percent higher than the 5½ percent cost of using the forward hedge technique. It is also 1½ percent higher than the cost of the money market approach to hedging for banks which have access to the interbank Europound's rate of 12 percent. In other words, the 1½ percent premium over the interbank rate which the non-bank firms must pay is reflected in the total cost of hedging in the money market, 7 percent. This exceeds the cost of the alternative, hedging in the forward market, by 1½ percent.

This difference in hedging costs is not surprising. Banks run a much larger risk when they lend money to a customer than when they close a forward exchange transaction with a customer. A loan represents a 100 percent credit risk to the bank for the entire ninety days. A loss in a forward exchange transaction will occur only if the bank fulfills its part of the transaction before the customer does, and then the customer refuses to fulfill his or her obligation. (This situation is explained further in Chapter 12.)

In summary, we can say that, for banks, the hedging cost is the same regardless of whether they use the forward or the money market approach because they can deal at interbank rates, and those rates are the basis for swap rates in the foreign exchange market. There may be other considerations guiding a bank to prefer one or the other technique. For a nonbank company, however, it is always better to use the forward exchange market for a hedge than to use the money market. An exception to this rule is made only at a time when, in addition to the hedging need, there is also a business need which could use the proceeds of the money market hedge. This is explained below.

Let's now assume a situation where the company not only does have a need to hedge a three-month pound receivable, but, at the same time, it also needs to borrow U.S. dollars. The company can solve this problem in one of two ways:

1. Sell forward pounds and borrow dollars, or

2. Borrow Europounds and convert them spot into dollars

In each case the company is selling pounds and, therefore, hedging its net exposure in that currency. Also, in each case it is generating the needed dollars. Let's now see which is the preferable approach.

In the first approach, the cost of selling forward pounds, as computed before, is 5½ percent. Borrowing domestic dollars would cost 9 percent, a combination of the domestic U.S. base rate of 7 percent plus a markup over that base rate and the cost of maintaining non-interest-bearing compensating balances. The total cost is 14½ percent. If, instead of domestic dollars, Eurodollars are borrowed, the cost of borrowing would be 8 percent (6½ percent interbank rate plus a markup of 1½ percent). Then, the total cost would be 13½ percent (8 percent + 5½ percent).

In the second approach, the company borrows Europounds at 13½ percent (1½ percent above the interbank rate) and sells the pounds spot against dollars. The spot sale represents a hedge, and the proceeds from this sale are dollars that can be used in lieu of borrowing dollars domestically. The total cost of borrowing and hedging is 13½ percent.

We see that borrowing Europounds and selling spot pounds is 1 percent cheaper than the combined cost of forward hedging and *domestic* dollar borrowing. It has the same cost as forward hedging and *Eurodollar* borrowing. The percentages in our example may be slightly exaggerated to facilitate making the point, but usually it can be said that the spot sale of a currency borrowed in the Euro-market is cheaper than the combined cost of forward hedging and *domestic* borrowing. The reason is that the banks' markups over interbank rates on Euro-loans are smaller than the banks' markups over interbank rates on domestic loans.[5] A company should always consider the money market approach to hedging whenever the need to hedge coincides with the need to borrow.

Using the domestic market. When there are controls on foreign capital flows, the difference between domestic interest rates and Euro-rates for that particular currency may be significant. If we look at the rate scenario in Exhibit 8.4, we see a 2 percent difference between the interbank rates for domestic pounds and Europounds—the British have controls on capital exports.

Let's assume that British entities may prepay for ninety days. Also, let's assume that the account payable which corresponds to the pound receivable we are trying to hedge is owed by a fully owned subsidiary of the multinational company. This subsidiary has access to the domestic pound market, and it can borrow domestic pounds at 11½ percent (10 percent interbank rate plus 1½ percent). These funds can then be used to prepay the subsidiary's liability to the parent company, the multinational company which has the pound receivable exposure. The parent company can then sell the pounds spot and invest the proceeds at 6½ percent.

The total cost of this hedging operation, using the domestic money market, is 5 percent. This is ½ percent below the cost of using the forward market approach to covering and 2 percent below the cost of using the Euro-market for the same purpose. Whenever we find controls on foreign capital flows, we shall discover that making use of the domestic money market provides the most desirable option for hedging. However, to make use of this route in the case of controls on capital outflows, two requirements must be met. The other party, in this case assumed to be a fully owned subsidiary, must be willing and able to borrow locally at

---

[5] Banks operating in the Euro-markets usually do a wholesale business. As a result, they have less overhead, and costs are easier to control. For this reason their markup is often smaller.

competitive rates and prepay the debt. Also, the government regulations must allow the prepayment of liabilities to nonresidents. This procedure for hedging is usually called "leading payments."

To complete the picture of the use of domestic money markets for hedging strategies, let's look at a case where "lagging," instead of "leading," is desirable. Lagging is a simple technique applied when a company is interested in hedging a currency that is a candidate for upvaluation. If there are capital inflow controls in the country, this currency will have significantly lower interest rates in the external market than in the domestic market. This was the case in West Germany in the early 1970s when domestic interbank rates for German marks approximated 8 percent, and Euromark rates were in the neighborhood of 3 percent. The parent company would then encourage a subsidiary in such a hard-currency country as West Germany to defer payments in local currency which otherwise would have to be made. Instead of paying its debt, the subsidiary would invest domestic marks at 8 percent. If the parent company needed funds, it could borrow Eurodollars at 8 percent (6½ percent interbank plus 1½ percent). The company then had marks invested at 8 percent and dollars borrowed at 8 percent. This situation is the same as would occur if the company had purchased forward marks against dollars at the spot rate, i.e., at no premium and no discount. However, the mark must have been selling at a forward premium of 3½ percent (Eurodollar at 6½ percent less Euromark at 3 percent). The lagging technique permitted the company to maintain a net overbought position in marks at no cost, while a buildup of such a position at market rates would have cost 3½ percent p.a.

If the company did not want to maintain a net overbought position in marks, it could still benefit from the segmented markets in marks. It could keep the marks invested in West Germany at 8 percent while simultaneously borrowing Euromarks at 4½ percent (3 percent plus 1½ percent) and converting them into dollars. This would eliminate the need to borrow dollars at 8 percent, thus saving 3½ percent. Through all this activity, the company could keep a zero net exchange position in marks.

The techniques of leading and lagging are used heavily by multinational companies whenever exchange controls permit their doing so and changes in currency values are expected. This use leads to tremendous pressures on spot exchange rates. The following is an illustration of the problem.

When the German mark was expected to upvalue against the dollar, American corporations instructed their West German subsidiaries to defer (lag) remittances to the United States. This delay decreased the supply of marks in the spot exchange market because conversions from marks into dollars, which otherwise would have been made, did not take place. At the same time, West German corporations instructed their sales offices in the United States to accelerate ("lead") their payments in dollars so that these dollars could be converted into marks before the mark appreciated in value. This activity increased the demand for marks in the spot exchange market.

If both American and West German corporations had continued business as usual, the supply and demand in the spot exchange market for marks might have been reasonably balanced. However, the German subsidiaries of American corporations reduced the supply for marks at the same time that the German corporations increased the demand for marks by selling the dollars received (buying the marks) as prepayments from their American subsidiaries.

We would like to emphasize that leading and lagging are perfectly legitimate vehicles when the exchange regulations of the countries involved permit acceleration and deferral of payments. The people responsible for hedging would not be doing their jobs if they did not take advantage of these alternatives. In any event, if leading and lagging were not permitted, the hedging operations would probably take place in the forward markets.

Swaps and nonbanks

Nonfinancial institutions deal in the foreign exchange market mostly with the intention to change their net exchange position. These businesses typically generate some form of exposure to foreign exchange rate fluctuations. Usually, they enter the exchange market to change or eliminate their net positions. The changes can be effected only through a simple purchase or sale of the exposed currency. A swap is a purchase and a sale of the same currency for two different maturities. Because we are purchasing and selling the same currency and the same amount, the swap can never change our net position. So, swaps are not often used by nonfinancial businesses.

Occasionally, however, situations arise in which a multinational company may want to use a swap in the course of its regular business. Take, for example, the following case:

Assumed rate scenario:

Spot rate	DM56.70 = FF100
Three-month swap rate	DM0.42/FF
	(3% p.a. discount on francs)

Money markets, three-months maturity

French francs	8%
German marks	5%

The German subsidiary has accumulated cash in German marks. These marks are needed in three months to pay an installment on a term loan in West Germany. At the same time, the French subsidiary needs funds immediately, and it is negotiating a French franc loan. However, funds will not be available until three months from now. We have a situation where the German company has money available for three months, and the French company needs money for three months.

According to the rate scenario in Exhibit 8.5, one alternative for the French company would be to borrow French francs from a French bank at 9½ percent (8 percent plus 1½ percent) and for the German company to invest German marks with a German bank at 5 percent. This action would solve the problem at a total cost of 4½ percent.

Another alternative would be to swap the German company's excess marks into French francs for three months. Thus, the German company would purchase spot French francs against German marks at DM56.70/100FF and sell French francs against German marks for three-month delivery at DM56.28/100FF, a discount of 3 percent p.a. on francs. The firm would pay for the spot purchase of francs with its excess German marks and then make an intercompany loan in francs for three months to the French subsidiary. At the end of the three-month period, the French subsidiary would repay the francs. These francs would be exchanged into marks at the agreed rate of DM56.28/100FF, and the installment on the German subsidiary's loan would be paid. Under this scheme the total cost is 3 percent—the forward discount on French francs against the mark. The overall saving is 1½ percent.

Nonbanks should always avoid borrowing and investing at the same time. The difference between the swap cost of 3 percent and the negative spread resulting from simultaneous borrowing and investing of 4½ percent is the 1½ percent premium paid by the French subsidiary when it

Exhibit 8.5
USE OF SWAP BY NONFINANCIAL BUSINESSES

RATE SCENARIO

Money Market, Three-Month Maturity

French franc	8%
German mark	5%

Foreign Exchange Market

Spot rate	DM56.70/FF100
Three-month swap rate	DM00.42/FF100 (discount on franc)
Three-month forward rate	DM56.28/FF100

PROBLEM:
For three months, German subsidiary has excess funds
For three months, French subsidiary needs funds

SWAP SOLUTION:
Purchase francs against marks spot at DM56.70/FF100
Sell francs against marks three-month forward at DM56.28/FF100

Cost <u>3% p.a.</u>

LESS DESIRABLE ALTERNATIVES:
Borrow francs at 9½%   (8% interbank plus 1½%)
Invest marks at 5%

Net cost <u>4½%</u>

borrows French francs. We should note that the company is temporarily switching German marks into French francs without changing the company's net exchange position in either French francs or German marks. It is swapping one currency into another, and a swap never changes the net position.

CHAPTER 9
Computing the effective cost or yield of funds

So far, we have conducted our discussions on the basis of a given rate scenario. In real life, one of the problems which the funds manager must confront is how to calculate the effective cost or yield of funds in a particular rate scenario. Fees, regulations, commercial practices, and many other factors make it difficult to compare interest rates and exchange rates at face value. To make a valid comparison, the funds manager must include all the relevant factors in the calculation.

In this chapter, we shall present some of the problems encountered in computing effective yields. To facilitate presentation, we have divided these problems into two major groups: those characteristic of commercial banks, and those encountered by nonfinancial businesses. The discussion is not intended to be exhaustive, but it should illuminate some of the factors which must be taken into account in order to compute effective rates.

Effective yields in commercial banks

To illustrate the factors which commercial banks must take into account in computing effective yields, we shall present three examples. In the first case, we estimate the return on float; in the second problem, we estimate the interest rates which a bank could pay on foreign deposits; and in the last problem, we estimate the value of keeping funds over a weekend when U.S. dollar "clearinghouse funds" are used.

The value of float

Let's assume that we are in Jakarta, the capital of Indonesia. We are managing a financial institution in that city. Customers present Indonesian rupias to be exchanged into Singapore dollar drafts. There is a large amount of business between Indonesia and Singapore. Normally, the Singapore dollar draft cannot be presented in Singapore until the following day, except when negotiated for immediate transfer. The accepted fee for negotiating this transfer is 0.1 percent flat.

We have as a rate scenario the one presented in Exhibit 9.1. We have to sell rupias to (purchase U.S. dollars from) the Indonesian Central Bank at the rate of R415/US$ and purchase Singapore dollars (sell U.S. dollars) at the rate of S$2.30/US$. What exchange rate between rupias and Singapore dollars shall we quote the customers so that we can obtain the desired 0.1 percent flat fee?

We shall have to quote the exchange rate in Indonesian terms, that is, rupias per Singapore dollar. To obtain the base exchange rate, we know:

$$R415/US\$ = S\$2.30/US\$$$

or

$$R415 = S\$2.30$$

Then,

$$\frac{R415}{2.30} = S\$$$

$$S\$ = R180.43$$

So, the base exchange rate is R180.43/S$. We wish to charge a 0.1 percent flat fee. This is equivalent to R0.18. However, we know that the demand draft on Singapore dollars will not be presented until the following day. Therefore, we sell the rupias and buy the Singapore dollars today for delivery tomorrow (at tomorrow's value), and we have the use of the rupias overnight. We can invest the rupias at the overnight rate of 12 percent p.a. In terms of absolute amounts, 12 percent overnight will earn R0.06. Then, if we want to charge only a 0.1 percent fee, the exchange rate should be the basic exchange rate, plus the fee, *minus* the interest earned on the float of overnight rupias. The exchange rate quoted to the customer should be R180.55/S$.

Exhibit 9.1
COMPUTING VALUE OF FLOAT

RATE SCENARIO

Money Market, Overnight Rates

Indonesian rupia	12%
U.S. dollar	6%

Foreign Exchange Market	*Spot rates*
Indonesian rupia	R415/US$
Singapore dollar	S$2.30/US$

Cost of Overnight Transfer from Rupia into Singapore Dollar

Base exchange rate	R180.43/S$
Plus 0.1% fee	0.18
	R180.61/S$
Less interest earned on overnight rupias float	0.06
Total cost	R180.55/S$

Cost of deposits

We are in the funds management department of a commercial bank in the United States. We have been requested to have a customer's time deposits denominated in German marks. What interest rate can we pay on these deposits?

We have as a rate scenario the figures presented in Exhibit 9.2. The rate on domestic dollars is lower than the one on Eurodollars because of the additional costs associated with maintaining deposits in the United States, namely, reserve requirements and insurance costs. We are assuming that there is no foreign exchange control which would affect the relationship between domestic and Euro-rates beyond the cost differential just mentioned.

If we accept the deposit in German marks, we shall be receiving German marks and be liable for German marks when the deposit matures. There are two ways of computing the rate that we can pay on such deposits:

1. We can use the domestic deposit rate and adjust it for the cost of covering the conversion of German marks into dollars and back into German marks. In this case, the cost will be:

Domestic dollar rate	6.00%
Swap rate—premium on forward mark (sell mark spot; purchase forward at premium)	2.50%
Deposit rate for marks in the United States	3.50%

2. We can use the Euromark rate as the base and subtract the reserve requirement and other costs which have to be incurred when the deposit is kept in the United States. In this case, the cost will be:

Euromark rate	4.00%
Cost of deposits in U.S.	0.50%
Deposit rate for marks in the U.S.	3.50%

In this case the two methods produce the same deposit rate. The reason for the identical rates is that we assumed that the swap rate fully reflects the interest differentials in the Euro-markets, and that the Euro-rates and

Exhibit 9.2
COMPUTING COST OF DEPOSITS

MARKET SCENARIO

Money Market, Three-Month Maturity

Domestic dollar	6.00%
Eurodollar	6.50%
Euromark	4.00%

Foreign Exchange Market

Spot rate	DM2.50/US$
Swap rate	DM0.0156/US$

$$\frac{.0156 \times 100}{2.50} \times \frac{12}{3} = 2.50\% \text{ p.a.}$$

(discount on dollars against German mark)

Regulations

Cost of reserve requirements and insurance on domestic deposits	0.50%

domestic rates differed only by the additional costs associated with domestic deposits. In practice, however, we often find that the Euro-rates are slightly higher than domestic rates for comparable maturities. A difference of 20 points is not unusual. Professional arbitrage usually begins at a disparity of 25 basis points. This is thought to reflect the difference in political risk associated with keeping the deposits in other countries. If this difference in rates prevails, the two methods of computing the cost of foreign deposits will yield different answers. Using the domestic rate as the base will yield a lower cost. If, for example, we change the domestic rate in this case to 5.80 percent, the deposit rate for German marks kept in the United States would be 3.30 percent, in contrast with 3.50 percent in the previous calculations.

Of course, we have assumed that nondollar deposits in the United States would be subject to the same regulations as dollar deposits. If these regulations were changed so that nondollar deposits were exempt from these costs, the rate which we could pay on these deposits would be the same as the Euro-rates.

From the above, it is clear that a depositor receives a lower interest rate on deposits held in the United States than in the Euro-markets. Only considerations relating to sovereign risk would motivate a depositor to keep funds in this country rather than with the same bank in the Euro-markets.

Value of funds over a weekend

The payments of checks in the United States are normally made in terms of clearinghouse funds.[1] The checks to be presented for payment are given to the clearinghouse. These clearinghouse funds become "Fed Funds" (funds deposited with one of the Federal Reserve Banks) the following day. It is not until then that the bank can make use of the funds. All settlement of worldwide foreign exchange and money market transac-

---

[1] Clearinghouse funds are U.S. dollar-denominated checks which have been presented for collection through a clearinghouse. These funds become available in the form of deposits with one of the Federal Reserve banks on the following business day. (These deposits with a Federal Reserve bank are usually referred to as "Fed Funds.")

There are two types of clearinghouses. The first type exists at the local and regional levels and is organized by participating private commercial banks. The other type is run directly in each of the Federal Reserve banks. Both types of clearinghouses "clear funds" in the same amount of time.

tions denominated in U.S. dollars are also made in terms of clearinghouse funds. In other words, the vast majority of payments made in the United States are not available in actual funds to the recipient until the following day. When the payment day is Friday, the funds are not available until Monday. This often requires an adjustment of the rate.

Let's say that a branch of our bank borrows Eurodollars overnight on Thursday. The repayment is due on Friday, and the branch pays interest on the funds borrowed for only one day. In practice, however, the proceeds of the loan are available in Fed Funds on Friday, and repayment of the loan, which is made in clearinghouse funds on Friday, is not available to the lending bank in Fed Funds until Monday. Effectively, we, the borrowing bank, have "good," investable funds available for three days—Friday, Saturday, and Sunday; the lending bank has actually loaned "good" funds for three days. Given that the rate quoted is for only one day, the rate has to be adjusted to reflect the reality of the transaction. The funds are available to the borrowing bank for three days, or 300 percent more time than the rate expresses. Thus, if the daily rate is 9 percent, the daily rate on Thursday should be 300 percent of 9 percent p.a., or 27 percent p.a. For example, $100 at 9 percent p.a. earns $0.025 in a day ($100 \times .09/360$). In three days the $100 will earn $0.075. Since we are quoting a per annum rate to be applied as though we lent the funds for only one day, the rate has to be adjusted by the same multiple as the number of days increased. In this case, 27 percent p.a. will produce $0.075 of interest per day ($100 \times .27/360$). (See Exhibit 9.3.)

If we place funds in the Eurodollar market from value Friday until value Monday, the next eligible value date, we have a three-day placement. In reality, however, the funds which we have placed will not become Fed Funds on the other bank's account until Monday. Effectively, the funds are available to the other bank for only one day. Then, the three-day rate should be adjusted to reflect the fact that the funds are available for only one-third the time for which the rate is given. If the three-day rate is 9 percent p.a., then the Friday placement should earn only one-third that rate, or 3 percent p.a. For example, $100 placed for three days at 9 percent p.a. would earn $0.075 in interest ($100 \times .09/360 \times 3$). But, in practice, the funds are available to the other bank for only one day, and the interest rate it collects per day is only $0.025. To adjust the per annum rate on three days to reflect this reality, we multiply the rate by the actual fraction of three days for which the funds are available, i.e., one-third. The three-day rate quote on Friday is 3 percent p.a. (See Exhibit 9.4.)

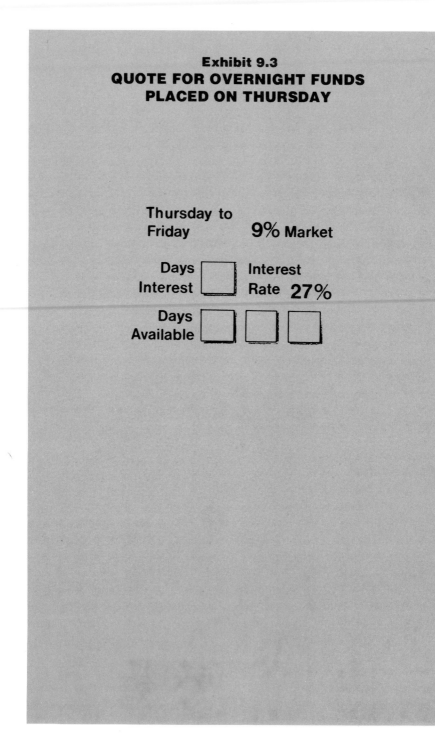

Exhibit 9.3
QUOTE FOR OVERNIGHT FUNDS
PLACED ON THURSDAY

Thursday to
Friday   9% Market

Days   Interest
Interest   Rate 27%

Days
Available

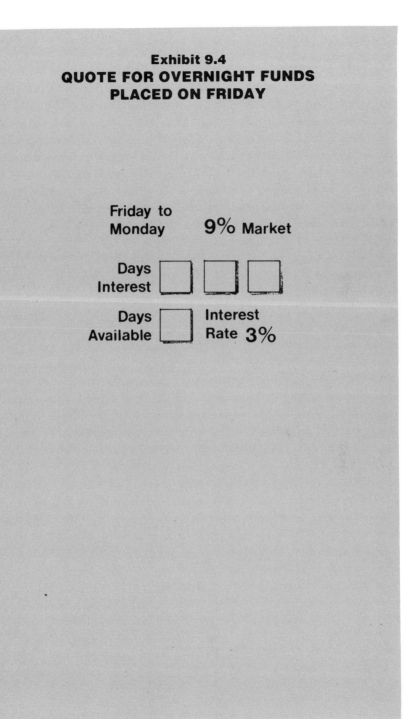

Exhibit 9.4
QUOTE FOR OVERNIGHT FUNDS
PLACED ON FRIDAY

Value of funds for one-month
and longer maturities

The same pattern applies to funds for longer maturity. For example, a one-month time deposit received on Monday, April 5, is due on Wednesday, May 5. The bank begins to pay interest on the deposit on Monday, April 5, although the proceeds of the deposit are not available to the bank in Fed Funds until Tuesday, April 6. However, at the other end, the bank stops paying interest on the deposit on Wednesday, May 5, but it does not lose the use of Fed Funds until Thursday, May 6. Since the number of days lost at the beginning is the same as the number of days gained at the end, the number of days when money is available equals the number of days for which interest is paid, thirty days. Therefore, the general market rate of 9 percent is not adjusted. (See Exhibit 9.5.)

In the previous example, if a Friday is involved, we shall have to make adjustments on the rate. Let's say that the one-month deposit is received on Wednesday, April 7, and matures on Friday, May 7. The bank begins paying interest on the deposit on Wednesday, April 7, although the proceeds of the deposit are not available in Fed Funds until Thursday, April 8. However, the bank stops paying interest on Friday, May 7, but it does not lose Fed Funds until Monday, May 10. The bank actually has the use of the money for thirty-two days. Therefore, the one-month rate of 9 percent must be adjusted upward. The number of days when money is actually available is two-thirtieths larger than the thirty days for which the 9 percent is quoted. Therefore, the 9 percent p.a. rate should be increased by a factor of 2/30. This yields a rate of 9.60 percent p.a. $(9 \times 2/30) + 9$. (See Exhibit 9.5.)

In a one-month deposit with a Friday start and a Monday ending, the situation is reversed. The bank receiving the deposit has the funds available for two days less than the number of days for which the rate is given. Therefore, the per annum rate must be adjusted downward. In this case, the rate would be 8.42 percent p.a. (See Exhibit 9.5.)

The rates found in the market will follow the international customs as to value dates, and when Fridays are involved, the rates will reflect this fact. For example, if the normal run for a one-month deposit is from Wednesday, April 7, to Friday, May 7, we shall find the one-month rate on April 5 to be 9.60 percent p.a. if the general one-month rate is 9 percent.[2] If a depositor should choose to depart from the normal run and wishes the

---

[2] On Monday, April 5, the standard spot value date is Wednesday, April 7.

Exhibit 9.5

QUOTE FOR ONE-MONTH FUNDS WITH DIFFERENT NUMBERS OF DAYS INVOLVED

From	Until	Days Available	Days' Interest		Interest Rate
Mon 4/5	Wed 5/5	30	30	——	9.00%
Wed 4/7	Fri 5/7	32	30	$\frac{9 \times 32}{30}$	9.60%
Fri 4/9	Mon 5/10	29	31	$\frac{9 \times 29}{31}$	8.42%

deposit to mature on Monday, May 10, then the per annum rate for the 32-day deposit would be 9 percent.

When periods longer than a month are involved, the adjustment to the per annum rate to reflect the precise number of days involved in the transaction is smaller in terms of percentage points. In our example of 9 percent p.a., the adjustment would be 30 points for two months, 20 points for three months, 15 points for four months, 12 points for five months, 10 points for six months, and so on. The adjustment in terms of dollars and cents paid or received in interest is always the same. These adjustments in terms of percentage points are larger the higher the interest rate, and smaller the lower the interest rate.

Effective yields in nonfinancial businesses

In this section we shall refer to two cases. One case illustrates the need to make sure that all costs are included in the computation of an effective exchange rate. In the other case, we point to the impact which controls on foreign capital flows can have on the effective yield of funds.

All-in cost of exchange transactions

When a company is comparing a foreign exchange rate of one bank with the rate of another bank, it is important to remember that the rate alone may not represent the all-in cost of the transaction. Some banks charge a brokerage fee or commission. It is also not uncommon for a bank to receive the currency purchased one or several days before it makes the currency it sold available to the customer. This float, negative for the customer and positive for the bank, must be taken into account, as well as fees and other charges when evaluating the overall attractiveness of an exchange rate.

Consider, for example, the case presented in Exhibit 9.6. If a company would like to purchase dollars and sell German marks, it would seem that Bank B has the better rate. It offers dollars at DM2.6095/$, whereas Bank A offers DM2.6103/$. However, Bank B charges a fee of .05 percent and delivers the dollars one day after it receives the German marks. The fee equals 13 points, and the one-day float equals 4 points. So, the total cost of buying dollars from Bank B is DM2.6112. Bank A has a higher exchange rate, but, in bottom-line terms, it has the more attractive offer.

Exhibit 9.6
COMPARATIVE EXCHANGE RATES

	Bank A	Bank B
Basic quote	$39.31/100DM	DM2.6095/$
Fee	none	0.05%
Value date	Today	tomorrow (@ 6% p.a.)
Adjusted Quotes in German Terms		
Basic quote	DM2.6103/$	DM2.6095/$
Fee	0	0.0013*
Float	0	0.0004†
All-in Cost	DM2.6103/$	DM2.6112/$

---

* $0.0005 \times 2.6095 = 0.0013$.

† $0.06 \times 1/360 \times 2.6095 = 0.0004$.

Impact of capital flow controls

Let's take the case of a United States multinational company which has been maintaining excess funds in German marks with its West German subsidiary. The recurrent appreciation of the mark against the U.S. dollar during the early 1970s has made this policy pay handsomely. However, by August 1973, management began to think that the appreciation of the mark had already peaked. Accordingly, it ordered the German subsidiary to transfer its deposits from German marks into dollars.

The market scenario at the time is presented in Exhibit 9.7. The substantial difference between domestic and Euromarks is the result of exchange controls in Germany. The free forces of supply and demand have driven down the interest rate for Euromarks to 3 percent, although the rate on domestic marks is 14 percent. Arbitrage between domestic and Euromarks is not possible because of foreign exchange controls. The forward exchange rate for U.S. dollars against marks, is, of course, based on interest rates for *Eurodollars* and *Euromarks* so that the U.S. dollar has a discount of 9 percent against the mark.

Given the interest level for domestic marks of 14 percent and a swap rate of U.S. dollars against marks of 9 percent, it follows that the value of U.S. dollars on a covered basis in Germany must be 23 percent. Persons who pay 23 percent in West Germany for U.S. dollars available in that country can sell these dollars spot against marks and purchase them back forward against marks at a discount in their favor of 9 percent. If we deduct the 9 percent swap profit from the 23 percent interest costs for the dollar borrowing, we arrive at a 14 percent cost for marks on a fully covered basis. This price is the going market rate for marks in West Germany. However, virtually nobody in that country has U.S. dollars, so the deposit market for U.S. dollars inside West Germany is very narrow.

The unusual thing in our case is that the American subsidiary in West Germany has excess funds in marks which it has been requested to transfer into U.S. dollars. The fact that the company is prepared to switch its net exchange position from the upvaluation-prone mark to the devaluation-prone dollar entitles it to a net yield of 23 percent. This yield could be achieved in either of two ways:

1. Maintain deposit in marks with German bank at   14%
   and sell forward marks against dollars at a
   premium of   <u>9%</u>
   for a total yield of   <u>23%</u>

Exhibit 9.7
COMPARATIVE NET EFFECTIVE YIELDS

RATE SCENARIO

Money Market, Three-Month Maturity

Eurodollar	12%
Euromark	3%
Domestic mark	14%

Foreign Exchange Market

Spot rate	DM2.7500/$
Three-month swap rate	DM0.0620/$ (discount on dollar)
Three-month forward rate	DM2.6880/$ (9% discount on dollar)

2. Convert spot marks into U.S. dollars and demand a deposit rate for these dollars of 24 percent. If the bank refuses to pay higher than 23 percent, then revert to the first alternative.

PART III

Controlling funds management operations

We have seen how to deal successfully as a funds manager in the money market and the foreign exchange markets. How can we evaluate how successful we have been and what risks have been taken? The answers to these questions are of particular importance when the functions of the funds manager must be delegated to one or more individuals.

Because the accounting for foreign exchange transactions involves some slightly different accounting practices, we dedicate Chapter 10 to this issue. In Chapter 11 we identify in detail the various risks which are involved in the transactions in the money market and the foreign exchange market. Finally, in Chapter 12, we discuss ways to control the risks which funds managers assume in their operations.

CHAPTER 10
Accounting for foreign exchange transactions

Throughout the book we have made extensive use of "cash flow boxes" to illustrate the currency, timing, and size of cash flows. By taking the balance among these boxes, we were able to compute the aggregate profit or loss for the transaction in question. Needless to say, these cash boxes, although pedagogically useful, are not a conventional way of keeping records and computing profits and losses.

We are familiar with the traditional way of keeping records and computing profits and losses for transactions in the money market. The balance sheet carries the level of investments among its assets, and the level of borrowings among its liabilities. The profit and loss statement shows the amount of interest earned on investments and the amount of interest expenses on borrowings. The net of the interest earned and the interest expenses provides the net profit or loss of the money market operation.

Ultimately, the profits and losses on foreign exchange transactions must also be shown in the conventional financial statements: the balance sheet and the profit and loss statement. However, because of the specialized nature of these transactions, it is necessary to keep some additional records and to make use of special techniques to value the transactions at market prices and to compute a net profit or loss. Clarification of these accounting requirements is the purpose of this chapter.

Before going any further, let's make it clear that we shall be talking only about the purchase and sale of spot and forward exchange. The problems associated with valuing real assets held in other countries are outside the scope of this book. As mentioned in the context of the discussion on hedging, nonfinancial businesses confront special problems in estimating the economic value of their net investments in foreign countries. In addition to the intrinsic difficulties of the problem, there are the problems associated with reporting practices which follow accountants' conventions in each country.

Our discussion is most relevant to the measurement of the performance of a foreign exchange trading room. Thus, it is more applicable to financial institutions than to nonfinancial businesses. On the other hand, nonfinancial businesses must also evaluate their performance in foreign exchange dealings, even if this activity is not a profit center in the company.

Special records

The position book

For each currency, a position book should be kept. We can think of the position book as a detailed record of the inventory which the business keeps in each currency. Every single transaction in that currency, regardless of its size or origin in the foreign exchange market (not in the money market, for example, not in loans and deposits), should be entered in this book. An example of a position book, in this case for pound sterling, is presented in Exhibit 10.1.

The position book registers every purchase and every sale in terms of two currencies: (1) the foreign currency for which the position book is kept (pound sterling in our example), and (2) the local currency, that is, the currency of the country in which the operation takes place (U.S. dollars in this case). Purchases are treated as debits, and sales as credits. Additional columns identify other particulars of the transaction, such as the date on which the transaction was closed, the rate (implicit in the expression of each transaction in terms of two currencies), the value date on which the transaction matures, and the name of the other party to the transaction, as well as the contract number. Then, at the end of the accounting period, a balance is taken for each column and a net balance is computed.

If the exchange transaction does not have a natural local currency equivalent, as is true when one foreign currency is purchased and another foreign currency is sold (multilateral or arbitrage contract), an artificial local currency equivalent is assigned to that contract. For example, if a bank in the United States purchases £1 million at DM5.50/£, the notation means that the bank has purchased £1 million and sold DM5.5 million. Both currencies are foreign currencies to the U.S. bank, and, therefore,

Exhibit 10.1
SAMPLE POSITION BOOK

CURRENCY: pound sterling

| | | | Name of Counterpart | | Foreign Currency £ | | Local Currency | |
| | | | No. of Contract | Rate | Debit (Buy) | Credit (Sell) | Debit (Buy) | Credit (Sell) |
Date	Value Date							
June 1	June 3		1	2.3900	110,000		262,900	
June 1	June 3		2	2.4000		100,000		240,000
June 1	Sept. 3		3	2.3820	200,000		476,400	
June 1	July 3		4	2.3940		1,000,000		2,394,000
June 1	Dec. 3		5	2.3640	1,000,000		2,364,000	
			Balances		1,310,000	1,100,000	3,103,300	2,634,000
			Net balance		210,000	—	469,300	—

there is no natural local currency equivalent. In this case, the trader assigns a rate of, say, US$2.40/£ to the contract and establishes a local currency equivalent of US$2.4 million. The transaction is then entered in the position book for sterling as a sterling purchase at DM5.50/£ and as a local currency amount of US$2.4 million. Likewise, a sale of DM5.5 million is recorded in the position book for marks at DM5.50/£ with a local currency equivalent of US$2.4 million. The economic effect is the same as if the bank had purchased sterling at US$2.40/£ and sold marks at US$0.4364/DM. The choice of the arbitrary rate is immaterial. For example, if the trader chooses a rate of US$2.30/£ to determine the local currency equivalent, the sterling purchase will be recorded at US$2.30. This will increase the earnings on sterling when the purchase price is compared with the market price. But, the same local currency equivalent of $2.3 million must be assigned to the mark sale which will be registered at US$0.4182/DM, instead of US$0.4364/DM. This transaction will appear as a loss when compared with the market. The overall profit, however, is not affected by the rate changes. But, if the arbitrary rate differs substantially from the market rate, we arrive at sharply higher earnings in one currency and sharply lower earnings in another currency. This is undesirable because it distorts a profit and loss analysis of the exchange department on a currency-by-currency basis.

In the position book in Exhibit 10.1, we have recorded the following transactions, which, we assume, have all taken place on June 1:

1. Purchase £110,000 spot at $2.39/£

2. Sell £100,000 spot at $2.40/£

3. Purchase £200,000 three-month outright at $2.3820/£

4. Sell £1,000,000 one month at $2.3940/£

5. Purchase £1,000,000 six months at $2.3640/£

The net balance line shows a net overbought position in the amount of £210,000, equivalent to $469,300.

We can net the entries in the position book by date and arrive at an inventory of outstanding foreign exchange transactions. This calculation can be done on the trading position work sheet as shown in Exhibit 10.2.

Exhibit 10.2
TRADING POSITION WORK SHEET

POUNDS POSITION ON JUNE 1

Maturity	Long (L) and Short (S) Position	Contract Rate
Spot	L 10,000	2.3900
Forward		
Sept. 3	L 200,000	2.3820
Swap Position		
July 3	S 1,000,000	2.3940
Dec. 3	L 1,000,000	2.3640

Trading position work sheet

Scanning the position book in Exhibit 10.1, we find the following:

1. The net of transactions 1 and 2 produces
   (a) a profit of $1000 from £100,000 bought and sold spot, and
   (b) an inventory of spot pounds in the amount of £10,000.

2. Transaction 3 is a net outright purchase of forward pounds in the amount of £200,000.

3. Transactions 4 and 5 reflect a swap position with the sale of pounds on July 3 and the purchase of pounds on December 3, both in the amount of £1 million.

These figures are shown in the trading position work sheet presented in Exhibit 10.2. The realized profits in the amount of $1000 are not shown on this sheet. They are past history. There is nothing the trader can do about the £100,000 already bought and sold. However, the final closing value for the transactions listed in the trading position sheet still remains to be determined. For example, consider the cost of the £10,000 spot purchased at $2.39£. We do not know precisely at what price we shall be able to sell these pounds. Tomorrow's spot price may be above or below the purchase price. The balances in the position book and the trading position sheet are combined in the so-called exchange profit work sheet (as shown in Exhibit 10.3) to arrive at the net profit or loss in each currency. This form is discussed in the context of the following section.

Measuring returns on foreign exchange transactions

A widely accepted method of accounting for foreign exchange earnings is the rebate system. This system simulates a complete squaring of all exchange positions. In other words, if a bank were to be liquidated, it would liquidate not only its assets and liabilities but also its contingent accounts, including unliquidated foreign exchange contracts outstanding. For every value date for which the bank has purchased foreign exchange, it would sell a like amount, and for every value date where the bank sold foreign exchange, it would purchase a like amount. Under the rebate

Exhibit 10.3
EXCHANGE PROFIT WORK SHEET

BRANCH _____ DATE _____

	1	2	3	4	5	6	7	8
	NET FOREIGN CURRENCY POSITION FROM POSITION BOOK	LONG OR SHORT	MIDDLE RATE	VALUE OF POSITION AT MIDDLE RATE	VALUE OF POSITION FROM POSITION BOOK	UNADJUSTED PROFIT (NET OF COLUMNS 4 + 5) (SHOW + OR −)	ADJUSTMENT FOR FUTURE CONTRACTS (SHOW + OR −)	ADJUSTED PROFIT (NET OF COLUMNS 6 + 7) (SHOW + OR −)
	£210,000	L	$2.40	$504,000	$469,300	+34,700	−22,400	+12,300

PROFIT FOR CURRENT MONTH

PREPARED BY _____
CHECKED BY _____
REVIEWED BY _____

system, one does not actually liquidate the position but applies rates to the open positions which one would very likely have to accept if the position were in fact liquidated. That is, foreign exchange positions are valued at market prices at the time of closing the books.

A standard procedure to arrive at the market valuation of the exchange position is, first, to value everything at the spot market rate, and then to adjust the forward transactions to reflect the appropriate market premium or discount. This is done above, using the exchange profit work sheet shown in Exhibit 10.3.

Columns 1, 2, and 5 in the exchange profit work sheet are copied from the position book in Exhibit 10.1. Column 1 shows the net foreign currency position of £210,000. Column 2 says that it is a long, or net overbought, position. Column 5 gives the value of the position in terms of local currency, $469,300. As we showed in the position book in Exhibit 10.1, this local currency value of the position is the result of assigning to each transaction a local currency equivalent. We can say that column 5 is the cost of acquiring the £210,000 position.

To translate the value of the £210,000 position at the spot rate, we establish first the current spot rate. This is indicated in column 3; it is $2.40/£. In column 4 we show the value of the pound position expressed at the current spot rate, $504,000 ($2.40/£ × £210,000). This is a crude current market value of the position; it assumes that the entire foreign currency position can be liquidated at the spot rate. The difference between this spot market value of the position, $504,000, and the value at which it was acquired, $469,300 (shown in column 5), provides a first estimate of the profit resulting from the foreign exchange transactions in pounds. This difference is shown in column 6 as "Unadjusted profits."

Now we have to adjust the open forward position for the difference between the spot rate which we initially applied to that position and the rate at which the respective forward positions can actually be liquidated. In our case, we estimated the market value of the entire position at the spot rate of $2.40. We know, however, that the forward sterling is selling at a discount against the dollar. The market rates on the outstanding forward contracts are below the spot rate of $2.40. Therefore, we must make adjustments to the profits computed in column 6.

Let's assume that the discount for forward sterling has been reduced from $0.0060 per month to $0.0040 per month. Thus, the trading position work sheet shown in Exhibit 10.4 presents the current market rates for each of the various value dates in the position book. Next, we compute the difference between the rate at which each of the transactions was

Exhibit 10.4
TRADING POSITION WORK SHEET

POUNDS POSITION ON JUNE 1

Maturity	Long (L) or Short (S) Position	Contract Rate	Market Rate	Adjustments
Spot	L 10,000	2.3900	2.4000	+ 100
Forward				
Sept. 3	L 200,000	2.3820	2.3880	− 2,400
Swap Position				
July 3	S 1,000,000	2.3940	2.3960	+ 4,000
Dec. 3	L 1,000,000	2.3640	2.3760	− 24,000
				−$22,300

initially valued (the current spot rate) and the current market rate for the various forward dates. We then enter the difference in the column called "Adjustments."

The adjustment required for the spot position is +$100. The September 3 maturity is three months away from spot and commands a 120-point discount. The position could be sold at $2.3880. Previously, it was evaluated at the spot rate of $2.40. Therefore, earnings were overstated by 120 points; this calls for a negative adjustment of US$2400. The July 3 sale of £1 million is one month away from spot. It could be covered at $2.3960. Previously, we assumed coverage at the spot rate of $2.40, which was 40 points higher than the actual rate available in the market. Therefore, we must make a positive adjustment of $4000. The December 3 purchase of £1 million is six months away from spot and could be sold at 240 points below spot at $2.3760/£. Previously, we assumed a sale price of $2.40. Therefore, we have to make a negative adjustment of $24,000. The total of the "Adjustments" column in Exhibit 10.4 is a negative figure of $22,300.

The negative net adjustment of $22,300 is inserted in column 7 of the exchange profit work sheet in Exhibit 10.3. The difference between the unadjusted profit in column 6 and the adjustment for future contracts in column 7 is the actual profit in pounds, $12,400. This figure appears in column 8. To repeat, these profits represent the difference between the cost of the position and its market value at the time that the books are closed.

The procedure just described for pounds is applied to all currencies for which we have entries in the position book, and the grand total of column 8 in Exhibit 10.3 will show total exchange earnings for the period.

Closing the books

The final step in accounting for the profits and losses in the exchange department is to incorporate the final results into the main financial statements of the business. An account usually called "Exchange gains and losses" is the one used for this purpose. This is a subaccount among the profit and loss accounts.

In our example, we found that we have a profit of $12,400. Since it is a profit, the exchange gains and losses account will be credited by this amount. The corresponding debit entry is an adjustment in the value of the inventory of pounds. The bookkeeping entry would look like this:

	Debit	Credit
Pounds position	$12,400	
Exchange earnings		$12,400

The adjustment in the value of the pounds position is also entered in the position book. Exhibit 10.5 shows, on the next-to-the-last line, the increase in the value of the sterling position, an adjustment on the debit side in the amount of $12,400. This brings the total value of the position, at current market rates, to the amount of $481,700. Of course, the value of the position in terms of pounds remains unchanged. Only the figures in local currency, dollars, are adjusted to reflect the market value of the position. The net balance after adjustments in the net position book reflects the asset value of that currency which will appear in the business's balance sheet.

If we had had a loss instead of a gain, the debit and credit in the entry just discussed would have been reversed. The exchange loss account would have been debited, and the pounds position would have been credited. In the position book, the credit to the pounds position would have been entered as a credit in the adjustment line. The net value of the pounds position after this adjustment would have been decreased.

Reporting covered interest arbitrage

We have discussed cases of covered interest arbitrage at some length. In Chapter 5, page 85, in particular, we examined a case where there was an interest differential between the pound and the dollar of 2¾ percent in favor of the pound. Simultaneously, the forward discount on the pound for a comparable period was 180 points, or 3 percent. To take advantage of this market disequilibrium, we sold spot sterling against dollars and purchased forward sterling against dollars at the 3 percent p.a. discount. The cash flows on the spot day, negative cash flow for sterling and positive cash flow for dollars, were squared in the money market through a sterling borrowing and a dollar placement. This was done at a net cost of 2¾ percent against us. The maturing of these two money market transactions squared the cash flows for the forward exchange transaction.

If we follow the accounting conventions described in this chapter, this transaction will be recorded in our books as a large exchange profit and a

Exhibit 10.5
POSITION BOOK

CURRENCY: pound sterling

Date	Value Date	Name of Counterpart No. of Contract	Rate	Foreign Currency £		Local Currency	
				Debit (Buy)	Credit (Sell)	Debit (Buy)	Credit (Sell)
June 1	June 3	1	2.3900	110,000		262,900	
June 1	June 3	2	4.4000		100,000		240,000
June 1	Sept. 3	3	2.3820	200,000		476,400	
June 1	July 3	4	2.3940		1,000,000		2,394,000
June 1	Dec. 3	5	2.3640	1,000,000		2,364,000	
		Balances		1,310,000	1,100,000	3,103,300	2,634,000
		Net balance		210,000		469,300	
		Adjustment				12,400	
		Net balance after adjustment		210,000		481,700	

slightly smaller interest loss. The difference between the two figures, ¼ percent, is the profit realized in the arbitrage. A large number of these transactions will distort the earnings picture shown under exchange and interest. A realistic picture of the total net profit gained through the exchange transactions and the money market transactions in a covered interest arbitrage situation can be shown by recording them together. One way of recording the exchange part of covered interest arbitrage together with the money market part is to earmark the exchange transactions. The so-called exchange transactions can have their exchange rate differentials converted into interest differentials and entered together with the money market transactions.

In our example, the 180-point discount translates roughly into a 3 percent interest differential. The bookkeeping department will recognize that the trader marked such a transaction as a finance swap. Therefore, it will not enter this transaction in the position book, and the profit of 180 points will not show as an exchange profit. Instead, the bookkeeping department will treat this particular finance swap as if it were a placement of pounds and a borrowing of dollars. The trader determined that the 180-point discount equaled an interest differential of 3 percent p.a. in favor of the pound. The bookkeeping department will apply interest rates to the placement of pounds and the borrowing of dollars which reflect this 3 percent interest differential in favor of the pound. It may use 13 percent for pounds and 10 percent for dollars. It may also use any other set of interest rates. As long as the interest differential remains 3 percent, any set of rates will be acceptable. In this fashion, the earnings from a finance swap will be accrued as normal interest over the life of the swap transaction just like the real money market transactions offsetting the finance swap, i.e., the pound borrowing and the dollar placement. Obviously, the "placements and borrowings" resulting from finance swaps are booked in a subsection of the "General placements and borrowings" section to identify them as finance swaps.

CHAPTER 11
Risks in money market and foreign exchange operations

In this chapter we shall discuss the various types of risk which must be considered in evaluating the performance of the funds manager or in choosing alternative strategies. First, we shall describe the nature of these risks; then, we shall evaluate them in a specific example.

Types of risk

We can identify three types of risk when operating in the money and foreign exchange markets: rate risk, credit risk, and liquidity risk.

Rate risk

We saw in previous chapters that the way in which one can profit in the financial markets is by anticipating changes in the rates currently prevailing. It is this anticipation that leads the funds manager to produce "mismatched" cash flow positions.

In the money market, the rate risk arises when the maturities of the placement and the borrowings are not matched. For example, when we lend funds for six months while borrowing with a one-month maturity, the interest rate on the six-month loan has been locked in from the beginning. However, at the end of the first month, additional borrowings are necessary to repay the initial debt or to roll over the debt. But, at the beginning of the transaction, we do not know with certainty what the interest rate will be at that time. Most likely, the funds manager in this situation is speculating that interest rates will decline after a month. If the assumption proves correct, the funds manager would have locked in a high interest rate on the loan for six months while refinancing the operation at a lower interest rate after the initial first month. (See Exhibit 11.1.) If the initial expectation proves to be wrong and interest rates actually increase and keep doing so for the remainder of the loan period, however, the funds manager will be forced to obtain financing (to borrow) at rates which might prove to be higher than the one at which the funds were placed or lent initially.

In foreign exchange transactions the rate risk appears in two forms: (1) in net exchange positions, and (2) in swap positions or mismatched maturities. The most obvious case of rate risk is the maintenance of a *net exchange position* in a given currency. If the position is long or overbought and there is a depreciation of the currency, a loss is sure to occur. On the other hand, if an upvaluation occurs while the funds manager is holding a long net exchange position, there will be a profit from such a change in exchange rates. The opposite result would occur if the net exchange position were short or oversold in that currency.

The other way in which rate risk appears when one operates in the foreign exchange market is through swap positions. As explained in previous chapters, a swap transaction does not affect the *net exchange position*. By definition, a swap involves a simultaneous buy and sale of currency for two different maturities. For example, the funds manager may buy German marks against U.S. dollars for three-month delivery and sell German marks against U.S. dollars for one-month delivery. Let's say that the forward mark is selling at a premium against the dollar. In this case, in order to make a profit, the funds manager must be expecting that, when the one-month transaction matures, it will be possible to square the two-month gap at a premium larger than the one that prevailed initially. That is, the spread on a per annum basis at which the marks were purchased for three-month delivery must increase after a month so that the marks are sold for two-month delivery at a premium larger than the one paid to acquire them on the initial three-month contract. If the mark had been selling at a discount, the funds manager, when entering into this specific swap, would have expected that the discount would decrease.

This expectation of an increase in the premium or a decrease in the discount of the mark against the dollar must be based on a change in the relative interest rates. The interest differentials must change in favor of the dollar. If the initial situation was one of a forward premium on the mark against the dollar, then, in this case, the interest differential was in favor of the dollar. In other words, the interest rate for dollars was higher than the one for marks, and the forecast implied that the interest differ-

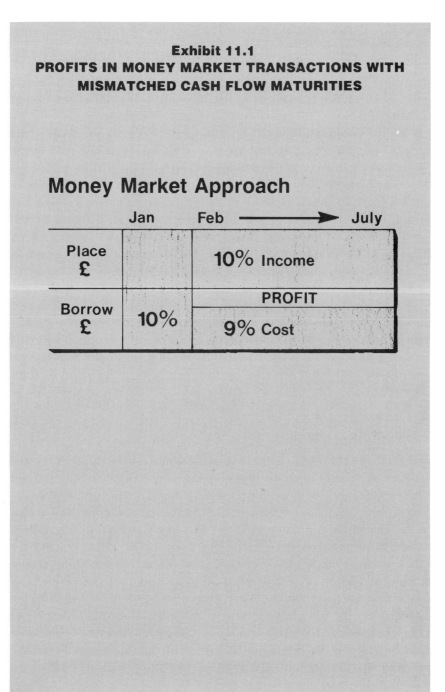

Exhibit 11.1
PROFITS IN MONEY MARKET TRANSACTIONS WITH
MISMATCHED CASH FLOW MATURITIES

ential would become even more strongly in favor of the dollar. If the initial situation was one of a discount on the mark against the dollar, then interest differentials must have been in favor of the mark. Therefore, the expectation behind the swap transaction described earlier must have been that the differential would narrow (become less favorable to the mark) either because the mark rate would decrease or the dollar rate would increase.

The previous paragraph clearly points out the connection between the forward exchange market and the money market. The rate risks in the forward exchange market, when one is dealing in swap transactions, are dependent on the same assumptions and outcomes as in the money market. A swap position, after all, is not really an exchange position. Profits and losses in a swap position depend exclusively on the development of interest rates for the two currencies involved. *A swap position is a money market position disguised with exchange contracts.* (For another example of a swap position, see the section "Swap Transactions" in Chapter 5, pp. 83–87.)

One major distinction between the rate risk in money market operations and swap transactions is that, when operating in the money market, we are forecasting only the rates for one currency. When operating in the foreign exchange, or swap, market, it becomes necessary to take into account the future interest rates for two currencies, a slightly more complicated task!

Credit risk

The credit risk has to do simply with the ability of the other party to a transaction to meet the agreed-upon obligations. Any time one operates in a market, a second party must be brought into the picture if a transaction is to be completed. In financial markets, the ability to meet a contracted obligation translates into the ability to pay when the obligation to deliver funds matures.

In the money market, the credit risk is very obvious. In this market, one borrows and lends, or places, funds. From our point of view, there is no credit risk when we do the borrowing; however, on the lending (or placing) side, there is always the risk that the borrower will be unable to repay the funds we have lent. In spite of a very profitable rate on the loan, if the borrower is not able to pay back the debt, the funds manager is sure to have a loss.

In the foreign exchange market, one can distinguish between two types of risk. The less serious one appears when the partner is unable or unwilling to fulfill a delivery of a currency promised under a forward contract. In this case, the funds manager is expecting a cash inflow in that currency to take place on the contracted date. Chances are that an outflow had already been planned to ensure the proper use of the inflow promised by the forward contract. However, if the other party to the transaction does not meet the specified obligation and the funds manager needs the funds, the party will have to go to the spot market to obtain those funds. The actual gain or loss in the spot transaction depends on the then-prevailing spot rate of the desired currency relative to the rate contracted through the now-defaulted contract. This risk has traditionally been called the 10 percent risk, though the term is quickly going out of style. The 10 percent refers to the size of the usual revaluation during the fixed-rate system which prevailed from the end of World War II until 1971. Note that this risk occurs when the other party to the transaction defaults *prior to maturity* of the contract.

A more serious credit risk in the foreign exchange market is the one that has appeared prominently in a few major losses in commercial banks. This situation occurs when the other party to a transaction goes bankrupt *on the day of maturity* and settlement of the contract and after the initial leg of the transaction has been completed. Given the time differences among various financial centers, one party may transfer the funds corresponding to his or her part of the transaction during regular office hours while the other party decides to declare bankruptcy before opening on the day on which the transaction is to take place. This loss amounts to 100 percent of the funds involved.

A widely publicized example which illustrates the credit risk in foreign exchange transactions is the failure of the German Herstatt Bank on Wednesday, June 26, 1974. The bank was very active in foreign exchange; in fact, it was this business that led, in large part, to the bank's failure. In a move which has led to much controversy, the German authorities closed the Herstatt Bank early in the afternoon of that Wednesday. The financial and nonfinancial institutions who had exchange business with Herstatt were divided into two groups: those that had exchange contracts outstanding with Herstatt maturing *after* June 26, and those with exchange contracts that matured *on* June 26.

Suppose the rate for marks at that time was US\$0.40/DM, and another bank had sold marks to Herstatt, maturing in July 1974, at US\$0.44/DM.

Herstatt did not perform under this contract, and the bank which sold to Herstatt at US$0.44/DM had to sell the marks again to another bank at the then-prevailing rate of US$0.40/DM. This is the 10 percent loss potential we mentioned earlier. Obviously, this kind of situation can lead to larger or smaller losses, as the case may be, or even produce a profit. In the latter instance, however, the bankrupt bank would probably file a claim.

Those parties who had exchange transactions with Herstatt maturing on June 26 were really in trouble, particularly if they had sold European currencies, including marks, to Herstatt and purchased U.S. dollars against them. The European currencies were paid to Herstatt on Wednesday morning, German time. However, Herstatt was closed before it had a chance to pay the U.S. dollars on Wednesday morning, New York time, which is Wednesday afternoon in Europe. Everybody having exchange transactions maturing that morning initially lost 100 percent of the amount involved in the exchange transaction and was treated just like the regular depositors of the bank.[1]

This *clean risk at liquidation* of exchange contracts prevails even when different time zones are not involved. The operations in financial institutions are automated to such an extent that a payment could probably not be stopped on the same business day even if one were to hear at some point in the morning that a partner in an exchange transaction was going bankrupt.

A subgroup within the credit risk is the *sovereign risk*. At any point in time, a given country has the prerogative of closing its foreign exchange window. Particularly in countries whose currencies are very sparsely traded in the market, the central bank can be the only source of foreign exchange. Thus, we can have the situation of a very good credit risk in a company located in a country with a high sovereign risk. For example, one can be fairly certain that the corporation will be able to generate the necessary local currency to repay a loan we have made in foreign currency. However, if the central bank makes it impossible to convert the local currency into foreign exchange, the proceeds from the repayment of the loan will not be available in the desired foreign currency.

The sovereign risk is even more direct when lending to governments themselves. The additional dimension of a possible change in the government or in the policies of the same government can easily invalidate any previous contract and, therefore, any hope of receiving a payment for the loan in hard currency.

---

[1] The eventual loss will usually be less than 100 percent. The amount recovered depends on the settlement of the bankruptcy proceedings.

Liquidity risk

The liquidity type of risk is closely associated with rate risk. Liquidity risks arise because the cash flows in a transaction are not "square." These cash flows are not balanced on purpose because of the expectation of a change in rate (hence the rate risk). However, there is also a risk which arises from the question of ability to obtain the funds when a cash inflow has not been prearranged; this is the liquidity risk.

In the money market, the liquidity risk appears when the funds are placed for a period longer than the source of funds which made the placement possible. Using the same example that we used in the discussion of the rate risk, if we lend funds for six months while borrowing for only one month, a risk exists that at the end of the month when refinancing must be arranged, it will not be found. One example of such a situation is seen if the initial source of funds is a certificate of deposit (CD) with one-month maturity. At the end of the month, the CD is presented for redemption, and funds must be found to pay the initial lender. The usual procedure is to issue another CD. However, in the intervening month the market for CDs may have disappeared because of regulations imposed by the central bank. In an extreme case, a very tight money market may make it impossible to raise funds in the market, regardless of the rate offered; this is liquidity risk. However, this risk usually is more relevant in terms of rate risk. There is always a price at which funds can be raised by creditworthy borrowers! Raising funds under these conditions (rate risk) might prove not to be very profitable, but bankruptcy because of loss of liquidity can usually be avoided. The exception, clearly, is any case in which the entity in question becomes a very poor credit risk and no one is willing to lend funds to it at any rate, nor are there any financial assets to be sold or pledged.

The liquidity risk in the foreign exchange market also arises from uncertainty of the ability to obtain the funds in the currency desired. This problem is much more acute in the foreign exchange market than in the money market. This imbalance between the risks in the two markets arises from two factors: (1) greater inclination on the part of monetary authorities to impose funds availability controls on the foreign exchange market than on the local money market, and (2) the narrowness and shallowness of foreign exchange markets when compared with the money markets for the same currencies. In the example we used in the discussion of rate risk, we described a swap transaction where we bought three-month marks against dollars and sold one-month marks against dollars.[2]

---

[2] See pp. 225–227.

At the end of the first month, in the absence of any further transactions, marks must be purchased in the spot market to fulfill the forward contract entered into one month before. If the Bundesbank (the West German central bank) decides to close its foreign exchange window because of instabilities in the market, we will be at the mercy of sellers of marks in the market. These other sellers are likely to be unable to deal in very large quantities. If the transaction is for a fairly large amount, say DM100 million or more, it may be very hard to complete the desired transaction. If it is completed, it will surely take place at disadvantageous rates (the rate risk). If the transaction is not completed, this may mean almost-certain bankruptcy to some financial institutions.

Evaluation of risks

We have seen that the various types of risk which attend transactions in the money market also affect transactions in the foreign exchange market. However, the degree is not necessarily the same in each market.

To illustrate the measurement of the various types of risk in money market transactions and foreign exchange transactions, we shall make use of the example discussed in Chapter 5 where an interest change was anticipated (pp. 87–92). In this case, the initial market is in equilibrium; interest rate differentials equal the premium/discount in the forward exchange market. However, a change in interest rate differentials is forecast. We have a case of the dollar and the pound sterling, with the initial interest differential being 3 percent in favor of the pound. It is forecast that the interest rate on the pound will decrease by 1 percent in a month, thus reducing the interest differential to 2 percent and changing the discount on the forward pound accordingly.

To take advantage of this information in the money market, we would want to lend, or place, pounds for a longer period at the present high rate and finance the transaction with borrowings of a shorter maturity. When the borrowings mature, we can refinance the transaction by borrowing for five months, now at the lower costs. The market scenario and the cash flow boxes accompanying this transaction are reproduced in Exhibit 11.2. In the example where we lend funds for six months at 13 percent and finance them initially with one-month borrowings, the profit is derived from the lower interest rate, 12 percent, obtained to refinance the loan for five months when the one-month borrowings mature. Dealing with £1 million, we can make a total profit of $10,000 with the interest differential of 1 percent p.a. in our favor for five months.[3]

---

[3] The profit is £15,000 (Box C) less £10,833 (Box B), equal to £4167. The profit of £4167 at $2.40/£ equals $10,000. For a more detailed discussion of this example see pp. 134–141.

The expected interest reduction on the pound translates into a smaller discount on the forward pound. We expect the swap rate of the pound against the dollar (a discount) to decrease. Therefore, we want to purchase the pounds now and sell them after the swap rate has decreased. To take advantage of this information in the exchange market without assuming a net exchange position, we must do it through swap transactions.

In the first swap position, we arrange the sterling purchase for a relatively long maturity. The sterling sale is arranged for a relatively short maturity. We hope that when the maturity of the sell transaction arrives, our forecast has come true, and that we can enter a new swap—purchase spot and sell forward sterling—at a lower swap rate. The market scenario and the cash flow boxes accompanying this transaction are reproduced in Exhibit 11.3. In this example, the initial swap transaction is:

Purchase pounds against dollars for
    six months

Sell pounds against dollars for one
    month

at a swap rate of
$0.0060 per month

At the end of one month, when the one-month contract matures and our forecast for the decline in the interest rate of the pound has proven correct, we enter another swap transaction:

Purchase pounds against dollars spot

Sell pounds against dollars for
    five months

at a swap rate of
US$0.0040 per
month

Again, the profit here originates from the $0.0020 difference in swap rate enjoyed for five months. The equivalent interest rate is 1 percent p.a. The total profit is also $10,000. Let's now analyze the various types of risk in each of these approaches.

Comparative rate risks

The expectation of profit in the above transactions is all predicated on the basis of a change in the pound interest rate. When we used the money market, we were concerned only with the interest rate for the pound. However, when we used the foreign exchange market, we were concerned with changes in interest differentials; therefore, we are susceptible to changes in two different rates, the rate for the pound and the rate for the U.S. dollar. In our example, we change only the interest rate for the

Exhibit 11.2
ACTING ON ANTICIPATED CHANGES IN INTEREST RATES: MONEY MARKET APPROACH

MARKET SCENARIO

Initial Situation:	Money Market (all maturities up to six months)	Foreign Exchange Market
Pound sterling	13%	
		3% discount on pounds
U.S. dollar	10%	

Anticipated Situation in One Month:

Pound sterling	12%	
		implies 2% discount on pounds
U.S. dollar	10%	

CASH FLOWS

Box A

Currency: Pound sterling

Date: January 1

Balance: − 1,000,000 (placement at 13% for six months)
          + 1,000,000 (borrowings at 13% for one month)

Net balance   Ø

Box B

Currency: Pound sterling

Date: February 1

Balance: − 1,010,833 (repayment of one-month borrowings at 13%)
          + 1,000,000 (borrowings at 12% for five months)

Net balance   − 10,833

Box C

Currency: Pound sterling

Date: July 1

Balance: + 1,065,000 (repayment of our placement at 13% on
          January 1)
          − 1,050,000 (repayment of five-month debt at 12%
          initiated on February 1)

Net balance   + 15,000

Exhibit 11.3
ACTING ON ANTICIPATED CHANGES IN INTEREST RATES: EXCHANGE MARKET SOLUTION

MARKET SCENARIO

Initial Situation:	Money Market (maturities up to six months)	Foreign Exchange Market
Pounds sterling	13%	Spot rate: $2.40/£ 3% p.a. discount on pounds
U.S. dollars	10%	One-month swap rate: $0.0060/£
Anticipated Situation:		
Pounds sterling	12%	Spot rate: $2.40/£ 2% p.a. discount on pounds
U.S. dollars	10%	One-month swap rate: $0.0040/£

CASH FLOWS

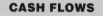

Box A

Currency: Pound sterling
Date: February 1
Balance: − 1,000,000 (initial compensating one-month contract entered on Jan. 1) + 1,000,000 (squaring spot transaction)
Net balance   Ø

Box B

Currency: U.S. dollar
Date: February 1
Balance: + 2,394,000 (initial compensating one-month contract entered on Jan. 1) − 2,400,000 (squaring spot transaction)
Net balance   − 6,000

Box C

Currency: Pound sterling
Date: July 1
Balance: + 1,000,000 (six-month contract entered on Jan. 1) − 1,000,000 (squaring five-month contract entered on Feb. 1)
Net balance   Ø

Box D

Currency: U.S. dollar
Date: July 1
Balance: − 2,364,000 (six-month contract entered on Jan. 1) + 2,380,000 (squaring five-month contract entered on Feb. 1)
Net balance   + 16,000

pound; however, one could have gained the same profit in the foreign exchange market if the U.S. dollar interest rate had increased by 1 percent. In either case, the interest *differential* would have decreased by 1 percent, and the discount for the pound would have decreased by 1 percent also. So, on the one hand, the foreign exchange market makes it possible to realize a profit even if a similar event takes place; on the other hand, now we are forecasting the behavior of two rates in contrast with the single rate involved when we operate in the money market. For example, even if the expected decrease in the interest rate for pounds from 13 to 12 percent takes place, it is possible that the interest rate for dollars will drop from 10 to 8 percent over the same period. Now, the interest differential will be 4 percent, producing a monthly swap rate of $0.0080 per month, a $0.0400 cost to close the five-month gap. This situation will cause a loss although the rate forecast for a drop in the pound interest rate was correct.

Comparative liquidity risks

In the money market, at the end of one month, we are forced to roll over our borrowings, i.e., to approach a lender. In the foreign exchange market, at the end of the first month, we have only to go to the spot market. There is almost always somebody willing to sell the desired currency although we may not like the rate, but that is a different type of risk. In addition, there is a cosmetic problem. When we use the money market, borrowings appear in the balance sheet. This may upset some of the multiple ratios which a financial institution must maintain to keep within the government regulations. Forward exchange transactions are, in a way, off the balance sheet.

Thus, it appears that, from the point of view of the liquidity risk, there is a slight advantage in using the foreign exchange market instead of the money market, particularly if one is anticipating not being such a good credit risk when the borrowings have to be rolled over!

Comparative credit risks

The credit risk depends entirely on the nature and abilities of the party with whom we are contracting to fulfill its part of the transaction. If the other party turns out to be a bad credit risk and one is using the money market route, one stands to lose 100 percent of the funds lent to that party. If one is using the forward exchange market, the 100 percent loss can occur only if the timing permits the other party to go bankrupt after we have completed our part of the transaction by transferring the necessary funds. In other words, using the money market approach produces a 100 percent credit risk for the entire life of the transaction. The exchange approach produces some risk for the life of the transaction. The exact amount of that risk is the difference between the rate in the forward contract which is not completed and the rate which we can obtain in the spot market. This so-called 10 percent risk prevails except on the delivery date itself when the clean risk of liquidation exposes the entire amount.

The following table gives an overview on a risk-by-risk basis. A positive sign indicates the approach that is preferable to take advantage of an expected change in an interest rate for a currency.

	Money market approach	*Exchange approach*
Credit risk	−	+
Rate risk	+	−
Liquidity risk	−	+

If we are dealing with first-rate institutions and are part of that select group ourselves, the liquidity and credit risks play a minor role as compared with the rate risk where anticipated profits may evaporate or even become losses because of a faulty forecast. Once we start dealing with anyone other than the very best names in the world, however, the credit risk becomes more important. Furthermore, if we are not among the most prestigious institutions, we have to be much more concerned with our liquidity risk.

CHAPTER 12
Control of money market and foreign exchange operations

We have described the risks in foreign exchange and money market operations and identified them as rate risk, credit risk, and liquidity risk. In this chapter we shall discuss ways of controlling these three risks as they apply to operations in the foreign exchange and the money markets. To facilitate presentation, we shall consider these risks in a different order from the one used in the last chapter.

Credit risk

In order to control credit risk, lines of credit must be established for each party with whom we deal. These lines should specify separate credit lines for exchange transactions and money market transactions. If several operators have authority to extend credit to a single party, as international banks operating in the international money market can do, it may be useful to establish at headquarters one global line for exchange transactions and one line for money market placements. The individual operators should then receive allocations from this total line.

Credit risk in the foreign exchange market

Credit risk in foreign exchange operations is either a so-called 10 percent or a 100 percent risk, depending on whether the other party to the contract defaults *before* or *at* the maturity date. Thus, any operator in the foreign exchange market should have both a limit on the aggregate amount of exchange contracts outstanding with a particular party to cover the so-called 10 percent risk and a sublimit on transactions maturing on any one day to cover the 100 percent clean risk at liquidation of the contract.

A bank might be willing to have a total of US$10 million outstanding in exchange contracts with a given customer and to bear the 10 percent risk on this total. However, the line might specifically stipulate that no more than US$2 million may mature on a single day. This means that the bank can have US$2 million worth of contracts maturing on every day of a week Monday through Friday. This would make an aggregate of US$10 million, and the total maturity per day would not exceed $2 million. A maximum loss in this situation would, in theory, be as follows: The customer defaults on Monday, and the bank suffers a 100 percent loss on the $2 million maturing on that day (assuming the bank has already paid for its part of the contract). Losses on the Tuesday through Friday maturities of the remaining $8 million would be limited to the extent to which the exchange rate has deteriorated since the time the original forward contract was made. If we assume that this deterioration usually does not exceed 10 percent, the loss would be $.8 million. The total loss on the entire US$10 million outstanding at the beginning of the week would be $2.8 million. The actual foreign exchange line could be worded: "US$10 million or equivalent, for aggregate exchange transactions outstanding with a sublimit of US$2 million, or equivalent, for transactions maturing on any one day." Of course, by defining the sublimit so that it controls contracts maturing on any one day, it is assumed that the bank has a system for assuring itself at the end of each day that "good" counterpart funds have been received in its depository. If it does not have such a system, or if liquidation is not made by direct credit to its account (e.g., if the bank receives payment by means of a check which has to be cleared to make sure the funds are good), the sublimit will have to be redefined so that it reflects the exposure more precisely.

The international trade practices of many businesses make it necessary for them to buy and sell certain currencies in order to settle their accounts in various countries. In these cases it is wise for a bank to have specific knowledge as to which currencies its customers must buy and sell as a result of their normal business. Then, the exchange lines can be more specific and may possibly be limited to transactions in these specific currencies. These sublimits will alert the bank whenever a customer decides to deal in currencies which are not related to that customer's usual commercial business transactions. The bank may very well honor the request, but it may be useful to note that such transactions are out of the ordinary for the customer.

Credit risk in the money market

The credit risk in money market operations is controlled simply by establishing lines for placements with banks or other business institutions. This can be done in the same way that credit lines are established for commercial loans. The wording of these lines is important. Supplementary clauses may be added to the statement of the total size of the line. For example, a line might read: "US$10 million, or equivalent, for money market placements up to six months, with a sublimit of US$5 million, or equivalent, for money market placements up to twelve months."

Sovereign risk

A bank extending credit in foreign countries must develop a system to measure the total amount of funds exposed to sovereign risk on a country-by-country basis. One way of doing this is, first, to establish a maximum amount of credit exposure allowed for each country. If there are several independent operators with authority to extend credit to businesses within a country or to the country itself, it may be practical to ask them to report transactions to a suitable central point at the end of each business day. This procedure can be continued until total outstanding credits for a given country are approaching, for example, 80 percent of the limit. At that time, all operators should be advised that they must obtain approval for additional transactions prior to extending credit to that particular country. This system permits instant decision making by all operators until the 80 percent limit is reached. After 80 percent of the credit line has been extended, the operators must use caution, and the bank is guaranteed that the credit limit will not be exceeded.

Rate risk

Rate risk in foreign exchange transactions

The first risk to be controlled is the size of the *net exchange position*. Changes in the spot rate and in forward outright rates may have a direct impact on the value of a net exchange position. A limit must be established for net overnight exchange positions in each currency, including the local currency of the home country. The reason for the overnight limit is that political and economic events occurring outside that particular country's business hours may have an important effect on exchange rates. The trader, not working at night, cannot react immediately to these changes and is, therefore, particularly vulnerable. During the day, traders should also be limited in their net positions, but they may be permitted larger positions than overnight. This larger limit is necessary to enable the traders to respond to the foreign exchange needs of their customers. The *daylight limit* is usually a multiple of the overnight limit.

Depending on the type of currency, the net overnight and daylight limits may be split, with different limits imposed depending on whether the position is a net overbought or a net oversold one in that specific currency. These distinctions may be particularly advisable if a currency is a strong candidate for devaluation, in which case the net overbought position limit would be smaller than the net oversold position limit. In case of an upvaluation-prone currency, the relationship of the limits would be reversed.

In addition to the limits just mentioned, some banks establish a so-called override limit. This is a limit for aggregate net positions in all currencies traded. For example, a trader may have a limit of US$1 million equivalent for each of ten different currencies with an override limit of $6 million for the aggregate of all positions. Without the override limit, the trader could have an aggregate net position of $10 million, which would be the case if the full $1 million limit in each of the ten currencies were to be used. The override limit prevents the trader from reaching the net position limit in all ten currencies and restricts that individual's aggregate net position to US$6 million. It is very important to impose a net position limit on the local currency and to include it within the override limit. Otherwise, traders can either buy or sell their maximum limit for all other currencies against local currency. This would, of course, create a very large net overbought or net oversold exchange position in local currency which, like any other currency, may be subject to devaluations or upvaluations.

Rate risk in money market operations

This risk can best be controlled through limits on cumulative cash flows. We shall discuss these limits in connection with our description of the liquidity report.

Liquidity risk

A very large net exchange position in spot may represent a liquidity risk if the currencies involved are not very marketable. This is particularly true in a floating rate environment, when central banks cannot be expected to buy or sell foreign currencies at a fixed rate. This risk is controlled and limited through the net overnight position limit described earlier. Swap positions, i.e., overbought positions for one maturity and offsetting oversold positions for other maturities in the same currencies, also present a liquidity risk. This risk, as well as the more obvious liquidity risk resulting from money market operations (from lending long and borrowing short), can be controlled through limits on maximum cumulative cash flows and should be reflected in the liquidity report.

The simplified liquidity report shown in the exhibits consists of four blocks. In each block the columns represent different currencies; the rows indicate different maturity brackets. (See Exhibit 12.1.) Block 1 shows maturing net assets and liabilities, currency by currency, on a noncumulative basis for each maturity. Block 2 shows the same type of information for net cash flows resulting from maturing forward exchange contracts. Block 3 is a consolidation of Blocks 1 and 2. It adds the cell in (Block 1) for a given currency and maturity for the net cash flow resulting from net assets and liabilities to the corresponding cell (in Block 2) for forward exchange contracts. Block 4 is the same as Block 3, but on a cumulative basis.

To illustrate how the form works, we will show how the cash flow gaps discussed in a previous case would be reflected in the liquidity report. We choose the case where the funds manager wishes to take advantage of an anticipated decline in the pound interest rate. (See Chapter 5, pp. 87–92, and Chapter 11, pp. 232–237.)

Let's begin with the money market approach. We place six-month pounds and borrow one-month pounds. (See Exhibit 12.2.) The net cash flow in Block 1 of these two money market transactions is an outflow of pounds after one month (repayment of the one-month borrowing) and an inflow of pounds after six months. There is no dollar cash flow in Block 1, and there are no cash flows in pounds or dollars in Block 2. Therefore, Block 3 shows the same cash flows as Block 1 since there was no cash flow in Block 2. Block 4 differs from Block 3 because it is cumulative. It clearly indicates that there is a negative cash flow for pounds for five months. However, the net cumulative cash flow for six months is zero (blank), because at that time our placement matures; that is, we get our money back, and there is no more negative cash flow.

Now let's depict the foreign exchange approach on the liquidity report. Exhibit 12.3 reflects in Block 2 the sale of one-month pounds against dollars (outflow of pounds, inflow of dollars) and the purchase of six-

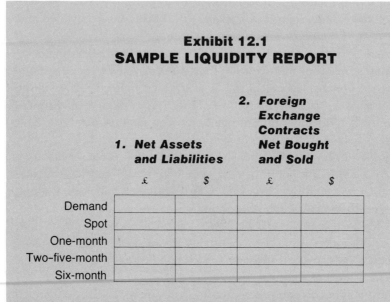

Exhibit 12.1
SAMPLE LIQUIDITY REPORT

	1. Net Assets and Liabilities		2. Foreign Exchange Contracts Net Bought and Sold	
	£	$	£	$
Demand				
Spot				
One-month				
Two–five-month				
Six-month				

	3. Consolidation		4. Cumulative		Total
	£	$	£	$	
Demand					
Spot					
One-month					
Two–five-month					
Six-month					

Exhibit 12.2
LIQUIDITY REPORT: MONEY MARKET CASH FLOW GAP

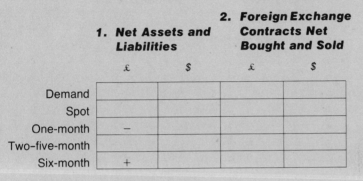

PLACE SIX-MO. £ BORROW ONE-MO. £

	1. Net Assets and Liabilities		2. Foreign Exchange Contracts Net Bought and Sold	
	£	$	£	$
Demand				
Spot				
One-month	−			
Two–five-month				
Six-month	+			

PLACE SIX-MO. £ BORROW ONE-MO. £

	3. Consolidation		4. Cumulative		
	£	$	£	$	Total
Demand					
Spot					
One-month	−		−		
Two–five-month			−		
Six-month	+				

Exhibit 12.3
LIQUIDITY REPORT: FOREIGN EXCHANGE CASH FLOW GAP

SELL ONE-MO. £/$ BUY SIX-MO. £/$

	1. Net Assets and Liabilities		**2. Foreign Exchange Contracts Net Bought and Sold**	
	£	$	£	$
Demand				
Spot				
One-month			−	+
Two–five-month				
Six-month			+	−

SELL ONE-MO. £/$ BUY SIX-MO. £/$

	3. Consolidation		**4. Cumulative**		
	£	$	£	$	Total
Demand					
Spot					
One-month	−	+	−	+	
Two–five-month			−	+	
Six-month	+	−			

month pounds against dollars (inflow of pounds, outflow of dollars). Block 3 is a repetition of Block 2 because there was no activity in Block 1. Block 4 shows the activity in Block 3 on a cumulative basis. It is very obvious that there is a negative cash flow for five months in pounds and a positive cash flow for five months in dollars. In month 6, the cumulative outflows equal inflows in each currency.

We know from descriptions in previous chapters that gaps, i.e., mismatched maturities for cash flows, can be established through exchange contracts and through money market transactions. Regardless of whether the exchange approach or the money market approach is used, this example shows that the impact on cash flows is the same. Thus, management can establish limits on maximum cumulative positive or negative cash flows for each currency traded, and it can check the figures for each currency in Block 4 against the established limits.

The liquidity report can be used to limit liquidity and rate risks at the same time. All positive cumulative cash flows represent a rate risk, and all negative cumulative cash flows represent a rate risk and a liquidity risk; i.e., funding is necessary.

On the extreme right side of Block 4, a column called "Total" is added. In this column, the report should show the net positive or negative cumulative cash flow of all currencies combined for the particular maturity bracket in that row. This is a true measure of liquidity because it will show the cumulative money market gaps regardless of the currency. Gaps resulting from exchange transactions will always be netted out because, as the word "exchange" suggests, on each occasion that there is a purchase of a currency, there is also a sale of another currency. Each maturing exchange contract creates two cash flows: a positive cash flow in the currency purchased and a negative cash flow in the currency sold. For "total" liquidity purposes the two flows are offsetting.

There are two major items which require special attention regarding their appearance on the liquidity report. The first is demand deposits. Any bank has substantial demand deposits which, theoretically, can be withdrawn on any day, but, as a practical matter, they are probably the most stable deposits in the bank. If all these demand deposits are shown in the demand column of the liquidity report, the entries will indicate a very large negative cumulative cash flow. This problem must be approached with common sense, and one solution is to classify demand deposits bearing interest at a rate close to the interbank money market in the demand column. Non-interest-bearing demand deposits, or those bearing interest at rates substantially below the interbank money market level, should be placed in the three- or six-month column.[1]

The second type of special item is the revolving Euro-term loan as described in Chapter 2. In order to measure their rate risk, such loans should be recorded in the liquidity report by rollover date, that is, the date on which the negotiated interest rate ceases to be in effect, and a new interest rate based on the then-prevailing interbank offered rate is set. We recommend that system because, from the viewpoint of a rate risk, the taking of a deposit matching the interest period chosen by the borrower is the most conservative form of borrowing or funding. However, for the measurement of liquidity, we should use the expiration date of the entire loan commitment, which is usually several years in the future. Banks with a heavy volume of revolving term loans should have two liquidity reports: one with revolving term loans recorded by interest periods (rate risk oriented) and one with revolving term loans recorded by ultimate expiration date (liquidity risk oriented).

If one bank or company has several independent operators in the international money markets and exchange markets, the enterprise will find it worthwhile to consolidate periodically their individual liquidity reports and to create a master report which will show the overall positive and negative cumulative cash flows for each currency. It is conceivable that each operator may have taken a position within the specified cumulative cash flow limits, but that the aggregate of all the operators' positions may seem excessive to senior management. In this case, orderly reductions of the respective positions may be initiated.

We have shown in the previous paragraph the value of the liquidity report to limit cumulative positive or negative cash flows and to control different operators in their adherence to established limits. There is an additional advantage associated with this report. In many cases, the liquidity report will reflect fundamental funding techniques of a specific country. This information can be useful to review personnel in the headquarters of international banks. We see, in Block 1 of Exhibit 12.4, a positive cash flow in one- to three-month local currency (DM). This is not surprising because a German branch naturally makes loans in German marks which it expects to collect a few months later; the collections create the positive cash flow in the DM column. We also see negative cash flows

---

[1] The charts for the liquidity report presented in the exhibits in this chapter have been simplified. The maturity brackets can be broken down into many more rows such as daily for the first week, weekly for the rest of the first month, and monthly for the rest of the year.

Exhibit 12.4
LIQUIDITY REPORT FOR A GERMAN BRANCH OF A BANK

FUNDING MARK LOANS WITH DOLLAR DEPOSITS

	1. Net Assets and Liabilities		2. Foreign Exchange Contracts Net Bought and Sold	
	DM	$	DM	$
Demand	(20)	(10)		
Spot			(15)	14
One-month	40	(37)	(38)	39
Two-month	50	(46)	(49)	47
Three-month	60	(63)	(61)	62

	3. Consolidation		4. Cumulative	
	DM	$	DM	$
Demand	(20)	(10)	(20)	(10)
Spot	(15)	14	(35)	4
One-month	2	2	(33)	6
Two-month	1	1	(32)	7
Three-month	(1)	(1)	(33)	6

for U.S. dollars in Block 1. They can only be the result of dollar deposits received which must be repaid over the next few months, thus creating the negative cash flows in the US$ column. At this point, the examiner of the liquidity report may be concerned because the German branch is apparently lending marks and borrowing dollars, which would make it necessary to maintain a very sizable net overbought position in marks against dollars. However, as we study Block 2, we recognize an outflow of marks in the one- to three-month area and an approximately corresponding inflow of dollars. These cash flows are the result of forward exchange transactions. Now the whole report begins to make sense. The branch made loans in marks, borrowed dollars, converted these dollars into marks in the spot exchange market, and covered in the forward exchange market, i.e., sold forward marks and purchased forward dollars. This means that the branch has no net exchange position and a cumulative cash flow position which results, by and large, from demand deposits. The cash flows from assets and liabilities and exchange purchases and sales are almost balanced. The explanation for this funding approach must be that the branch finds it cheaper to borrow dollars and swap them into marks than simply to borrow marks. (See Chapter 7, pp. 151–153.)

Miscellaneous controls

Aggregate limit

We have described tools to limit and control the credit, rate, and liquidity risks. The aggregate limit proposed here does not control any particular risk which would not be controlled already by one of the above-mentioned limits. The aggregate limit is a limit for total unliquidated exchange contracts outstanding with all other banks, corporations, and individuals. It is strictly a volume indicator and functions as a red flag whenever there is an increase in unliquidated exchange contracts. For example, if the aggregate contracts outstanding increase without a corresponding increase in earnings and without any other good explanation, and if this increase in volume is accompanied by a general increase in operating costs such as telephone and telex expenses, a careful examination of the entire operation seems advisable.

On the other hand, there may be a good reason for changes in outstanding balances and, therefore, in limits. For example, the volume of unliquidated exchange contracts rose substantially when floating rates became a reality after August 1971. Importers and exporters who had previously handled their exchange needs on a spot basis whenever they needed a certain currency then began to protect their interests through forward purchases and sales. A spot contract is settled within a few business days, but a forward contract, by definition, is not settled until several months in the future. Therefore, the aggregate limit for unliquidated exchange contracts had to be substantially increased, and there was a very good reason to do so.

Confirmations

Whenever wholesale exchange and money market transactions are closed, a confirmation is sent to the other party to the contract. If the other party is a bank, there will usually be an incoming confirmation from that bank which can be compared with a copy of the outgoing confirmation. If such an incoming confirmation is not expected, or if transactions are carried out with commercial customers and individuals, it is wise to send out a confirmation in duplicate and request a return copy signed by the other party. The importance of this process cannot be emphasized enough. Operating errors of any kind can usually be detected in the period between the day the contract is closed and the settlement date. These details include the name of the other party, the rate, the amount placed/borrowed or purchased/sold, the currencies involved, the value date of the transaction, and the account and/or banks where amounts should be received or paid.

In the hectic atmosphere of a trading room, it is inevitable that some of these details will, on occasion, be recorded improperly. The confirmation slip makes it possible to identify these errors and to avoid substantial costs and penalties.

Protection against fraud

Generally, foreign exchange and money market operations are no exception to the rule that if enough smart people gang up against an institution, no rule or control will totally protect it against such an assault. However, there are a few guidelines which provide reasonable protection and make life at least more difficult for the fraudulent operator. The incoming confirmations of exchange and money market contracts play a key role in this context. All business partners should be advised that these confirmations must be sent to the attention of an auditing (or some other) department which is completely unconnected to the trading room. The incoming information should be compared in detail with the outgoing confirmation, and any discrepancies should be carefully appraised. If the discrepancy is significant, it should be investigated independently. If the discrepancy is small, a copy of the confirmation may be given to the trader for clarification with the counterparty, since the trader will probably have daily contact with the other party anyhow. In any event, it is important for the audit department to follow up on all these discrepancies and to ensure that new confirmations are obtained for any agreed changes in terms.

The importance of this procedure is that it makes it impossible for a trader to enter into a contract, mail out the original of a confirmation, and then destroy all copies. This technique would enable a trader to build up positions without the knowledge of the bank's management. If the incoming confirmation is directed to the trader, it could be destroyed as well, and nobody would ever know about the position. The trader, when selling this position, will make up a ticket for the originally destroyed contract and pass it on together with the sales contract so that the position is square again. Receipt of the incoming confirmation by an independent audit department will immediately uncover this kind of activity.

An additional protection is the use of serially numbered manifold forms for confirmations. There should be exact accounting and comprehensive explanation for any forms not used.

Another form of fraud is to deal at off-market rates with cooperating parties who are willing to share the resulting profits or provide other forms of kickbacks. To protect against this, a daily rate sheet should be maintained where, on an hour-by-hour basis, the exchange rates, interest rates, and key forward rates (one, three, and six months) are recorded. In a jumpy market, these entries should be made whenever there is a significant change in rates. In addition, the handwritten contract should be time-stamped by the trader immediately after preparing the ticket and before passing it on for entry in the position book. This procedure permits retroactive comparison between the market rates recorded on the rate sheet and the rates at which business was closed on an almost minute-by-minute basis.

This system not only protects against deliberate transactions at off-market rates, but it is also useful in solving rate discrepancies in transactions with other banks and customers. For example, the rate for pounds against dollars moves during a given day between $2.3800/£ and $2.4000/£; a customer buys pounds at $2.3950/£. The customer may think that the pounds are being bought at $2.3850/£ instead of $2.3950/

£. The rate sheet described earlier will be helpful in clarifying the discrepancy to the satisfaction of both parties involved.

We have only touched upon some of the necessary controls. It cannot be stressed enough that a sound operational backup department and an effective control system are essential for any institution which is actively engaged in operations in the foreign exchange and money markets.

Bibliography

The following publications (most of them produced by governmental or international agencies) are sources for the economic, financial, and trade data necessary to make decisions relating to the foreign exchange and money markets. This list is divided into two parts. The first part gives sources of information for a variety of areas; the second part gives sources for particular countries. In addition, most major international banks regularly publish newsletters and other periodicals which contain useful information.

A. General

Bank for International Settlements, *Annual Report*. Basel.

Commission of the European Communities, *Economic Situation in the Community*. Brussels (quarterly).

The Economist. London (weekly).

Economist Intelligence Unit, *European Trends*. London (quarterly).

————, *Quarterly Economic Review:* (selected countries). London.

The Financial Times. London (daily).

International Monetary Fund, *Balance of Payments Yearbook*. Washington (annual with monthly updates).

————, *International Financial Statistics*. Washington (monthly).

Organization for Economic Cooperation and Development, *Main Economic Indicators*. Paris (monthly with quarterly and irregular supplements).

————, *OECD Economic Outlook*. Paris (semiannual).

————, *OECD Economic Survey:* (selected countries). Paris (annual).

————, *OECD Financial Statistics*. Paris (semiannual with bimonthly supplements).

Statistical Office of the European Community, *Basic Statistics of the Community*. Brussels (annual).

————, *General Statistics*. Luxemburg (monthly).

United Nations, *Monthly Bulletin of Statistics*. New York.

————, *Statistical Yearbook*. New York.

B. Specific countries

Austria

Austrian Economy in Figures. Vienna: Creditanstalt-Bankverein (annual).

Austria's Monetary Situation. Vienna: Oesterreichische Nationalbank (monthly).

Der Oesterreichische Betriebswirt. Vienna: Hochschule fur Welthandel (quarterly).

Oesterreichische Nationalbank, *Bericht Uber das Geschaftsjahr mit Rechnungsabschluss*. Vienna (monthly).

Oesterreichisches Bank-Archiv. Vienna: Oesterreichische Bankwissenschaftliche Gesellschaft (monthly).

Statistiches Zentralamt, *Statistisches Handbuch fur die Republik Oesterreich*. Vienna (annual).

Belgium

Banque Nationale de Belgique, *Bulletin*. Brussels (monthly).

————, *Rapports*. Brussels (annual).

Institut National de Statistique, *Annuaire Statistique de la Belgique*. Brussels (monthly).

Canada

Canada: The Annual Handbook of Present Conditions and Recent Progress. Ottawa: Statistics Canada.

Canada Year Book. Ottawa: Statistics Canada (annual).

Canadian Statistical Review. Ottawa: Statistics Canada (monthly).

Economic Council of Canada, *Review*. Ottawa (annual).

System of National Accounts: Aggregate Productivity Measures. Ottawa: Statistics Canada (annual).

System of National Accounts: The Canadian Balance of International Payments. Ottawa: Statistics Canada (annual).

France

Banque. Paris (monthly).

Banque de France, *Bulletin Trimestriel*. Paris (quarterly).

Banque Nationale de Paris, *Revue Economique*. Paris (quarterly).

Institut National de la Statistique et des Etudes Economiques, *Annuaire Statistique de la France*. Paris (annual).

_____, *Bulletin Mensuel de Statistique*. Paris (monthly).

Italy

Banca d'Italia, *Bolletino*. Rome (bimonthly).

Instituto Centrale de Statistica, *Annuario Statistico Italiano*. Rome (annual).

Japan

Bank of Japan, *Economic Statistics Annual*. Tokyo.

_____, *Economic Statistics Monthly*. Tokyo.

_____, *Monthly Economic Review*. Tokyo

Ministry of Finance, *Monthly Finance Review*. Tokyo.

Netherlands

Centraal Bureau voor de Statistiek, *Statistical Yearbook of the Netherlands*. The Hague (annual).

Nederlandsche Bank, *Report Presented to the Annual Meeting of Stockholders*. The Hague.

Switzerland

Schweizerische Nationalbank. *Rapport*. Berne (annual).

Schweizerische Nationalbank, Statistisches Bureau, *Monatsbericht*. Zurich (monthly).

United Kingdom

Bank of England, *Quarterly Bulletin*. London.

_____, *Report*. London (annual).

Great Britain Central Statistical Office, *Economic Trends*. London (monthly).

_____, *Financial Statistics*. London (monthly).

Overseas Trade Statistics of the United Kingdom. London: Her Majesty's Stationery Office (monthly).

United States

Department of Commerce, *Survey of Current Business*. Washington (monthly).

Department of the Treasury, *Treasury Bulletin*. Washington (monthly).

Federal Reserve System, Board of Governors, *Federal Reserve Bulletin*. Washington (monthly).

————, *Selected Interest and Exchange Rates*. Washington (weekly).

West Germany

Deutsche Bundesbank, *Monatsbericht, Statistische Beiheft*. Frankfurt (monthly).

————, *Monthly Report*. Frankfurt.

————, *Report*. Frankfurt (annual).

Glossary

Aggregate limit The total volume of all unliquidated contracts allowed to be outstanding at any one time. This limit is only a total volume indicator and is not affected by the characteristics of the particular parties involved in a contract. See "Miscellaneous Limits," p. 252.

Appreciation A gradual increase in the value of a currency, usually occurring over several days or weeks as the result of market forces of supply and demand in a system of *floating exchange rates*. By contrast, an *upvaluation* is an official government act which produces a substantial increase in an exchange rate, usually overnight.

Arbitrage The process of taking advantage of the existence of different prices for the same product (or its substitute) at the same time but in different markets. The different markets can be different geographic locations for the same financial asset or different financial assets in one or more geographic locations. Arbitrage between different locations can involve two or more currencies and occurs, for example, when the price for Swiss francs against U.S. dollars in Zurich is higher than the price for Swiss francs against U.S. dollars in New York. In this case profits can be obtained by purchasing Swiss francs against U.S. dollars in New York and, at the same time, selling Swiss francs against U.S. dollars in Zurich. More than two currencies could be involved if the price for Swiss francs in Amsterdam expressed in guilders were higher than the price for Swiss francs in New York expressed in U.S. dollars. Profits in this case could be derived from purchasing Swiss francs against U.S. dollars in New York and, simultaneously, selling Swiss francs against guilders in Amsterdam. Since, at this point, there is a net *long* position in guilders and a net *short* position in dollars, an additional transaction is necessary: Guilders must be sold against U.S. dollars to eliminate any risk. For an example of arbitrage between different financial assets, see *Covered interest arbitrage*.

Asian currency unit A trading department of a bank in Singapore which has received a license from the monetary authority in Singapore to deal in *external currencies*. Although the unit is called Asian Currency, it trades in all external currencies, not just Asian ones.

Asian dollar See *External dollar*.

Asian dollar market See *External dollar market*.

Ask rate See *Offer rate*.

Balance of payments A financial statement prepared for a given country summarizing the flows of goods, services, and funds between the residents of this country and the residents of the rest of the world during a certain period of time. The balance of payments is prepared using the concept of double-entry bookkeeping where the total of debits equals the total of credits (total sources of funds equal total uses of funds).

Balance of trade   The net of imports and exports of goods and services reported in the *balance of payments*.

Balloon payment   The simultaneous return of the principal and interest on a loan at the end of the loan period.

Bankers' acceptance   A *money market instrument* providing relatively low interest rate credit to the borrower and a marketable security to the bank. Bankers' acceptances are created as follows: First, a bank's customer draws a bill or draft on the bank. Second, the bank "accepts" the bill. By this acceptance, the bank promises to pay the face value of the bill to its holders. The resulting instrument is a two-name paper (the customer's and the bank's are on it); thus, it is highly marketable. The bank charges an "acceptance fee" for accepting the draft; so, the cost of a banker's acceptance to the customer is the going *discount rate* for bankers' acceptances in the market plus the fee charged by the bank. The discount rate for bankers' acceptances is approximately the same as the rate for *commercial paper* and *certificates of deposit*.

Basic balance   The net of the following accounts in the *balance of payments*: exports and imports of goods and services, *unilateral transfers*, and long-term capital flows.

Bid rate   The price at which the quoting party is prepared to purchase a currency or accept a deposit. If the bid rate is accepted by the party to whom it was quoted, then that party will sell currency or place/lend money at that price. The opposite transaction takes place at the *offer rate*. See p. 63.

Bilateral exchange contract   An exchange contract for a local currency against a foreign currency. See also *Multilateral exchange contract*.

Bond   A security which shows the liability of the issuing party. It is usually a negotiable instrument with a fixed *interest rate* and a fixed maturity date which is longer than a year.

Break a deposit/loan   The advancement of the maturity date of a deposit or a loan upon the request of a customer. In the case of a deposit, the maturity acceleration means that the customer would like his money back prior to the originally negotiated maturity date. In the case of a loan, the customer would like to repay the loan prior to the originally negotiated maturity date. Banks will usually charge a penalty for breaking a deposit or a loan, especially if interest rates have moved up (in the case of a deposit) or down (in the case of a loan).

Break-even exchange rate   The particular spot *exchange rate* which must prevail at the maturity of a deposit or debt in a foreign currency (which has not been *covered* in the *forward market*) so that there will be no advantage to any party from *interest rate differentials*. For example, if the Swiss franc interest rate is 5 percent, and the pound interest rate is 12 percent, it may be desirable for the holder of Swiss francs to convert the Swiss francs into pounds and invest them at 12 percent. If this is done without a forward *cover*, an interest gain of 7 percent will be derived. Then, the investor can afford an exchange loss of up to 7 percent which might result from a *depreciation* of the *exchange rate* of the pound against the Swiss franc. Thus, the break-even exchange rate for this transaction would be that spot rate which is 7 percent p.a. below the exchange rate at which the original conversion from Swiss francs to pounds took place.

Bretton Woods conference A meeting of representatives of non-Communist countries in Bretton Woods, New Hampshire, in 1944. The participants agreed on the characteristics of the international monetary system which prevailed through 1971. This system was called the "Bretton Woods System" and was a *fixed exchange rate system.*

Broker An individual who introduces the two parties in a transaction to each other. The parties could be a buyer and a seller of foreign currencies or a borrower and a lender of a given currency. The broker charges a fee for this service. Brokers never take a position for themselves; they only arrange for transactions among other parties. In dealing with brokers, financial institutions should insist that the broker disclose the name of the other party to the transaction immediately after the deal is closed. This procedure ensures that the broker does not take a position on his own account, even if only for a few minutes.

Brokerage fee The charge made by a *broker* for his service.

Call money Funds placed with a financial institution without a fixed maturity date. The money can be "called" (withdrawn) at any time with a telephone call. There is "same day" call money, which means that the call must be made (usually) before 10 o'clock in the morning. There is also "24-hour," "48-hour," and "7-day" call money, which means that the money must be called 1, 2, or 7 calendar days prior to the actual repayment date. While these are the most common varieties of call money, two parties can obviously agree on different types.

Capital accounts The accounts in the *balance of payments* which measure the changes in liabilities and financial claims of local residents on foreigners and of foreigners on local residents. For example, the purchase of a *bond* issued by a German company by a U.S. resident increases liabilities to foreigners in the German balance of payments. In the U.S. balance of payments, foreign financial assets, or claims on foreigners, have increased.

Cash flow The increases and decreases in an institution's or an individual's balances in a particular currency. See p. 37.

Central bank A bank acting on behalf of a country's government with the right to issue the country's currency and the responsibility to manage the country's money supply, *interest rate* levels, and credit availability. It also manages the level of the country's *foreign exchange reserves* and the external value of its currency.

Certificate of deposit (CD) A placement of funds for a certain period of time with a bank for which the depositor of the funds receives a confirmation which makes the deposit receipt a negotiable instrument. Investment bankers create a secondary market where CDs can be purchased and sold prior to maturity. Investors usually accept a smaller interest rate on CDs than on regular time deposits because the investment is more liquid, that is, the CD can be converted into cash at any time without asking the bank to *break the deposit*. CDs were originally invented in the United States in the early sixties and were used in the domestic U.S. money market. They were later also used for *external dollars* in several financial centers. The technique is so attractive that the instrument has also been introduced into the *domestic money market* of several other countries. See *Near-money*.

Chain A method of calculating *cross rates*. For example, if a trader knows the *exchange rate* for marks against dollars and for French francs against dollars, the chain makes possible a calculation of the *cross rate* for marks against French francs. See p. 72.

Clean risk at liquidation A type of *credit risk* which occurs when exchange contracts mature. There may be a brief interval (usually no more than a few hours) during which one of the parties to the contract has fulfilled its obligations, but the other party has not. During this period, the first party is subject to a 100 percent credit risk, on the chance that, in the interval, the second party may become bankrupt and its assets become frozen before it can fulfill its part of the contract. See p. 230.

Clearinghouse funds U.S. dollar checks deposited with a local or regional clearinghouse. These funds become available on the business day following the one on which they are deposited in the form of *Fed funds*. See p. 198.

Commercial paper A *money market instrument* which shows that there has been a *money market* transaction between two nonfinancial institutions. For example, a petroleum company with excess funds may purchase commercial paper issued by an automobile company which needs funds. In this case, the petroleum company is, in effect, lending funds to the automobile company for the period during which it holds the commercial paper. Only the largest companies have access to the commercial paper market. It is particularly developed in the United States because bank regulations do not allow interest to be earned on bank deposits for periods of less than a month. Consequently, the main activity in the U.S. commercial paper market is for periods between 1 and 29 days. The very largest companies *place* their commercial paper directly with investors. Other companies use the services of a *broker*, who places the commercial paper for a fee. Usually, companies borrowing in the commercial paper market have confirmed back-up lines of credit with commercial banks. These lines can be used for borrowing if money is not available in the commercial paper market.

Compensated value date A day on which both parts of a *foreign exchange* contract are supposed to be consummated. By contrast, a contract with *noncompensated value dates* requires the delivery of one currency on a different day from the delivery of the other. In the latter transaction, the party which receives delivery first can avoid any *clean risk at liquidation* and can possibly obtain further profits from the *float* resulting from receiving and investing one currency a day or more before paying out the other.

Confirmation A record of the terms of a *foreign exchange* or *money market* transaction sent out by each party to the transaction to each other before the actual consummation of the transaction itself. The confirmation contains the exact details of the transaction and thus serves legal, practical, and antifraud purposes. See pp. 253–254.

Correspondent bank A bank located in one geographic area which accepts deposits from a bank in another region and provides services on behalf of this other bank. Internationally, many banks maintain one account with a correspondent bank in each major country so as to be able to make payments in all major currencies. Correspondent banks are usually established on a reciprocal basis, with the two banks maintaining local currency accounts with each other. For example, American Bank "A" maintains a pound account with British Bank "B", and in turn British Bank "B" maintains a U.S. dollar account with American Bank "A". Both banks usually maintain reasonable working balances in their accounts so that "A" can receive and make payments in pounds and "B" can receive and make payments in U.S. dollars.

Country limit An amount of money which a financial institution has established as the maximum it is willing to lend borrowers in a given country regardless of the type of borrower or the currencies involved.

Cover To fix by transactions in the *foreign exchange market* an *exchange rate* on funds which will mature or be required at some future date. For example, if an American company has a deposit of funds in pounds which will mature in three months, it can sell those pounds for U.S. dollars in the *foreign exchange market* for delivery on the date of the maturity of the deposit. By doing so, the company is setting in advance the exchange rate at which it will convert its pound deposit into dollars; it is thus protected against any decline in the value of pounds against dollars during the intervening three months.

Covered interest arbitrage The process of taking advantage of a disparity between the *net accessible interest differential* between two currencies and the forward exchange *premium* or *discount* on the two currencies against each other. For example, if the interest rate for pounds is 10 percent and 7 percent for dollars, while the *swap rate* between them equals 3.5 percent, it is possible to borrow pounds at 10 percent, *swap* them through the *forward exchange market* at a discount of 3.5 percent (which provides dollars at 6.5 percent), and invest the dollars at 7 percent, for a profit of 0.5 percent. See pp. 59 and 85.

Crawling peg system An *exchange rate* system in which the exchange rate is adjusted every few weeks, usually to reflect prevailing rates of inflation. In between adjustments, a *fixed exchange rate system* prevails. In Brazil, for example, where a crawling peg system has been in use for some time, the Brazilian cruzeiro *devalues* about ten times a year.

Credit risk In lending operations, the likelihood that a borrower will not be able to repay the principal or pay the interest. In *foreign exchange* operations, the *clean risk at liquidation*. See p. 228.

Cross currency risk The risk associated with maintaining opposite *net exchange positions* in two different currencies as the result of one transaction. For example, if an operator borrows Swiss francs at 5 percent and invests the proceeds in pounds at 12 percent, the cross currency risk is the chance that the pounds will *depreciate* in value against the Swiss francs to such an extent that there will be a loss on the transaction in spite of the favorable *interest rate differential*.

Cross rate An *exchange rate* calculated from two other bilateral exchange rates (two different currencies compared to the same third currency). For example, if we know the exchange rates for both marks and French francs against U.S. dollars, we can compute the exchange rate for marks against French francs. See p. 69.

Current account balance The net of the following accounts in the *balance of payments*: exports and imports in goods and services, and *unilateral transfers*.

Daylight limit The maximum net exchange position which an institution will allow during business hours. See *Overnight limit* and p. 244.

Deflation A price decrease for the same type and amount of goods and services.

Demand deposit Funds in a currently active account (a checking account) which can be withdrawn at any time without notice. Depending on local regulations demand deposits may or may not be interest bearing.

Depreciation A decline in the value of a currency. Depreciation is a gradual decline, usually occurring over several days or weeks on account of market forces of supply or demand. *Devaluation*, by contrast, is an official government act which produces a substantial decline in *exchange rates*, usually overnight.

Devaluation See *Depreciation*.

Direct investment The purchase of enough shares of equity ownership in a company in a foreign country to involve some degree of managerial control.

Dirty float A *floating exchange rate* system in which some government intervention still takes place. A government may announce that it will let its currency *float*, i.e., it will let the currency's value be determined by the forces of supply and demand in the market. However, the government may secretly allow its *central bank* to intervene in the exchange market to avoid too much *appreciation* of the currency (hurts exports) or too much *depreciation* (increases *inflation*). This is also called a *managed float*. See *Floating exchange rates*.

Discount (noun) The amount (usually expressed by a *per annum* percentage rate—the *swap rate*) by which the *forward exchange rate* of one currency against another currency is less than the *spot exchange rate* between the two currencies.

Discount (verb)   To subtract from a loan, when it is first made, the amount of interest which will be due when the loan has to be repaid.

Discount rate   The *interest rate* used to *discount* a loan (see preceding definition). The discount rate most commonly discussed is the rate at which a *central bank* is prepared to purchase eligible *money market instruments* or to lend to *commercial banks* against eligible collateral. Through upward and downward adjustments of the official discount rate, and through increases and decreases in the rediscount lines established for commercial banks, a central bank can influence the general level of interest rates and the lending capacity of the banking system.

Domestic money market   The places where a local currency is borrowed and deposited by financial institutions and other major corporations.

Domestic U.S. dollars   The assets and liabilities denominated in U.S. dollars on the books of financial institutions in the United States.

Effective interest rate   The amount of money, expressed as a *per annum* percentage, actually paid on a loan or deposit. The effective interest rate may differ from the *nominal interest rate*, depending on interest payment schedules. For instance, when the interest is deducted from a loan when the loan is first made (see *Discount*), the actual proceeds available to the borrower are less than the nominal loan principal used to calculate the interest payments. The effective interest rate in this case is the interest payments expressed as a percentage of the actual proceeds on a *per annum* basis.

Eligible value date   A normal business day on which a payment to settle a *money market* transaction can be made. An eligible value date for a *foreign exchange* transaction must be a business day in the home countries of *both* of the currencies involved. See p. 41.

Engineered swap transaction   A *spot* transaction and an offsetting *forward* transaction (e.g., sell pounds for dollars spot; buy pounds for dollars forward) in which each of the two transactions is carried out with a different party. See p. 84.

Euro-bond   A *bond* denominated in an *external currency* and traded in an *external market*. See *Bond*.

Euro-currency   See *External currency*.

Eurodollar   See *External dollar*.

Eurodollar market   See *External dollar market*.

Euro-market   See *External market*.

Euro-rate   See *External interest rate*.

European currency band   See *European Monetary Union*.

European Monetary Union   An agreement among some of the countries of the European Common Market and some other European countries to restrict the fluctuations among participating currencies to a given maximum spread. Since March 1973, this maximum has been 2¼ percent. In addition, the participating currencies have been allowed to *float* jointly against the U.S. dollar. The maximum allowable change in the *exchange rate* between two participating currencies, 2¼ percent since March 1973, is usually referred to as the *European Currency Band* or *"the snake"*. See p. 120.

Exchange controls   The regulation of *foreign exchange* transactions by a government/*central bank* to avoid an excessive expansion of the local *money supply* or depletion of the country's *exchange reserves*. Such controls are usually imposed when a country has undesirably large capital inflows or outflows.

Exchange profit work sheet   A record of *foreign exchange* gains and losses. See p. 217.

Exchange rate   The amount of one currency that can be bought by or sold for a certain amount of another currency. See p. 28.

Exchange rate differential   The difference between the two *exchange rates* in a *swap transaction*. See p. 79.

Exchange reserves   The total amount of freely convertible foreign currencies held by a country's *central bank*.

Explicit interest rate   See *Nominal interest rate*.

Exposure   The amount by which inflows in a given currency are less or greater than outflows in that currency. See *Net exchange position*.

External currency   A currency which is an asset or liability in a financial institution outside its home country. For example, pounds on deposit in Paris are external pounds. Such funds are also called *Euro-currencies* or *offshore currencies*. See p. 8.

External dollar   The U.S. dollar assets or liabilities on the books of financial institutions outside the United States. These funds are also called *Eurodollars*, *Asian dollars*, or *offshore dollars* to indicate that they are being held outside of the country. Thus, they are not subject to the same government regulations as *domestic U.S. dollars*. See p. 9.

External dollar market   The places where *external dollars* are traded. Also called *Eurodollar market*, *Asian dollar market*, or *offshore dollar market*.

External interest rate   The *interest rate* applicable to *external currencies*. See p. 23.

External market   Any place where a currency is traded outside of that currency's home country, i.e., a place where *external currencies* are traded. See p. 8.

Fed funds   Money deposited with the U.S. Federal Reserve Bank, the United States' *central bank*. This money is available immediately. Purchases of *U.S. Treasury bills* and other *money market instruments* in the *domestic U.S. dollar money market* can be made only with Fed funds. See p. 198.

Financial center   A city or country where a large number (relative to other places in the world) of financial transactions take place. International financial centers arise in places with little or no governmental regulation constraining the inflow or outflow of foreign currencies and with an adequate amount of political stability.

Fiscal policy   The management of government expenditures and income to accomplish desired economic goals.

Fixed exchange rate system   A system in which the values of various countries' currencies are tied to one major currency (such as the U.S. dollar), gold, or *special drawing rights*. The term should not be taken literally because fluctuations within a range of 1 or 2 percent on either side of the fixed rate are usually permitted in such a system. The *Bretton Woods conference* set up such a system. See *Floating exchange rate system*.

Flat interest rate   A simple percentage interest rate which ignores the element of time. For example, 5 percent flat of $100 is $5. If a flat interest rate is charged over a certain period of time, then it can be converted into a *per annum interest rate*. Thus, 5 percent flat of $100 over three months would equal 20 percent p.a. See p. 20.

Float (noun)   The money available between the actual receipt of funds and the scheduled payment of those funds (usually for only a day or two). During this interval, the beneficiary of the float can deposit the funds in the *money market* and earn interest. Thus, it can be said that a positive float earns money and a negative float costs money.

Float (verb)   To move the value of *exchange rates* up or down according to the forces of supply and demand in the market.

Floating exchange rate system   A system in which the values of various countries' currencies relative to each other are established by the forces of supply and demand in the market without intervention by the governments which are behind the currencies. See *Dirty float*. Frequently, when a currency under a *fixed exchange rate system* is under pressure to *upvalue* or *devalue*, its government will allow it to *float* for a period of time in order to let the market determine the level at which the currency should be fixed again.

Foreign exchange   In any one country, the currencies of all other countries.

Foreign exchange market   The places where one country's currency can be bought with or sold for another country's currency. This market, as well as the *money market*, is not a geographic location, as the term might suggest; instead, the market is the collection of *foreign exchange* and *money market* traders with offices in their respective banks who are connected with each other around the world via telephone and telex.

Forward exchange rate   The price of foreign currencies for delivery (on a *value date*) some time in the future. Normally, transactions which mature within a calendar week are called *spot* transactions. Any transaction with a longer value date is a *forward exchange* transaction. See p. 12.

Gap The period, in *foreign exchange* transactions, between the maturities for purchases and the maturities for sales of each foreign currency (exchange gap). In *money market* transactions, the period between the maturities of placements (loans) and the maturities of borrowings (deposits) of each currency (money market gap). The former occurs when a currency is purchased against one currency and sold against another, each time for different maturities. The money market gap is created by lending a certain amount of a certain currency for a longer or shorter period than the same amount of the same currency is borrowed. See *Swap position* and pp. 87–97.

Hard currency The currency of a country with large *exchange reserves* and a surplus in its *balance of payments*. The *exchange rates* of such a currency would be apt to be stable or possibly candidates for *upvaluation*.

Hedge The elimination of a *net exchange position* through an offsetting exchange transaction. See p. 180 and *Cover*.

Inflation A price increase for the same type and amount of goods and services. If a country consistently has a higher rate of inflation than other countries, its products will become less competitive in the world markets, and the country may have to *devalue* its currency.

Interest period The period for which an *interest rate* is fixed for a *revolving term loan*. See p. 26.

Interest rate The amount (generally expressed as a *per annum* percentage) of money charged for allowing another party the use of one's money.

Interest rate differential The difference between the *interest rates* on two different currencies. Also the *swap rate* between two currencies expressed as a *per annum* percentage premium or discount. The formula for calculating it is

$$\frac{\text{Swap rate} \times 100 \times \text{time}}{\text{Spot rate} \times \text{time}}$$

It is essentially the annualized *net accessible interest differential* between the two currencies.

Interest withholding tax The amount of money which, in some countries, must be withheld by the borrower from any interest the borrower pays. This tax is levied, for the most part, on interest paid to foreigners.

International Monetary Fund (IMF) An international organization created under the *Bretton Woods Agreement*. The IMF's resources are composed of money received from member countries. These resources constitute a pool which participant countries can draw upon during short-term *balance of payments* difficulties. During the period of *fixed exchange rates* that prevailed until 1971, the IMF was supposed to be consulted before a country *upvalued* or *devalued* its currency.

Intervention The actions of a *central bank* designed to influence the *foreign exchange* rate of its currency. The bank can use its *exchange reserves* to buy its currency if it is under too much downward pressure, or to sell its currency if it is under too much upward pressure.

Lag To defer payment of a debt. A company with a subsidiary in a *hard currency* country which has capital inflow controls will often encourage the subsidiary to lag its payments in order to take advantage of higher interest rates available in the *domestic money market* (as opposed to the *external markets*) and a possible *upvaluation* of the hard currency. See p. 188.

Lead To prepay a debt. A company with a subsidiary in a *soft currency* country which has capital outflow controls will often encourage the subsidiary to prepay any money due to the home office to avoid the risk of the soft currency's *depreciating* relative to the home currency. See p. 188.

LIBO See *London Interbank offered rate*.

Liquidity The ability to meet financial obligations without delay.

Liquidity report A record of an institution's inflows and outflows of funds in a particular currency, whether the flows are created by *money market* contracts or *foreign exchange* contracts. See p. 245.

Liquidity risk The chance that it may be impossible to meet financial obligations without delay. Even though a corporation may have a sufficient amount of total assets, it will be exposed to liquidity risk whenever there is a difference between the maturities of assets and liabilities, i.e., a *gap* resulting from *foreign exchange* or *money market transactions*. Thus, if a bank *covers* a six-month placement of funds with only a three-month deposit (borrowing), it may be difficult or impossible for the company to *rollover* that deposit for an additional three months if it suffers a deterioration of its credit standing or a tightening of the *money market*. See p. 231.

London Interbank offered rate (LIBO) The *interest rate* at which prime banks offer foreign currency to other prime banks in London. This rate is often used as the basis for pricing *Eurodollar* and other *Euro-currency* loans. The lender and the borrower agree to a mark-up over the *LIBO* rate, and the total of LIBO plus the mark-up makes the *effective interest rate* for the loan. See p. 26.

Long To have greater inflows than outflows of a given currency. In *foreign exchange* operations, long positions arise when the amount purchased of a given currency is greater than the amount sold. In *money market* operations, a long position arises from investing a given currency for a shorter period of time than it is borrowed. See *Short*.

Make a market To deal so frequently and in such volume in a given asset as to make it possible for others to buy or sell that asset at almost any time.

Managed float See *Dirty float*.

Monetary policy The management of several tools at the disposal of a *central bank* in order to achieve desired economic goals. The tools of monetary policy include control of *reserve requirements*, the *discount rate*, and *open market operations*.

Money market The places where funds can be borrowed or deposited.

Money market instruments The negotiable documents which show someone's obligation to pay a certain amount of money on a specific date, usually within a year. The most popular money market instruments are *bankers' acceptances, treasury bills, commercial paper,* and *certificates of deposit.*

Money supply The currency in circulation plus *demand deposits* at *commercial banks.* Broader definitions of money supply also include different types of *time deposits.*

Multilateral exchange contract An exchange contract involving two foreign currencies against each other, e.g., a contract for U.S. dollars against French francs which is made in London or a contract for pounds against marks made in New York. Also called an *arbitrage exchange contract* perhaps because of the need for such a contract whenever *arbitrage* between locations involves more than two currencies. See *Bilateral contract, Chain,* and p. 73.

Near-money (near-cash) Securities which, while not actually currency themselves, are almost as negotiable as currency, e.g., *Treasury bills.*

Negative interest A fee charged by a bank for accepting a deposit from a customer. This can happen when a currency is under pressure to *appreciate.* A *central bank* in this situation can establish capital import controls and limit the amount of deposits which a bank can receive from nonresidents. If market participants want to deposit more money in the country than the central bank will allow, *interest rates* will drop initially to zero, and, if the pressure continues, produce negative interest. Any taxes which a central bank may impose on foreign deposits can also create negative interest.

Net accessible interest differential The difference between the *interest rates* which can actually be obtained on two currencies. This difference is usually the basis of the *swap rate* between the two currencies and, in most cases, is derived from *external interest rates* rather than domestic interest rates. These *external rates,* or *Euro-rates,* are free from *reserve requirements* (which would increase the interest rate) and from *exchange controls* (which would limit access to the money). See p. 60.

Net exchange position An imbalance between all the assets and purchases of a currency, on the one hand, and all the liabilities and sales of that currency, on the other hand. This imbalance is not affected by maturity dates. See p. 226.

Nominal interest rate The *interest rate* stated as a percentage of the face value of a loan. Depending on the frequency of interest collection over the life of the loan, the nominal rate may differ from the *effective interest rate.*

Noncompensated value date See *Compensated value date.*

Offer rate The price at which a quoting party is prepared to sell or lend currency. This is the same price at which the party to whom the rate is quoted will buy or borrow if it desires to do business with the quoting party. The opposite transactions take place at the *bid rate.* See p. 64.

Offshore currency See *External currency.*

Offshore dollar   See *External dollar.*

Offshore dollar market   See *External dollar market.*

Offshore rate   See *External interest rate.*

Official reserves   See *Exchange reserves.*

Open market operation   The actions of a *central bank* in its local *money market* to reduce or increase the *money supply*. For example, the purchase of government *bonds* and *treasury bills* will increase the money supply while the opposite actions will decrease it.

Option exchange contract   A contract for *foreign exchange* without a fixed maturity date. In this type of contract, a period of time is stated during which the person who has the option can choose any day for liquidation and settlement of the contract. The contract must state which party has the option (the buyer or the seller) and is usually employed when the date on which foreign exchange will be needed or will be available for sale is not known precisely. This can happen when the availability of foreign exchange depends on uncertainties regarding the production of goods or the arrival of a ship. These options are different from options in securities trading because option exchange contracts must be carried out by the final date of the contract. A security option need never be exercised.

Outright forward rate   A *forward exchange rate* which is expressed in terms of the actual price of one currency against another, rather than, as is customary, by the *swap rate*. The outright forward rate can be calculated by adding the *swap premium* to the *spot rate* or by subtracting the *swap discount* from the spot rate. See p. 53.

Overall balance   The net of all accounts in the *balance of payments* excluding transactions in *official reserves.*

Overbought   The position of a *foreign exchange* operator who has bought a larger amount of a certain currency than he has sold.

Overnight position   A *foreign exchange* or *money market* position maintained overnight. There is more risk involved in such a position than one maintained during the day because political and economic events may take place at night, when the operator cannot react immediately to them.

Overnight position limit   The maximum *exposure* an institution is willing to maintain in a given currency after business hours. See *Overnight position* and p. 243.

Override limit   The total amount of money (measured in terms of an institution's domestic currency) which the institution is willing to commit to *all foreign exchange net positions*. See p. 244.

Oversold   The position of a *foreign exchange* operator who has sold a larger amount of a certain currency than he has bought.

Per annum (p.a.)   Over the period of a year.

Place   To lend; usually this term refers to one bank lending to another.

Political risk   See *Sovereign risk*.

Portfolio investment   In the *balance of payments,* the acquisition of the bonds which have a maturity of more than a year or the stocks of a foreign business.

Position   A situation created through *foreign exchange* contracts (exchange position) or *money market* contracts (money market position) in which changes in *interest rates* or *exchange rates* could create profits or losses for the operator.

Position book   A detailed, on-going record of an institution's dealings in a particular currency. See p. 212.

Premium   The amount (usually expressed as a *per annum* percentage rate—the *swap rate*) by which the *forward exchange rate* of one currency against another currency is greater than the *spot exchange rate* between the two currencies.

Price quotation system   A method of giving *exchange rates* in which a certain specified amount of a foreign currency (1 or 100, usually) is compared to the proper amount of local currency. See p. 34.

Rate risk   In the *money market,* the chance that *interest rates* may rise when an operator has a negative money market *gap* (a *short* position), or that interest rates may go down when the operator has a positive money market gap (a *long* position). In the exchange market, the chance that the *spot rate* may rise when the operator has a net *oversold* position (a *short* position), or that the spot rate may go down when the operator has a net *overbought* position (a *long* position). See pp. 225–228 and 233–238.

Reciprocal rate   The price of one currency in terms of a second currency, when the price of the second currency is given in terms of the first. See p. 33.

Repurchase agreement   A contract in which the seller of an asset agrees to buy back the asset he sold on a specific date. This technique is frequently used when a bank, for regulatory reasons, cannot accept a deposit from a customer and pay interest on such a deposit. In such a case, the bank can sell a security, a *treasury bill* or a *bond*, for example, to its customer and agree in writing to repurchase this security on the date the customer wants to have his money back.

Reserve requirement   An amount of money (usually a percentage of commercial deposits) which *commercial banks* in most countries are required to keep on deposit with the *central bank*. Originally, these requirements were designed to protect the solvency of banks; today, central banks adjust requirements, for the most part, as a tool to affect the *money supply* and the *liquidity* of the entire banking system, i.e., its ability to make loans.

Revaluation   See *Upvaluation*.

Revolving term loan   A loan commitment from a bank to lend money for a number of years with the *interest rate* undergoing periodic adjustments. The revolving feature refers only to the interest rate and not to the actual availability of the money. See p. 24.

Rollover The extension of a maturing *foreign exchange* contract in the exchange market or of a loan or deposit in the *money market.*

Rollover date The end of an *interest period* in a *revolving term loan*.

Seven-day-notice money See *Call money.*

Short To have greater outflows than inflows of a given currency. In *foreign exchange* operations, short positions arise when the amount of a given currency sold is greater than the amount purchased. In *money market* operations, a short position arises from borrowing a given currency for a shorter period of time than it is invested. See *Long.*

Smithsonian Agreement An agreement reached at the Smithsonian Institution in December 1971 by the major nations of the non-Communist world. This agreement set new parity rates after the general floating period which prevailed between August and December of that year. This attempt to maintain a *fixed exchange rate system* was abandoned in March 1973. See *European Monetary Union*.

"The snake" See *European Monetary Union.*

Soft currency The currency of a country with low *exchange reserves* and a deficit in the *balance of payments*. The *exchange rate* of such a currency would be considered to be a candidate for *devaluation*.

Sovereign risk The risk that the government of a country may interfere with the repayment of a debt. For example, a borrower in a foreign country may be economically sound and capable of repaying the loan in local currency. However, his country's government may not permit him to repay a loan to a foreign bank because of a lack of *foreign exchange* or for political reasons. The bank making the loan in the first place must take this sovereign risk into account and reflect it in the *interest rate*. See p. 230.

Special drawing rights (SDRs) International paper money created and distributed by the *International Monetary Fund* to governments in quantities and at times dictated by special agreements among IMF member countries. The value of SDRs is determined by the weighted value of a "basket" of major currencies.

Spot exchange rate The price of foreign currencies for delivery in two business days. In practice, spot rates also refer to transactions with *value dates* within a week.

Spread The difference between the *bid rate* and the *offer rate* in an *exchange rate* quotation or an interest quotation. This difference is not identical with the profit margin because traders seldom buy and sell at their bid and offer rates at the same time. In another sense (for example, *Eurodollar* loans priced at a *mark-up* over LIBO), spread means a *mark-up* over cost, and in this context the spread *is* identical with the profit margin.

Square exchange position See *Square-off.*

Square-off   To make the inflows of a given currency equal to the outflows of that currency for all maturity dates. This produces a *square exchange position* in that currency.

Swap   The purchase of one currency against another currency for one maturity date and the simultaneous reversal of that exchange contract for a different maturity. Usually, a swap transaction involves a *spot* maturity date against a *forward* maturity date, and its net effect is the same as two *money market* transactions. See p. 83.

Swap position   A situation in which the scheduled inflows of a given currency are equal to the scheduled outflows, but the maturities of those flows are purposely mismatched (for example, the *forward* sale of a million pounds against dollars for six months, and the forward purchase of a million pounds against dollars for only one month). The expectation in a swap position is that the *swap rate* will change, and that the *gap* can be closed at a profit. See p. 87.

Swap rate   The difference between the *spot exchange rate* of a given currency and its *forward exchange rate*. See p. 79.

Swap-swap   A *swap* transaction involving one *forward* maturity date against another forward maturity date.

Take down   The receipt of the principal of a loan by the borrower.

Terms   The currency in which an item (including another currency) is priced. Thus, if 1 U.S. dollar equals 4 French francs, the price of a dollar is 4 francs in French terms. See p. 29. Also refers to the maturity in a *money market* transaction, e.g., a short-term loan.

Time deposit   The placement of funds with a financial institution for a fixed period of time, usually at least a month.

Trade accounts   Those parts of the *balance of payments* which reflect money spent abroad by the citizens of a country on goods and services and the money spent by foreigners in the given country for goods and services.

Trading position worksheet   A record of incomplete transactions in a particular currency. See p. 215.

Treasury bills   The obligations of a country's treasury department. Because of the unquestioned quality of their issuer and their usually short-term maturities, treasury bills are the most marketable *money market instrument*.

Two-way rate   An *exchange rate* or an *interest rate* quotation which contains both a *bid rate* and an *offer rate*. The size of the *spread* between the two rates indicates the relative quality of the quotation. See p. 66.

Unilateral transfers   The account in the *balance of payments* which reflects money sent out of a country and money sent into the country from abroad which is not in exchange for goods, services, or financial assets. Usually, this account reflects money sent by workers in one country to their families in another country.

Upvaluation   Also commonly called *revaluation*. See *Appreciation*.

Value [or] **Value date**   The day on which a financial transaction is to be settled, i.e., on which payments are actually made and received. The specification of a value date is an important part of any *foreign exchange* or *money market* transaction. See p. 40.

Volume quotation system   A method of giving *exchange rates* in which a certain specified amount of local currency (usually 1 or 100) is compared to the proper amount of foreign currency. The most prominent country using the volume quotation system is Great Britain. See p. 34.

Wash   A transaction which produces neither profit nor loss.

Index

Index